Subversive Subjects

Marguerite Yourcenar as a young girl, c. 1910.
Photo by permission of Houghton Library, Harvard University.

Subversive Subjects

Reading Marguerite Yourcenar

Edited by
Judith Holland Sarnecki
and Ingeborg Majer O'Sickey

Madison • Teaneck
Fairleigh Dickinson University Press

© 2004 by Rosemont Publishing & Printing Corp.

All rights reserved. Authorization to photocopy items for internal or personal use, or the internal or personal use of specific clients, is granted by the copyright owner, provided that a base fee of $10.00, plus eight cents per page, per copy is paid directly to the Copyright Clearance Center, 222 Rosewood Drive, Danvers, Massachusetts 01923. [0-8386-3992-5/04 $10.00 + 8¢ pp, pc.]

Associated University Presses
2010 Eastpark Boulevard
Cranbury, NJ 08512

The paper used in this publication meets the requirements of the American National Standard for Permanence of Paper for Printed Library Materials Z39.48-1984

Library of Congress Cataloging-in-Publication Data

Subversive subjects : reading Marguerite Yourcenar / edited by Judith Holland Sarnecki and Ingeborg Majer O'Sickey.
    p. cm.
Includes bibliographical references and index.
ISBN 0-8386-3992-5 (alk. paper)
    1. Yourcenar, Marguerite—Criticism and interpretation. I. Sarnecki, Judith Holland, 1944– II. Majer O'Sickey, Ingeborg, 1944–
PQ2649.O8Z89   2004
848'.91209—dc21   2003013434

PRINTED IN THE UNITED STATES OF AMERICA

In Memory of Elaine Marks

    Teacher
    Scholar
    Friend

In Memory of Daniel

Beloved child, cherished friend, lyrical polylinguist,
who loved Asterix, Rin Tin Tin, and Apollinaire.

Contents

Preface	9
JUDITH HOLLAND SARNECKI	
Introduction	11
Part I	11
INGEBORG MAJER O'SICKEY	
Part II	16
JUDITH HOLLAND SARNECKI	

Part I. Repositioning the Self: (Im)Postures

Achilles on the Field of Sexual Politics	33
KATHERINE CALLEN KING	
Autobiography and Matricide: Marguerite Yourcenar's *Dear Departed*	62
LEAKTHINA CHAU-PECH OLLIER	
Reading Prohibited: The Politics of Yourcenar's Prefaces	77
CAROLE ALLAMAND	
Is There No Body on the Scene of Writing?: Contemporary Conceptions of Textual Practice in/and Yourcenar's Paratexts	101
MIEKE TAAT	

Part II. Beyond History: The Politics of Desire

Coup de grâce as Male Fantasy: On the Sexual Politics of Fascism	125
MICHAEL ROTHBERG	
Questions of *genre*: History and the Self in Marguerite Yourcenar's *Mémoires d'Hadrien*	148
KSENYA KIEBUZINSKI	
The Essays of Marguerite Yourcenar: Analogy and Eternity	166
HENK HILLENAAR	

Part III. Transpositions: Reading the Self, Reading the Other

Good Intentions: Marguerite Yourcenar's American Translations	179
FRANCESCA COUNIHAN	

Performing the Masculine Voice 203
ELÈNE CLICHE
Death-defying Acts: Performing Gender in Marguerite
Yourcenar's "Sappho ou le suicide" 214
JUDITH HOLLAND SARNECKI

Bibliography 228
Contributors 241
Index 244

Preface

THIS PROJECT ON FRENCH WRITER MARGUERITE YOURCENAR—WHO SPENT the years between 1943 and her death in 1987 alternating between her cozy cottage on Mount Desert Island off the coast of Maine and traveling all over the world with her female or male companions—needs some explanation. In this brief preface I hope to give the necessary background information that will place our collection of essays in its historical and cultural context. When Ingeborg Majer O'Sickey began in the mid-1990s to collect articles on Marguerite Yourcenar that reflected the influence of feminist and poststructuralist theories, I was simply an aspiring contributor. Ingeborg turned the project over to me in 1997 when she received a yearlong fellowship to work on women filmmakers in Germany. We continued, however, to work together throughout the late 1990s as we communicated with contributors, and, in some cases, translators. We had collected essays from colleagues in the United States, Europe, and Canada, all of whom were interested in Yourcenar's labyrinthine texts. We worked on adding contributors' revisions and sought retranslations for two of the essays because we felt that the initial translations we had commissioned were not good enough to include in this volume. For newer translations of the articles by Cliche and Hillenaar I must thank Gervais Reed, professor emeritus of Lawrence University, who is currently editor of creative works for the *French Review*. His thoughtful translations capture and preserve the spirit and tone of the originals. Chantal Rodais took on the task of translating Mieke Taat's dense and highly theoretical article, and I commend her for its outcome. While working on this project I have acquired a newfound admiration for translators, including Yourcenar herself, who translated British and American authors as well as various Negro spirituals.

Finally, the process of putting together this collection of articles took far longer than anticipated; thus, I wish to thank our ever-patient contributors. I am delighted to present to an English-speaking audience on the one-hundredth anniversary of Yourcenar's birth these long overdue viewpoints on a fascinating and often overlooked French writer. I cannot fail to mention the fine work on Marguerite Yourcenar that has already been published in French, primarily by the Société Internationale d'Etudes Yourcenariennes under the competent direction of Rémy Poignault. To the society's members and their insightful texts I owe a large debt of gratitude. Similarly, if Ingeborg Majer O'Sickey had not remained on board to help with this project, I doubt that it would have come to fruition. Although we have never met, we have forged a close bond that comes from sharing our passion for reading and writing about a formidable female author.

The secretarial and technological support I received from Joanne Johnson and Dana Rose-Schmalz in formatting and reformatting this volume was invaluable. All too often the women behind the scenes who facilitate our lives and our work go unmentioned. I am most grateful to them and for them.

Finally, I want to thank Christine Retz, our editor at Associated University Presses, for her invaluable help in preparing this manuscript for publication.

JUDITH HOLLAND SARNECKI

Introduction

Part I
Ingeborg Majer O'Sickey

MARGUERITE YOURCENAR WAS THE FIRST WOMAN[1] TO BE INDUCTED INTO the Académie Française in this institution's more than three-hundred-year-long history. The Académie, founded by Cardinal de Richelieu in 1635, has forty sitting members, some of whom meet every Thursday to occupy themselves with the creation and maintenance of the French dictionary. The *immortels* (so called by virtue of a seal upon which "À l'immortalité" is inscribed that was given by Richelieu to the Académie) wear a *habit vert* with a two-sided hat, a cape, and a sword.[2] They are inducted in a solemn ceremony under the "Coupole" at Quai Conti in Paris and cannot be removed from their posts except for gravely dishonorable acts.[3] Each member occupies a numbered seat that becomes vacant when he or she dies; Yourcenar was elected on March 6, 1980, to Roger Caillois's *fauteuil* [chair] (number three), and her official induction took place on January 22, 1981.[4]

When the Académie was founded in 1635, women had just begun to play a central role in French literature and culture by way of a literary movement that would be called *l'école précieuse* in distinction and opposition to *l'école classique*. Literary history would judge women's writings and participation in the French salons of the seventeeth century negatively, as laughable. Donna Stanton explains: "[I]n selecting the term *précieuse* to depict the ridiculous female, seventeenth century male writers could exploit an ironic dichotomy between the apparent and the real. . . . The term, *préciosité*, is not listed in the seventeenth-century dictionaries of Richelet, Furetière or the Académie Française. The rare textual instances of the abstract noun date from the last third of the century, and refer almost exclusively to the ideas and behavior of certain women, who are characterized as finicky, disdainful, arrogant." Literary historical commentary (by Y. Fukui, especially) "serves to underscore the phallogocentric strategies of literary history: Preciosity or the précieux has been masculinized as a poetic tendency, while the female specificity of *la précieuse* has been effaced."[5] With the exclusion of the term *Préciosité* from its seventeenth-century dictionary, the Académie began a time-honored tradition of misogyny. A few hundred years later, in 1982, François Weyergans would write of *Oeuvres romanesques*: "She [Yourcenar] is a précieuse. I'm not making this up: she talks about it herself. I'm merely adding the adjective 'ridiculous.'"[6] Christiane Rochefort's terse assessment comes to mind: "A man's book is a book. A woman's book is a woman's book."[7]

By the time the Académie elected Yourcenar to join, the *lingua materna* had been so thoroughly discredited in and by the *lingua paterna* that there seemed to be no longer a need to exclude women: the institution had reached its goal. Yourcenar could either be called "ridiculous" or, at the other extreme, be praised or condemned for her "masculinist" works, her so-called "male talent." Neither represented a threat to the Académie's phallogocentric position.[8] Nevertheless, Jean d'Ormesson, who proposed her candidacy, would not have an easy time of it: "I had the traditionalists against me. And a few leftists, like André Chamson, who thought she was right-wing, which wasn't true. And Claude Lévi-Strauss, who was ardently opposed to her candidacy, 'because you don't change the rules of the tribe.'"[9] There were other problems, too, of course, some of them not so metaphysical; d'Ormesson described these with some irony: "The Académie is founded on a series of rites. One of the rituals is that we are all equal, the only order being that of seniority. An immutable order. So what would we do with a woman? Would we stand back and let Madame Yourcenar come in or go out ahead of us?"

Since appearance is an important element of the ritual, the men asked in some consternation: "What uniform would Madame Yourcenar wear?"[10] "In the Académie we grow old with one another. How could we be able to stand watching a woman grow old?"[11] Yourcenar, of the opinion that "a good woman is worth just as much as a good man, and that an intelligent woman is worth just as much as an intelligent man,"[12] would feel the fallout of these views, and reacted by celebrating the event with Jerry Wilson (companion to Yourcenar after Grace Frick's death) and other friends rather than, as was expected, in the company of her fellow *Académiciens*.

Expressions of negative attitudes were not limited to members of the Académie, however; Matthieu Galey, who had "collaborated" with Yourcenar on the volume of interviews *With Open Eyes*, evidently fuses his personal grudge against Yourcenar at the time of her induction[13] with his general misogyny as he describes his reception of the induction ceremony:

> Naturally, it takes me a week to get around to recording the only historic event I ever attended. For her reception truly was a show, entirely out of the ordinary. Not at all an academic reception: along the lines of a *Tastevin* installation ceremony, or Queen Victoria's jubilee. In her ample, black-velvet greatcoat, with a white collar, and a shawl, also white, on her head, Marguerite's entrance was quite stunning.
>
> A consecration, to the sound of a drum. A Franciscan tertiary, followed by a priest (the Reverend Father Carré), or an old empress being judged in the High Court by all these strange magistrates with green tails. With their insect-like appearance, one also got the impression of some mysterious confrairy; it was as if a large termite, inseminated by her insects, which were buzzing excitedly around her, were going to lay some eggs, beneath the gaze of the presidential couple, impassively perched on their Louis XV chairs. After which a heavy bundle, wrapped in velvet, propelled itself to a little table, underneath the platform of the director's office, and started to read a fine speech—but a long one—on Caillois, in which it was a question of diamonds, but this must have been unintentional. . . . At the end, the entire room rose to its feet to applaud. Except the Giscards, who take themselves for hereditary monarchs.[14]

Galey's vision of Yourcenar's relationship to her physical space in terms of an insect, a termite no less, is not only of interest in that it betrays his politics of representation (and how he sees this woman writer vis-à-vis her environment as destructive), it also betrays a fairly derivative imagination. His choice of image of the woman as the life-giver of death was by this time already quite commonplace.[15] Galey's psychophysical parallelism claims for Yourcenar a particular space in which she takes up the subject's identity as lure *and* source (as active and passive) and thus has everything to do with the psychosocial dilemma Yourcenar would find herself in as a member of the body of *immortels*.

Yourcenar, for her part, was not impressed with most of her fellow *immortels*. She judged them to be "a bunch of aging little boys who get together on Thursdays to have fun. I don't see much of anything a woman can do there."[16] The latter part of this statement may surprise quite a few of those readers who are familiar with her general stance relating to questions of gender. What may have caused her to make such a "radical" statement? Her biographer, Josyane Savigneau, proposes this reason: "The Académie was probably for Yourcenar the first site of confrontation with men. For the first time, perhaps the only time in her life, she felt their—

irrational—reprobation. It was a reprobation founded uniquely on her belonging to the other sex. Their hostility toward her was, and remains greater still than the hostility borne women who fight for women's rights. For Yourcenar didn't even clash with men socially. She ignored them. And this they could never tolerate."[17]

How very surprised or, perhaps, more aptly put, how dismayed the gentlemen must have been who had supported her candidacy and who had made possible this "progressive" move of inviting Yourcenar into the circle of the *immortels*. Indeed, how affronted those gentlemen who had opposed her candidacy must have been when they heard the opening remarks of her acceptance speech:

> You have welcomed me, as I was saying. This uncertain, floating self, this entity whose existence I myself have contested, which I only feel to be truly delimited by the several works that I have happened to write, here it is, such as it is, surrounded and accompanied by an invisible troupe of women who should, perhaps, have received this honor much earlier, to the point where I am tempted to step back to let their shadows pass. Nonetheless, let us not forget that it was only a little more or a little bit less than a century ago that the question of the presence of women in this assembly could have arisen. In other words, it was toward the middle of the nineteenth century that literature became in France for certain women both a vocation and a profession, and that state of affairs was perhaps still too new to attract the attention of a society such as yours. Madame de Staël would no doubt have been ineligible by virtue of her Swiss ancestry and her Swedish marriage: she contented herself with being one of the best minds of the century. George Sand would have caused a scandal because of her turbulent life, because of the very generosity of her emotions, which made her such an admirably womanly woman; the person even more so than the writer was ahead of her time. Colette herself thought that it was not for a woman to go calling on men soliciting their votes, and I can only agree, not having done so myself.[18]

The rhetorical move Yourcenar performs is quite astonishing. She posits and de-posits an "I" all at once as she historicizes it. She begins by radically undermining the logocentric notion of a unitary self. Then, in a genealogical parade of sorts, she makes material the written word, which is usually seen as an abstraction and the basis for philosophy. In this sense, one might say that Yourcenar rejects the central concept of Western metaphysics, the basis of the *lingua paterna,* which was designated in the Middle Ages "litteraliter" in opposition to "maternaliter." It is, after all, curious that she would place herself outside that body of Académie at the very moment when she delivers her acceptance speech ("society such as yours"—*d'une Compagnie comme la vôtre*) and instead, insert herself in a women writers' genealogy.

Our reference to "maternaliter" does not wish to claim, in a revisionist gesture, that Yourcenar was sympathetic to feminist critique or gynocritique.[19] Likewise, it does not claim that she had any affinity with either the school of *parler femme* [speaking the (female) body] or *ecriture feminine* [women's language]. Indeed, Yourcenar had not thought much about the heterogeneous voices of feminism in France or, indeed, as an international movement. If Yourcenar claimed affinity to any group at all, it would have been based on the French language, a language she did not see as a gendered language. As we have mentioned, the fact that the dictionary of the Académie Française constituted a specific, highly ideological context was most likely not recognized by Yourcenar until she came into contact with its members and until she experienced their treatment of her as thoroughly misogynistic. Thus, her reference to language in its limiting function and her deconstruction of the metaphysics of identity must be seen as decidedly masculinist-poststructuralist. Indeed, her notion of the "floating I" may be said to be Lacanian: the "I" as a product of the symbolic, of an abstract "other," which would have as a consequence that the "I" is really an ICH, ungraspable. Nevertheless, she admits here what she had for so many years vehemently denied: that being a woman was a political matter, having to do with positionality, with the space where one found oneself.[20]

Thus, for a fleeting moment, Yourcenar opposes to Lacan's play with the Nom-du-Père/Non-du-Père a decisive Non-au-Père. That she does this from the pulpit of the Académie Française is, of course, of enormous importance. She seems to have gone some distance, in her opening remarks that we cite above to articulate the irony of her position, by positing a historical, gendered I surrounded, as she puts it, "by an invisible troupe of women." And she very clearly *names* the body, the institution, that rendered nineteenth-century women writers invisible: the *Académiciens*, a *Compagnie comme la vôtre*.

We can only speculate on how different her working method might have been, had she had these experiences earlier in her working life. Would it have decreased her penchant for revisions and paratexts (both pre- and postfaces); would it, in other words, have made needless the obsessive installation of a Cartesian subject that does not *in praxis* allow the notion of the floating subject-in-process, such as been theorized by Julia Kristeva? It is perhaps wishful thinking that had she found herself in such a psychosocial dilemma much earlier in her career, Yourcenar would not have had to resort to her specific kind of megalomania toward a purely transcendent, completely self-sufficient subject.

Ironically, all the more the need for readings that refract the author's reading of her own work through a variety of critical screens. All the more need for an anthology of criticism on Marguerite Yourcenar's work when this writer appears to have written all her own criticism. As is known, Yourcenar was one of the few living authors to be included in the Pantheon of the Pleïade; it is remarkable that she forbade the inclusion of a customary critical apparatus.[21] Thus, Yourcenar's desire to control the reception of her work will itself be the point of departure for many inquiries into Yourcenar's oeuvre.

Part II
Judith Holland Sarnecki

We are gratified to be able to present a collection of articles that approaches Yourcenar's oeuvre from a variety of critical perspectives. Each author we have included ventures beyond traditional readings of Yourcenar's complex texts, pushing against the boundaries of interpretation that the Belgian-born writer carefully established. You will discover that although the essays represented in this collection work well together, they at times contradict one another in interesting ways. The anthology, therefore, creates a conversation that we invite the reader to join. Our goal is not to pigeonhole our author, but to interrogate her writing. It has never been easy to position Marguerite Yourcenar within the context of twentieth-century French literature. She willfully escapes categorization as she assumes the roles of both insider and outsider. Our hope is that this collection will enhance understanding and appreciation of a writer that clearly deserves a closer look.

In "Achilles on the Field of Sexual Politics," Katherine Callen King teases out the differences between what she calls "Western culture's originary war poem," the *Iliad*, and Yourcenar's lyric rendering of Achilles' story in "Achille ou le mensonge," and "Patrocle ou le destin." Her in-depth reading foregrounds the ambiguities in Yourcenar's prose poems as they relate to gender and sexual politics. Reproducing the feminine-masculine opposition that characterized her generation's view of the sexes, Yourcenar attempted to escape the boundaries of sexual identity by creating for each poem an androgynous figure (or third sex). King contends, however, that the androgynous figure cannot escape the binary that always already exists in language and culture. Thus, the only way out of sexual identities carved out for us before birth seems to be through death, a death chosen "with open eyes."

I would add here that the importance of death, heroic or otherwise, cannot be underestimated; it permeates Yourcenar's fictional universe. How one dies often summarizes how one lived: each character's death indicates how that character is to be read. Hadrian, for example, uses death to reflect on his life and to instruct his successor how to rule wisely. Zénon, hero of *L'oeuvre au noir*, watches the blood flow from his self-inflicted wounds before his enemies can put him to death; he remains the lucid master of his fate. Misandra, the masculine female in "Achille ou le mensonge," dies a living death, imprisoned in that closest of women's quarters, the female body. Penthesileia, the Amazon queen killed by Achilles, fares better only in that she dies an "honorable" death on the field of battle. The mask that Achilles discovers under her helmet stands as a reminder of the mystery of sexual identity that we find in many Yourcenarian texts.

King's essay captures the significance of death, the failed attempt at masculine glory, and the bitter aftertaste of war so evident in Yourcenar's rendering of Achilles. King artfully weaves together criticism of both Homer and Yourcenar as she develops her own more feminist scholarly take on the poems. Furthermore, she shows how "Achille ou le mensonge" and "Patrocle ou le destin" of the 1939 edition of *Feux* differ from earlier versions penned by Yourcenar. For King, Yourcenar's pessimism reflects the total submission of the feminine to the masculine: classical "heroism" seems to depend on the conquest of the feminine as well as the female in order to attain (or maintain) masculine identity and virility. Yet King acknowledges and demonstrates—through a close and careful reading—that the search for (sexual) identity in Yourcenar's short but complex texts is never simple or straightforward. Readers who deem these prose poems among the finest work produced by Yourcenar will delight in the scrupulous attention to detail and the fine translations King gives.

In "Autobiography and Matricide: Marguerite Yourcenar's *Dear Departed*," Leakthina Chau-Pech Ollier zeroes in on the "matricide" she perceives in the first volume of *Le labyrinthe du monde*. As Ollier reads it, Yourcenar's "matricide" turns out to be a double murder as well as an aborted birth. Ollier contends that Yourcenar, by refusing to accord subjectivity to her mother, unwittingly prevents her own emergence as a whole self. This in turn explains why the author appears so rarely as a character in her own autobiographical trilogy. Taking French theorists such as Kristeva and Irigaray into account, Ollier traces Yourcenar's failed attempt at separation from Fernande, who, she says, continues to haunt her daughter's writing even when ostensibly absent from the text. Ollier states that by refusing autonomous selfhood to her mother, Yourcenar smothers herself as well, thereby locking them both in a labyrinthine text from which there is no exit.

Ollier points out the ways in which Yourcenar struggles throughout the trilogy with her ambivalent feelings toward her mother. One example that Ollier gives is how, at one point, Yourcenar tries to reverse the mother-daughter roles, perceiving herself as mother and Fernande as daughter. But this configuration is no better than its opposite, ending in an aborted attempt to give birth to herself and her mother as separate subjects. Ollier perceptively observes that Fernande is most "alive" in *Dear Departed* when she is represented on her deathbed. The photograph of a pale Fernande on her deathbed—complete with bloated stomach—stands out as the reader's (and the author's) clearest image of Fernande. The reasons Ollier gives for this phenomenon are numerous. First, Yourcenar's primary source (her father) almost never spoke about Fernande; in fact, Yourcenar never saw a photograph of her mother until she was a grown woman. Furthermore, she realizes only too well that the occasion of her birth is the event that precipitated her mother's death—it seems as if Fernande can only exist for Yourcenar as a character in one of her books. Finally, since her mother was absent during the all-important "mirror stage" (as theorized by Lacan), Yourcenar—who both desires and fears her mother's gaze—remains stuck in an approach-avoidance mode throughout the work. Never given voice by her daughter in the family chronicles, Ollier contends, Fernande remains as a ghostly presence in *Dear Departed* that prevents Yourcenar from emerging as the subject of her own autobiography.

Carole Allamand takes on the paratext of Yourcenar's oeuvre in her essay "Reading Prohibited: The Politics of Yourcenar's Prefaces." She encourages us to read against the grain of Yourcenar's unusually long prefaces, which function as a shield to protect the author from undesirable interpretations of her texts. In Yourcenar's attempt to foreclose unwanted readings, she distances herself from her reader as well as her own writing.[22] Allamand has a fascinating take on Yourcenar's paratexts. Not only do they make of Yourcenar a disembodied voice—Allamand points out that there is no*body* behind the famous pseudonym—they also tend to authorize her as the only qualified reader of her oeuvre. Allamand engages with a variety of literary theories to read Yourcenar from several perspectives as she examines both how and why the author went to such pains to cover over the gaps in her texts by extensively reworking her prefaces.

And to what end? Allamand asks. Why the need for such control, such mastery? What does Yourcenar want or need to cover over? One avenue that Allamand explores is a possible textual link to Yourcenar's own origins and her mother's tragic death from childbed fever several days after the author's birth. Might the obsessive reworking of texts and paratexts be related to Yourcenar's outward rejection of the importance of her mother's death and her distinct distaste for the prospect of maternity? By distancing herself from her literary creation and struggling for control over her literary production and persona, does Yourcenar place herself in the position of "father" vis-à-vis her texts, repressing the maternal? Do all her prefaces function to ensure that her readers will see only Yourcenar the writer and not Marguerite de Crayencour, the person behind the pen? These are just some of the questions Allamand raises as she probes the ways in which Yourcenar positions herself as a "universal humanist." We feel confident that Allamand's insights into Yourcenar's prefaces will inspire scholars to continue to uncover the richness and complexity of this work within a work.

In her essay "Is There No Body on the Scene of Writing?: Contemporary Conceptions of Textual Practice in/and Yourcenar's Paratexts"—ably translated from the French by Chantal Rodais—Mieke Taat addresses Yourcenar's paratextual writings from another angle. She makes a theoretically sophisticated argument for a movement in the Yourcenarian paratext "towards a differently 'woman' form of genetics." After closely considering various prefaces, notes, interviews, and letters that span the author's life and writing career, Taat critiques the notion that Yourcenar positioned herself alongside phallocratic (post) modernists to establish herself as a virile writer. Instead, Taat pursues the possibility of reading Yourcenar's paratext "in the feminine."

She begins by signaling the "phallacious" writings of Barthes, Derrida, and Deleuze as they seek to announce the death of the author and dismantle the preface as an author-ity. Taat reads the symbolic death of the Father, heralded by these male authors, as another, albeit different, act of matricide, one that can be traced through the maternal or womb metaphors they use. Reading through Kristeva's texts that posit an abject, archaic Mother, Taat views much of French male postmodern theoretical writing as a cathartic rite that seeks to purify the text from the stain of the woman's in-body (her reproductive functions) as well as to protect themselves from her sexual and creative powers.

Next Taat turns her attention to the Yourcenarian paratext in order to demonstrate how differently this supposedly masculine female author approaches the creative act of writing. According to Taat, Yourcenar, in her prefaces, rare interviews, and notes, does not set herself up as the guiding force of the writing process. Instead, she distances herself from virile metaphors, preferring to use womb metaphors to refer to the complex process of bringing a novel to fruition.[23] In her interviews with Matthieu Galey, for instance, Yourcenar speaks of the evolution of her characters through a gestational process that allows *their* voices to emerge. For Taat, the long periods of gestation for many of Yourcenar's texts only reinforce her argument that they become, little by little, revealers of the *otherness* that Yourcenar seeks to find and communicate. To distance oneself from the ego, to avoid the trap of narcissism, this is Yourcenar's slow and difficult task as she, like the psychoanalyst, attempts to listen to and interpret the Other's story.

One of Yourcenar's rules in the genesis of her works of fiction, Taat reminds us, is to "read everything." The author tends to view herself as a kind of medium who allows the Other to speak through her if, that is, she has conscientiously prepared the way by reading everything that pertains to her subject. Wary of the way in which historians tend to systematize their material, Yourcenar seems always to keep in mind the ephemeral nature of "truth" and the fragmentary nature of "facts." Consequently Taat reads Yourcenar's prefaces as "narratives of genesis" fashioned according to a womb economy. The movement Taat perceives in the paratext is one that crosses frontiers, specifically from the head to the body, effectively deconstructing the Cartesian mind/body split. Yourcenar's visceral intelligence, Taat claims, does not deny the body, as some critics have claimed, but rather reconnects physiology to knowledge.

While I would argue that Yourcenar's maternal metaphors emerge as an unconscious subtext because of the repression (in the Freudian sense) of mothers and motherhood—basing my argument primarily on the three volumes in *Le labyrinthe du monde*—Taat sees this process as both conscious and voluntary on the part of Yourcenar, who, she contends, was very aware that she owed her existence to a mother who died of puerperal fever shortly after the author's birth. As Taat reads her, Yourcenar very much intended to make her readers aware of an internal realm that not only tolerates, but actively cultivates otherness and difference.

Michael Rothberg begins his piece, "*Coup de grâce* as Male Fantasy: On the Sexual Politics of Fascism," with a quotation that places Yourcenar firmly on the side of those writers who consistently counter the darker forces at work in European politics and economics. He then proceeds to question this traditional interpretation of Yourcenar's oeuvre, reading *Coup de grâce* alongside Klaus Theweleit's *Male Fantasies*. Rothberg carefully draws parallels between the actions of Yourcenar's problematic narrator, Erick von Lhomond, and the fantasies of the men of the *Freikorps,* proto-Nazi soldiers for whom World War I never really ended. He interrogates, in particular, Yourcenar's 1962 preface that instructs the reader how to judge or, more accurately, how not to judge Erick, the novel's protagonist.[24]

In order to read Yourcenar's 1939 novel in light of Nazi Germany, anti-Semitism, and the Holocaust, Rothberg first examines Theweleit's theory of fascist ego-construction. The social formation of the fascist soldier, according to Theweleit, necessitates repressing the production of desire by projecting it onto the bodies of marginalized others: Jews, women, communists, homosexuals, and gypsies. Such constraint of desire and policing of bodily borders leads inevitably to the act of killing off the disturbing Other. While Rothberg concedes and critiques the oversimplification of Theweleit's arguments, he finds them useful in reading Yourcenar's representation of one such soldier and his trajectory toward a "final solution"—that of killing his own troubling other or counterpart, Sophie de Reval. By killing the Medusa-like Sophie (a Communist sympathizer and double of her brother Conrad), Erick attempts to extinguish her frightening sexuality and his own forbidden (homosexual) desire in one blow, *le coup de grâce* of the title. By demonstrating Erick's misogyny and homophobia, Rothberg exposes the sexual politics both of fascism and of Yourcenar's (sub)text.

By rewriting her preface during the Cold War in her adopted country, Yourcenar adheres to the dictum of the day—an end to ideology—laying claim to an apolitical stance. In so doing, Rothberg astutely notes, she also writes over the anti-Semitism of Erick and others like him, demanding that her readers collaborate with her in forgetting the atrocities of the Holocaust just at the moment when their full extent is being revealed. Bringing to light Yourcenar's "collaboration" to forget the past, Rothberg makes us aware of our own when we obey the author's strict instructions and admonitions in her 1962 preface without question or critique.

Ksenya Kiebuzinski offers new insights into Yourcenar's *chef d'oeuvre*, *Mémoires d'Hadrien* in her essay "Questions of *genre*:

History and the Self in Marguerite Yourcenar's *Mémoires d'Hadrien*." She revisits much of the scholarship already done on this "master" work in order to investigate Yourcenar's stated and unstated goals in her adoption (read *creation*) of the second-century Roman emperor's voice to relate both his place in history and his more personal story. Kiebuzinski discusses the ambiguities inherent in a project that mixes writing history with writing fiction. Although a fictional memoir, Hadrien's story lays claim, if not to complete accuracy, to historical authenticity and universal truths.

Kiebuzinski is concerned with how and why Yourcenar turns to Roman history to take up the "I" of first-person narration. In other words, why does Yourcenar use Hadrien's voice to meditate on questions of power, authority, dominance, sacrifice, and love? And to what extent is Hadrien's memoir part of Yourcenar's intellectual and intimate autobiography? In comingling her narrative voice with that of an imperial hero, does the author successfully hide or reveal herself? Kiebuzinski demonstrates how Hadrien's "mémoire" and the "Carnet de notes" that accompanies it raise far more questions than they answer. What does it mean, for example, to assume an "imperial" voice after Hitler and the Holocaust, during the very period of France's struggles to keep its empire intact? What kind of political messages does Yourcenar send when she discusses the possibility of a beneficent world ruler in her celebrated interview with Matthieu Galey, *Les yeux ouverts?*

Kiebuzinski's essay problematizes Yourcenar's use of both *genre* and gender in writing a male memoir that crosses the traditional boundaries of History into the libidinal territory of dreams and desires. Perceiving both the historical conditions of women and the feminist movement as narrow and inevitably bound to the female body, Yourcenar seems to want to bypass this "destiny" when she adopts Hadrien's voice—a voice that strives to reach a spiritual plane that transcends time and place. Kiebuzinski asks whether Yourcenar, in her drive to achieve a metaphysical harmony or sense of self-acceptance, rejects the female as well as the feminine. Or, on the other hand, does she transgress all boundaries of gender and genre to arrive at a new destination that would incorporate male and female in nonoppositional and nontraditional ways? Much of Yourcenar's complexity as a writer lies, Kiebuzinski suggests, in weaving together strands of text that are anachronistic and reactionary at the same time that they are risk-taking and gender-bending.

In his article "The Essays of Marguerite Yourcenar: Analogy and Eternity"—skillfully translated by Gervais Reed—Henk Hillenaar takes Yourcenar's numerous essays as his point of departure. Yet he also manages a global reading of her oeuvre, zeroing in quickly and astutely on what he calls "the lost center," discernible in all her major works. Yourcenar's pessimism, Hillenaar contends, is linked to her obsession with death, an omnipresent theme that the author confronts in two ways, through idealization and defense. The concept of "eternity," for example, offers a way out of the usual opposition of life and death. Using myth and metaphysics as her accomplices, Yourcenar moves, Hillenaar notes, from the temporal to the atemporal, thereby skirting personal history and introspection, and using History to advance her own agenda. In her rare interviews and her reworked prefaces, she erected a wall—like Hadrien's defenses—destined to keep the "barbarians" at the gate. But as Hillenaar sympathetically points out, Yourcenar was probably fending off her own anxieties as much as unsympathetic readers.

Hillenaar penetrates some of these defenses when he uncovers Yourcenar's use of analogy as her modus operandi. Returning to a prescientific and preanalytic mentality, Yourcenar forges her sweeping generalizations by searching for similarities among her objects of study rather than remarking on what is peculiar to them.[25] In so doing, she widens her field of vision until the original subject is surrounded by an ever-expanding constellation of "stars" carefully chosen from world history and literature. Dazzling us with the breadth of her knowledge, this autodidact craftily deflects our attention from her observations's lack of depth. Ever seeking "Universal Man," she skirts her own past for a past that all humanity shares. Finally, Yourcenar steers us away from an in-depth look at her relationship to the women in her texts, particularly mother figures, as she rejects Freudian psychoanalysis in favor of Jungian archetypes.

Hillenaar finds that the author repeatedly evokes her mother's death—a death that involved an involuntary sacrifice of her life from complications following the birth of her only child. To counterbalance this womanly sacrifice, Yourcenar identifies with the male heroes she constructs, many of whom choose their own death— often for a lost cause—to demonstrate their freedom from the kind of constraints that bind women's lives. The epitome of this sacrifice is, of course, Antinoüs, Hadrien's young lover. Zénon too chooses his own death rather than accommodate his persecutors. Another way that Yourcenar deals with death, Hillenaar notes, is to relegate it to a realm outside of time and history, turning it into myth or abstraction. But whatever way the author approaches it, the twin themes of death and sacrifice, according to Hillenaar, remain at the heart of Yourcenar's oeuvre.

In "Good Intentions: Marguerite Yourcenar's American Translations," Francesca Counihan takes a look at a largely ignored portion of Yourcenar's oeuvre—her translations of American texts. Counihan first mentions how Yourcenar presented these translations to the public: by placing her work in the context of the struggle for civil rights in the United States. Counihan reminds us that Yourcenar undertook these translations as an "alien" herself, one who came to the United States at the beginning of World War II with very few financial resources. Yourcenar admired the Negro spirituals, and in a curious sense seemed to identify with the displaced former slaves who composed them. But in spite of Yourcenar's genuine desire to open herself to another culture, Counihan contends, she inadvertently compared the products of Black American culture to her own grounding in European civilization; hence, she never overcame her sense of the European as universal. Because of her European cultural model of reference, Yourcenar never achieved the kind of border crossing she hoped for.

Counihan also examines Yourcenar's prefaces to her translations of Negro spirituals, *Fleuve profond, sombre rivière*, and James Baldwin's *Le Coin des «Amen.»* In those prefaces, Counihan asserts, Yourcenar traces a tacit distinction between "high" and "low" culture and constantly makes value judgments about African Americans and their (mis)use of language. Stereotypes of Africa, classic oppositions between light and dark (or black and white) are clearly reproduced. Furthermore, religious practices of black Americans are considered simple, fundamental, and homogeneous. Yourcenar appears to take her own cultural and religious background as the "norm," whereas everything else is marked as an exception. The author functions as the authority conveniently located outside the culture under examination and thus uniquely able to make "objective" judgments.

Examining the translations themselves, Counihan points out the ways in which Yourcenar misreads both the Negro spirituals and Baldwin's play. According to Counihan, Yourcenar fails to see black English as a form of resistance to "standard English," a deliberately separate linguistic system with its own internal logic. This fundamental misapprehension leads to translations that miss their mark in two ways: first, they are unable to give the sense of coherence that the original texts convey because they do not grasp the linguistic system at work; second, they often interpret meaning in ways that distort the original because they have only a cursory understanding of the cultural context. Counihan gives several convincing examples, such as a misuse of "tu" and "vous" by one of the characters in Baldwin's play *The Amen Corner*. She concludes that Yourcenar, herself a somewhat unwilling *émigrée*, attempts to assimilate an otherness she seemingly identified with by placing it within her own linguistic and cultural domain.

In her essay "Performing the Masculine Voice" (translated by Gervais Reed), Elène Cliche introduces the "paradox of sexual ambiguity" that allows Yourcenar to assume various masculine voices throughout her oeuvre. Cliche discovers a "floating subject" when she compares Yourcenar's sexually ambiguous heroes to Virginia Woolf's *Orlando*.[26] Clearly attracted to Woolf's theory of the androgynous author (as Woolf expressed it in *A Room of One's Own*), Yourcenar creates memorable characters in her various works that appear to belong definitively to neither sex. Cliche specifically mentions Sophie of *Coup de grâce*, Sappho in *Feux*, Alexis, Hadrian, and Nathanaël.[27] For Cliche, Yourcenar's style is neither masculine nor feminine; it simply opens itself up to the Other, giving free rein to sexual border crossings.

Through a carefully constructed argument that makes use of several of Yourcenar's texts, Cliche demonstrates how the author upsets the binary logic of masculine-feminine. Characters that can be both at once, or first one and then the other, create the kind of gender trouble that Judith Butler has theorized. Cliche also notes the homosexualization of desire in both "Sappho ou le suicide" and *Mémoires d'Hadrien*. She examines Sophie's resemblance to her brother, Conrad, and remarks how Erick's desire for Conrad transforms Sophie into a male figure.

Cliche reads *Mémoires d'Hadrien* as an example of how Yourcenar performs the masculine voice. But the performative here, Cliche notes, signals that there is no essential being behind the performance. In other words, Yourcenar uses the performance to create the very kind of floating subject that Cliche sees as characteristic of Yourcenar's writing. Cliche goes on to demonstrate how the materiality of Hadrian's male body is constructed through language. She notes how Hadrian's story, from its inception, is a narration of the sensual and sexually ambiguous body. Cliche concludes that Yourcenar's Hadrian throws into question that which makes a body masculine or feminine in any given culture at any moment in time.

In my essay, "Death-defying Acts: Performing Gender in Marguerite Yourcenar's "Sappho ou le suicide," I focus on one short prose poem chosen by Yourcenar to conclude *Feux*. Not only is this slender volume the most lyric text in Yourcenar's oeuvre, it is in some ways the most tantalizing. The author "hooks" us in her introduction when she declares (rather disingenuously) that she hopes these poems will never be read. What better invitation could one receive to play hide-and-seek? It is up to the readers to locate and recognize the author behind the various masks—masks that are both male and female—for Yourcenar clearly felt constrained by boundaries of sex and gender.

Yourcenar rewrote the preface to *Feux* twice (in 1957 and 1974), rendering her textual mask more impenetrable with each rewrite. In a draft of a translation of Yourcenar's original preface (from the 1936 Plon edition), Grace Frick, Yourcenar's longtime companion, wrote:

> Possibly this book is like a house with only one door, carefully hidden, so that the building appears to a stranger as if utterly without entry. Behind its walls a masked ball is in progress, a travesty where one wears the disguise which is his true self.
> If the reader is ready to understand and feel in sympathy with the type of human architecture to which this structure belongs its arches and vistas will open to him as naturally as some flower. (*Fires*, bMS Fr 372 (1317), reprinted here with the kind permission of Houghton Manuscript Library.)

Yourcenar's French is even more forceful:

> Peut-être en est-il de ce livre comme de certains édifices qui n'ont qu'une porte secrète et dont l'étranger ne connaît qu'un mur infranchissable. Derrière ce mur se donne le plus inquiétant des bals travestis: celui où quelqu'un se déguise en SOI-MEME. Si le lecteur est destiné à comprendre et à aimer l'ordre auquel obéit cette architecture humaine, ces colonnades pour lui s'ouvriront d'elles-mêmes comme des fleurs. (Yourcenar's emphasis, quoted in Savigneau, *Marguerite Yourcenar, L'Invention d'une vie,* 114)

> [Perhaps this book is like certain edifices that possess a secret entry, where a stranger would encounter only an impassable wall. Behind this wall one finds the most troubling of costume balls: where the mask one wears is the mask of ONESELF. If the reader is destined to understand and appreciate this particular human construction, the columns, like flowers, will open for him of their own accord.]

Thus the poems in *Feux* expose the fiction of a "normal" sexuality with fixed and stable (hetero) sexual identities. They strongly suggest that the sexual roles we play are masks that we are either forced to wear or choose to wear to conform to certain gender stereotypes. Through a close reading of "Sappho ou le suicide" I attempt to show how—by subverting fixed categories of sexual identity—Yourcenar exposes oppositional genders as a lie.

Taken as a whole, the essays in our anthology help to trouble the more classic readings of Yourcenar often proposed by her ardent fans. Clearly she took great pains during her lifetime to secure her place in literary history, forming literary alliances that, along with her prefaces and notes, have helped protect her oeuvre from "wayward" interpretations. By encouraging such wayward interpretations, this grouping of articles poses the question of whether the reader is bound to respect the interpretation insisted upon by the author, or whether a literary scholar has the right—indeed, the obligation—to submit any and all texts to the scrutiny of close readings demanded by literary theory (and especially French literary theory). By answering "yes" to the latter, the composers of these essays shed new light on a writer who clearly deserves such thought-provoking discussion of her complicated authorly persona and confounding texts. It is in that spirit that we dedicate these essays to her.

Notes

1. Jacqueline de Romilly would be the second; elected on November 24, 1988, she would occupy André Roussin's chair. The first female professor at the College de France, her work concerned itself mostly with Greek literature. In 1990, Helene Carrère d'Encausse, a professor at l'Institut d'Etudes politiques in Paris, was the third woman to be elected.
2. Women and clergy are exempted from carrying the latter.
3. To date, there are seven hundred members.
4. After her death, she was succeeded by Jean-Denis Bredin *(http://www.academie-francaise.fr/immortels/base.html)*.
5. Colette Gaudin et al., eds., "The Fiction of 'Préciocité' and the Fear of Women, in *Feminist Readings: French Texts/American Contexts* (New Haven: Yale French Studies, 1981), 109–10.
6. "En effeuillant la Marguerite Yourcenar" [Leafing through the Venerable Marguerite Yourcenar], in *Le Matin des livres,* 24 November 1982. Cited in Josyane Savigneau, *Marguerite Yourcenar: L'invention d'une vie* (Chicago: University of Chicago Press, 1993).
7. Elaine Marks and Isabelle de Courtivron, eds., *New French Feminisms* (University of Massachusetts Press, 1980), 183.
8. A victory, of sorts, and ironic by-product of this election would be that from that moment on the word "Academicienne" was pronounced. I am grateful to Chantal Rodais for pointing this out to me.
9. Jean d'Ormesson, cited in Savigneau, *Marguerite Yourcenar: L'invention d'une vie,* 388.

10. They need not have worried. Yourcenar had her own very definite ideas about her "habit." She wore an elegant ensemble, designed by Yves Saint Laurent. See Savigneau, *Marguerite Yourcenar: L'invention d'une vie*, 396.

11. Savigneau, *Marguerite Yourcenar: L'invention d'une vie*, 388.

12. Marguerite Yourcenar, *With Open Eyes: Conversations with Matthieu Galey*, trans. Arthur Goldhammer (Boston: Beacon Press, 1984), 221.

13. Galey's displeasure had to do with Yourcenar's intransigence relating to the volume of interviews. Galey believed that it had a negative effect on the sale of the volume.

14. Cited in Savigneau, *Marguerite Yourcenar: L'invention d'une vie*, 399.

15. The most terse of those statements is surely Beckett's (in *Waiting for Godot*): "birth astride the grave." The most protracted one is to be found in pop culture: it took three films (*Alien I, II,* and *III*—made in 1979, 1986, and 1992 respectively) to bring the message of woman (Lieutenant Ripley) giving birth to a creature that will eventually destroy everything.

16. Savigneau, *Marguerite Yourcenar: L'invention d'une vie*, 389. Yourcenar, not feeling particularly welcome, and as we have seen, not having a great regard for the Académie's members, would stay away from their regular meetings.

17. The *Academiciens* would pay her back in, as Savigneau puts it, "a particularly crude way: there was no one representing the Académie Française at the funeral service held in her memory on 16 January 1988 on Mount Desert Island," 389.

18. Savigneau, *Marguerite Yourcenar: L'invention d'une vie*, 401.

19. The distinction was made in the late 1970s by Elaine Showalter; feminist critique makes its object of study the woman as reader, while gynocritique concerns itself with women as writers. *A Literature of Their Own* (Princeton: Princeton University Press, 1977).

20. In *Le labyrinthe du monde's Archives du Nord* she recounts (speaking of herself in the third person) that as a young girl, "She would not be hampered, as so many women still are in our time, by the fact of being a woman, perhaps because it did not occur to her that she ought to be hampered by it" (613–14). We could cite many instances, especially from her statements to Matthieu Galey, collected in *With Open Eyes*, where she adamantly refuses to say that being female has limited her.

21. See Savigneau, *Marguerite Yourcenar: L'invention d'une vie*, 413.

22. Yourcenar almost convinces us that her texts somehow wrote themselves. I am thinking particularly of *Les songes et les sorts*, but also of *Feux*.

23. Although Taat makes no mention of it, I cannot help but think of *Le labyrinthe du monde*, Yourcenar's semiautobiographical family chronicles, as an example.

24. Rothberg notes his debt to Elaine Marks's influential essay.

25. Poeticially speaking, an anti-Ponge approach.

26. We know, in fact, that Yourcenar met with Woolf in England to discuss her translation of *The Waves*.

27. Zénon, the wandering hero of *L'Oeuvre au noir*, also comes to mind.

Subversive Subjects

Part I
Repositioning the Self: (Im)Postures

Achilles on the Field of Sexual Politics

Katherine Callen King

MARGUERITE YOURCENAR, THE WOMAN CHOSEN TO END THE FRENCH Academy's three hundred years of male exclusivity, vehemently denied that she was a feminist, and her most famous work focuses on male heroes. It comes as no surprise, then, that Yourcenar introduces *Feux (Fires)*,[1] an early less famous work that does largely focus on women, with the assertion that its nine startling revisions of classical myth were intended only "to glorify . . . or perhaps exorcise" [glorifier . . . ou peut-être exorciser] an intense love relationship.[2] Yourcenar turned to ancient myth not to perform a feminist revision of the conscious type Alicia Ostriker discusses,[3] but because it represented for her "une approche de l'absolu. Pour tâcher de découvrir sous l'être humain ce qu'il y a en lui de durable, ou . . . d'éternel" [a way of approaching the absolute, a way of delving beneath the human surface to discover what was durable, or . . . eternal].[4] Nonetheless, what is *éternel* emerges from her 1930s female consciousness remarkably altered from its appearance in centuries of male tradition: Yourcenar's gender-charged transformations of traditional plot detail and imagery infect "the absolute" with festering feminist questions.[5]

I will examine here the production of these feminist questions through analysis of the classical and modern elements in "Achille ou le mensonge" and "Patrocle ou le destin," which were originally published together in 1935 as "Déidamie" and "Penthésilée" under the general title "Deux amours d'Achille" ["Two Loves of Achilles"].[6] The *Iliad*, Western culture's originary war poem, is of paramount concern to these stories' exploration of gender-identification and violence, but as the original subtitles indicate, Yourcenar approaches her heroic absolute circuitously through Achilles' pre- and post-Iliadic relationships with women: Deidamia, whom he loves and leaves, and Penthesileia, whom he kills and loves.[7] Yourcenar weaves these disparate works together on a loom of current events[8] and psychoanalytic theory, shuttling back and forth between war as literal social event and war as an image for conflict between male and female in society, masculine and feminine in the psyche. This artful weaving of classical and modern, of epic heroism and the Freudian unconscious, of ancient misogyny and contemporary fascism, earns these and the other seven stories in *Feux* a place among the most beautiful and powerful works in Yourcenar's corpus.[9]

ACHILLE/DÉIDAMIE

"Achille" ["Déidamie"] is based on a story that has survived most fully in Statius's *Achilleid*. In order to prevent her teenage son from joining the Greek army and dying in the Trojan War, Achilles' mother Thetis dresses him in women's clothing and persuades the unsuspecting king of a distant island to educate him among his daughters. Deidamia, the oldest, most beautiful of these daughters, provides Achilles' motivation for going along with his mother's emasculating wishes. After becoming good friends with her, he simultaneously reveals his true sex and initiates their sexual relationship by raping her. She gives birth to their child secretly. Then Ulysses and Diomedes, who have been sent to find this warrior without whom the Greeks cannot win, come to the island posing as merchants. After trying and failing to recognize Achilles among Lycomedes' daughters at a banquet, they display a supply of dresses and jewelry among which Ulysses has placed a sword and shield. As Ulysses had planned, the true females all rush for the feminine merchandise, but Achilles grabs the sword and shield. Ashamed when he sees his girlish reflection in the bloody shield, Achilles tears off his feminine clothes to assume his warrior role.

This story of transvestism may well have originated, as Vidal-Naquet believes, in a Greek rite in which the passage from boyhood to adult manhood—to participation, that is, in both war and marriage—was dramatized by means of symmetrical inversion.[10] In this rite of separation from the feminine, feminine dress either affirmed the feminine principle just before the young man rejected it (Jeanmaire, 321) or it encoded the uninitiated male's current lack of masculine nature (Sargent, 52). Statius's first-century C.E. Latin literary version, on the other hand, depicted the feminine not as a preliminary stage but as an ever-present danger to the masculine realm of being. The *Achilleid* aimed a clear sociopolitical message at a male audience: uncontrolled love *strips* a man of his masculine identity; aggression—expressed in rape and war—restores it.[11]

Yourcenar's treatment evokes the anthropological interpretation—the conscious attempt temporarily to become female as a prelude to assuming full masculine status—and at the same time, like the *Achilleid*, explores the relationship between masculine identity, love, and war. The combination produces ambiguous implications that might best be characterized as psycho- (rather than socio) political. Very much concerned with the dynamic of power in the interaction of man with woman, she is equally interested in the interaction of the masculine and feminine within the psyche of the individual (male) human being.[12]

Yourcenar sharpens her psychic focus by substituting boredom and repressed femininity for lust as the motivation for Achilles' acquiescence in his mother's emasculating scheme:

> il venait de sortir du collège des Centaures; fatigué de forêts, il rêvait de chevelures; las de gorges sauvages, il rêvait à des seins. (43)

> [he had just graduated from the Centaurs' high school; tired of forests, he dreamed of heads of hair; tired of savage *gorges*,[13] he dreamed of bosoms.]

The adolescent regards his enclosure in Lycomedes' palace as an opportunity to break with normative relations between male and female, to enter, protected by corset and dress,

> dans ce vaste continent inexploré des Femmes où l'homme n'a pénétré jusqu'ici qu'en vainqueur, et à la lueur des incendies de l'amour. (44)

> [into this vast unexplored continent of women where man had not penetrated until now except as a conqueror, and by the glimmer of love's fires.]

With "jusqu'ici" [until now] Yourcenar raises the possibility of breaking with a past in which men have come to women guided only by passion (that is, *heterosexually*) and only in order to establish relationships of domination. Achilles, deserter from the "camp des mâles," takes "la chance unique d'être autre chose que soi" [the unique chance to be something other than himself] (44).[14] The alternative to dominating the Other, Yourcenar tentatively suggests, is becoming the Other.

Yourcenar, however, raises this hopeful possibility of achieving psychic androgyny and nondominating interaction only to demolish it. Achilles' female companions refuse to believe in "cette fille trop pareille à l'image idéale qu'un homme se fait des femmes" [this girl too close to the ideal image of women created by men] (44) and proceed to introduce him to the "réalités de l'amour" (44). One of the women, Deidamia, becomes his lover; Misandra, a character newly created by Yourcenar whose name means Manhater, becomes his rival for her cousin's love. Interaction in these sexually focused roles, we are told, changes Achilles back into "the hard opposite of a girl" [L'amour de Déidamie, la jalousie de Misandre, refaisaient de lui le dur contraire d'une fille] (44). In its hardness, masculinity is confirmed to be not just different than but rigidly opposed to the female.

With the acceptance of (hetero)sexuality comes hostility. Achilles' lovemaking with Deidamia is described as an "apprentissage des luttes, des râles, des subterfuges" [apprenticeship in struggles, groans, subterfuges] (44)—all words that could equally well describe what he would be experiencing on the battlefield at Troy had he not fled the "camp des mâles." In this context, Yourcenar's use of the traditional analogy between sexual climax and death[15] takes on added significance both political and psychological:

> son évanouissement sur cette tendre victime servait de substitut à une joie plus terrible qu'il ne savait où prendre, dont il ignorait le nom, et qui n'était que la Mort. (44)
>
> [his swooning on this tender victim served as a substitute for a more terrible joy whose provenance and name he did not know, but which was nothing else but Death.]

The substitution of the joy of sex for the "more terrible joy" of death evokes Freud's explanation of sadism as the death instinct directed away from the self and subsequently alloyed with the reproductive instinct.[16] In the context of Achilles' traditional military career, however, the "more terrible joy" for which this sexual "death" currently substitutes is the literal extermination of others.[17] Heterosexual intercourse, Yourcenar implies, both displaces and prevents homicide.[18]

Achilles and Deidamia "se haïssaient comme ceux qui s'aiment" [hated each other like those who love] (45). The rivalrous relationship between Achilles and Misandra is equally paradoxical but paradoxically less negative. In contrast to the fundamental emotion of hate between the sexual lovers, the fundamental emotion between the rivals is love: "Misandre et Achille s'aimaient comme ceux qui se haïssent" [Misandra and Achilles loved each other like those who hate] (45). Yourcenar's language implies that the explanation for this paradox is that Achilles and Déidamie relate to each other as the Other biological sex while the androgynous[19] Misandra and Achilles relate to their own sex in each other: Achilles' "ennemie musclée" becomes "l'équivalent d'un frère"; Misandra's "rival délicieux" functions "comme une espèce de soeur." Since they are like sisters or like brothers, not like brother and sister, the reader infers that Achilles can love only brothers, Misandra can love only sisters. Each creates of the other an equal based on a perception of same-sexedness.[20]

With the failure of Achilles' attempt to become "autre chose que soi," Lycomedes' palace changes from a "feminine shelter" [abri féminin] (44) to a "women's prison" [prison de femmes] (46). But the young man, still in a transitional stage toward full masculinity, does not yet want to escape:

> La gloire, la guerre, vaguement entrevues dans les brumes de l'avenir, lui faisaient l'effet de maîtresses exigeantes dont la possession l'obligerait à trop de crimes: il croyait échapper au fond de cette prison de femmes aux sollicitations de ses victimes futures.[21] (45–46)

> [Glory, war, vaguely glimpsed in the haze of the future, looked to him like demanding mistresses whose possession would compel too many crimes: in the depths of this prison of women he trusted to escape the solicitations of his future victims.]

Now sexually active, Achilles interprets everything in terms of unequal and agonistic sexual relationships. His winning glory in war, a traditional concept introduced here for the first time, becomes the equivalent of an illicit heterosexual relationship [maîtresses] marked by ownership of the female [dont la possession] and criminality [obligerait à . . . crimes]. The word "victimes" links the men he will murder on the battlefield with Deidamia, the "tendre victime" he swooned upon in lieu of experiencing the joy of Death, and it thus reinforces the equivalency of destructive violence and sex. The word "sollicitations" associates the future murder victims with prostitutes, and it also evokes rape victims, who are often accused of having "asked for" their own violation.[22] From Achilles' point of view, his weaker victims are to blame for his use of force—a point of view that suggests an increasingly masculist mind embracing relations of increasing domination. Nonetheless, it is important to note that at this point Achilles judges murder a crime and chooses to avoid it by sharing women's confinement. His choice will change—the women will *become* a prison—as soon as a wholly male love object comes on the scene.

This love object, Patroklos, whom Yourcenar adds to Ulysses' search party, replaces the sword that had traditionally revealed Achilles' identity. In Yourcenar's story, the weapons buried among the dresses and jewelry fail to provoke the expected "masculine" behavior. On the contrary, the powerful femininity of the women's space transforms the tools of war into accessories of female activity: helmets become hair dryers, war belts become sashes, a shield becomes a cradle (47). Patroklos, who is described in hard, metallic imagery throughout,[23] is alone proof against the "charme" of this insidious femininity. He breaks it "comme une épée nue" [like a naked sword] (48); he attracts Achilles to him as a "vivante épée" [living sword] (48); his head, which Achilles clasps, is "dure" [hard] and "ciselée comme le pommeau d'un glaive" [chiseled like the hilt of a sword] (48). This walking phallic symbol clarifies Achilles' masculine consciousness:

> La loyauté, l'amitié, l'héroisme cessaient d'être des mots servant aux hypocrites à travestir leurs âmes: la loyauté, c'étaient ces yeux demeurés limpides devant cet amas de mensonges. . . . (48)

> [Loyalty, friendship, heroism ceased to be words used by hypocrites to costume their souls: loyalty meant these eyes remaining clear before this heap of lies. . . .]

The words loyalty, friendship, and heroism take on a reality they lacked before, as Achilles is suddenly concerned and able to discriminate between truth and falsehood. "Mensonge," the word Yourcenar attached to the title of the story when she separated "Déidamie" from "Penthésilée" and renamed the former "Achille," appears in the text only at this critical juncture. Before Achilles was drawn to Patroklos there was only adventure, escape, and the free use of metaphor. Now, with his swerve toward masculinity, there is a need for the label "lie."[24] Most important, at this moment "la gloire" loses its associations with illicit heterosexual love and criminality and becomes instead the men's "double avenir" [double future] (48). Martial glory and oppositional demarcations (truth/falsehood),[25] Yourcenar implies, are phenomena of an exclusively masculine interaction, or, as we might call it today, male bonding.

Heterosexual relations now become a barrier to the men's bonded future of martial heroism, but they function differently in "Achille" than they did in Statius's *Achilleid*, where Achilles' concern for Deidamia undermined his masculine *virtus* (*Ach.* I.888, 2.29–30). Yourcenar's Achilles' concern is for Patroklos only—the threat posed by Deidamia and normative heterosexual relations is an external one. The unequivocally masculine Patroklos repulses Achilles' spontaneous embrace, embarrassed by what he thinks is the transport of an amorous woman (48), but he responds more positively to Deidamia's more acceptably feminine flirtation—almost drowning, as Yourcenar puts it, in her waves of inviting glances and laces (49). Their stereotypic gender-specific heterosexual behavior enrages Achilles, who, in yet another startling innovation to the traditional story, kills Deidamia and thus puts himself in jeopardy of being arrested or executed for murder instead of going to Troy.

Just before the murder, Yourcenar suggests that women, like men, bear an ideal image of the opposite sex:

Ce garçon vêtu de bronze éclipsait les images nocturnes que Déidamie conservait d'Achille, autant qu'un uniforme primait à ses yeux de femme le pâle éclat d'un corps nu. (49)

[This young man clothed in bronze eclipsed the nocturnal images that Deidamia preserved of Achilles, as much as a uniform surpassed in her woman's eyes the pale splendor of a naked body.]

Earlier, Yourcenar had implied that women mistrust femininity that comes too close to men's ideal image of it. But Achilles' response to Patroklos, when Deidamia's admiration has brought this metallic marvel to his attention, implies that men do not equally mistrust such approximations to women's ideal image of masculinity. Does the text thus suggest that the ideal of masculinity (piercing hardness) is in some sense real, while the ideal of femininity (flowing emotionality) is false? Or does it suggest that men are less aware of the genderization of behavior than are women? Or that for men the ideal is the only reality?

Deidamia's genderized preference for bronze over skin, cultural masculinity over natural humanness, creates a certain sympathy for Achilles, whose more appealing androgyny is stressed by his spontaneous tears of confusion over Patroklos's rejection (48). A less appealing manifestation of his androgyny occurs during his attack on Deidamia: he drops the sword he had seized "maladroitment" and instead strangles her with "ses mains de fille envieuse du succès d'une compagne" [his hands of a young woman jealous of a girlfriend's success] (49), thus employing a feminine enclosing rather than a masculine piercing to extinguish her life.[26] This method of murder suggests that we may want to read the episode as a modern *psychomachia*. Anyone familiar with Greek tragedy is probably aware that strangulation is the preferred means of killing a woman;[27] Jocasta, Antigone, and Phaedra come immediately to mind. What also comes to mind is that these women strangled themselves, committed suicide by hanging. Such associations support interpreting Deidamia's murder as a symbolic murder of the feminine part of Achilles' psyche, or, in Jungian terms, his anima.[28] So too does Yourcenar's description of Achilles' reaction to the murder:

> il se sentait plus séparé que jamais de cette femme qu'il avait essayé, non seulement de posséder, mais d'être: devenue de moins en moins proche à mesure qu'il resserait son étreinte, l'énigme d'être une morte s'était ajoutée chez elle au mystère d'être une femme. (50)

> [he felt himself more separate than ever from this woman whom he had tried not only to possess but to be: becoming less and less close as he tightened his grip, with her the enigma of being dead was added to the mystery of being a woman.]

Note that Achilles feels no guilt, just separation from the feminine and a sense of mystery.

For Yourcenar's Achilles as for Freudian psychology, women remain a "dark continent."[29] For all his optimistic beginning, Achilles has failed in his goal to penetrate the "continent of women" except, like all men, physically as a lover. The social/political ramifications of this psychic failure are clear. The above passage suggests that the dynamic between femininity and death, which remain linked in Achilles' mind, has changed: embracing the feminine no longer substitutes for the criminal murder of others; instead, murder rids one of femininity. Now that Achilles has passed beyond heterosexuality, his interest in avoiding crime has been replaced by the desire to achieve glory in the society of men. We can identify the following progression: (1) monosexual innocence produces boredom; (2) (hetero)sexual initiation and relationships with women give rise to the concept of criminality, specifically vis-à-vis homicide; (3) masculine bonding exempts from criminality homicide (and feminicide) committed in the service of masculine glory.[30]

Having progressed to full masculine identity by killing off Deidamia/femininity, Achilles is desperate to escape Lycomedes' palace, a space that now appears to him to have no exit [les murs où ne s'ouvrait plus aucune issue] (50), that lacks frontage on glory [sans façade sur la gloire] (51), and where movement is circular and equivalent to immobility [ses mille pas autour de ce cadavre composeraient désormais l'immobilité d'Achille] (51).[31] He is helped to leave by his fellow androgyne, rival, and alter ego Misandra, who literally pushes him out the door while she herself, "prisonnière de ses seins" [prisoner of her breasts], remains behind "l'ensevelie vivante" [buried alive] (53).[32] This last phrase closes out the series of images used to describe the palace of Lycomedes in "Achille": shelter to the would-be woman; welcome prison to the male androgyne; grave to the female androgyne, who, despite her masculine hardness and heart,[33] is forbidden exit.

Before Achilles races from the palace, Yourcenar re-creates one last scene from the tradition, the scene in which Achilles is shown his reflection in a shield and is so ashamed of the effeminate image he sees there that he immediately tears off his feminine clothes and reassumes his male persona (Statius, *Ach.* 2). Yourcenar evokes this traditional scene by having Misandra hold out a mirror to Achilles as if she meant to inflict on him "la preuve blême et fardée de sa non-existence de dieu" [the pale and painted proof of his non-existence as a god] (52). But, as in the earlier scene in which the weapons that traditionally revealed Achilles' masculinity were themselves transformed by the overwhelming femininity of the women's room, the unexpected happens:

> Mais sa pâleur de marbre, ses cheveux ondoyants comme la crinière d'un casque, son fard mêlé de pleurs collant à ses joues comme le sang d'un blessé rassemblaient au contraire dans ce cadre étroit tous les futurs aspects d'Achille.... (52)

> [But his marble pallor, his hair waving like the crest of a helmet, his rouge mixed with tears sticking to his cheeks like blood on a wounded man instead assembled in this narrow frame all the future aspects of Achilles.]

In a reversal of the earlier dynamic, the masculine here sweeps all before it: it turns the pale complexion, long hair, and tear-streaked rouge of a housebound woman into the accoutrements and casualties of war.[34] The feminine, which the earlier scene suggested is antiwar by nature, is powerless against such dedicated masculinity.

Having stripped off his belt and scarf but leaving on his "mousselines asphyxiantes" [asphyxiating drapery] to guard against possible fire from the sentries,[35] Achilles leaps onto a Greek ship described as a girl "en qui naissait un dieu" [in whom a god was coming to birth] (53).[36] When he lands on the ship, the sailors worship him as the goddess of Victory, sculptures of which his draped figure no doubt resemble [Les matelots s'agenouillerèrent, s'exclamèrent, saluèrent de jurons émerveillés l'arrivée de la Victoire] (54–55). The last line of the story states that "personne ne se doutait que cette déesse n'était pas femme" [no one doubted that this goddess was female] (55). What conclusions can we draw from these final images of Achilles' deity? In order to answer, we must look at Yourcenar's use of the term "god" elsewhere.

"God" or "divinity" is an image that recurs several times in "Achille." At one point Yourcenar uses it very much as the ancient Greeks would, that is as the source of beauty (specifically Achilles') and as representing the immortality Achilles cannot inherit because of his mortal father (43). But, as in the passages quoted above and again in "Patrocle" (66–67), divinity also represents an acquirable status or state of being. Given this acquirability, it is easy for readers to accept godhood as in some way equivalent to the immortal glory that was Achilles' traditional goal.

Achilles' desire to be a god is mentioned for the first and only time just after he has killed Deidamia and is afraid he has lost "his only chance to be a god" [sa seule chance d'être un dieu] (50). Soon after, the pale and painted face that reflects his indoor existence as a woman is associated by Yourcenar with "his nonexistence as god" [sa non-existence de dieu]. Then, as Misandra brings Achilles to the margins of the palace, Yourcenar terms her "la plus dure de ces deux femmes divines" [the harder of these two divine women] (53). After a brief vision of Achilles' bloody future at Troy [Troie en flammes, et . . . Patrocle vengé], which Misandra considers assuming, Yourcenar continues: "le plus perspicace des dieux ou des bouchers n'aurait pu distinguer ce coeur d'homme de son coeur" [the shrewdest of gods or butchers would not have been able to distinguish this man's heart from her heart] (53). Since "dur" is the characteristic that earlier signified the opposite of female (44) and since both of these "women" with masculine hearts yearn to escape feminine enclosure, it would appear that "divinity" in some way contradicts "female." In combination with Achilles' being described as a *naissant* god upon completing his escape to the Greek navy, these passages create a firm link between masculinity, fighting at Troy, and godhood.

The first confrontation between divinity and femininity in "Achille" portrays women as having an instinctual fear of godhood. When Achilles, in whom "toutes les femmes flairaient un dieu" [all the women scented a god], arrived on the island, fear arrived too "comme une ombre couchée sous les pieds de la beauté" [like a shadow beneath the feet of beauty]. This fear brought by Achilles' incipient godhood transforms the women's world:

Le jour n'était plus le jour, mais le masque blond posé sur les ténèbres; les seins de femmes devenaient des cuirasses sur des gorges de soldats. (42)

[The day was no longer day, but a blond mask set on the shadows; women's breasts became cuirasses on the chests of soldiers.]

As soon as the women smell a god, shadows become their reality, while daylight is denatured to a "masque blond," a phrase that evokes the god Apollo, source of light personified as male arbiter of truth; nurturing breasts become signifiers of danger, either by functioning metaphorically as armor—as protection in a context of male aggression—or by being literally supplanted by armored male chests.

Subsequent events confirm and clarify the women's fear. When Achilles' born-again masculinity/divinity impels him to flee, he achieves "solar" status [bel être solaire] (53) for himself, but he leaves behind, as a direct result of his love for the bronze-clad Patroklos, "une obscurité suffocante, interne, qui n'avait rien à voir avec la nuit" [a suffocating internal obscurity that had nothing to do with night] (50). In other words, unbridled masculinity forcefully asserting its claims to the sun *creates* shadows. Later, the Amazons' story in "Patrocle" teaches that breasts will not deflect masculine force and that the cuirasses that supplant them when women adopt masculine ideals cannot effectively resist it. Pure masculine force represents absolute power and is absolutely to be feared by women, who are inherently alien to it.

What is a source of fear for women is, in Yourcenar's polarized world, the object of desire for men. When Achilles is welcomed by the sailors as the goddess of Victory, the Jungian definition of God comes to mind: God as our own longing to which we pay divine honors.[37] Achilles is the sailors' desire deified: the essential male force that lies behind every martial Victory. Why does no one doubt that "cette déesse" is "femme"? Because, we may feel encouraged to speculate, a sexually charged oppositional male supremacist culture imagines the objects of male desire—*la gloire, la guerre, la Victoire*—as feminine. Despite Thersites' laughter, however, Yourcenar's readers cannot doubt these "goddesses'" fearsome masculinity.

Patrocle/Penthésilée

Patroklos's corpse may be lying on the beach covered with blue flies, or it may be lying next to Achilles in his shadow-strewn tent, or it may be already burned and buried. The only thing that is totally clear about this seemingly ubiquitous corpse is that it and death are the only things that have any reality for Achilles. The living world has disappeared along with "cet ami qui tout à la fois avait rempli le monde et l'avait remplacé" [this friend who both filled the world and replaced it] (63), which is a recasting of the Homeric Achilles' assertion that he "valued Patroklos above all other companions, equal to my own self" (18.81–82).[38] This and several other recastings of Achilles' grief and martial valor distill the *Iliad*'s meditation on mortality into the question of how heroism relates to bodies, specifically dead bodies and female bodies, and thus continue in "Patrocle"/ "Penthésilée" the exploration of masculinity and aggression begun in "Achille"/ "Déidamie."

In "Achille," Achilles' simultaneous embrace of Patroklos and heroism had involved adopting categorical distinctions (between truth and falsehood, male and female). Now, on Yourcenar's Trojan plain, ten years of war have produced a landscape in which both heroism and distinctions have been lost. The story opens in an eternal twilight in which the creations of culture—towers, lipstick—seem to merge with the products of nature—mountains, blood (61–62). People have settled into a "routine rouge ou la paix se mélangeait à la guerre comme la terre à l'eau dans les puantes régions" [red routine, in which peace blended with war like earth with water in stinking swamplands] (62). This "red routine" with its "stinking" absence of demarcation between war and peace represents the third stage of war: an age of heroes mowed down by scythe-chariots[39] and an age of dutiful self-sacrificing soldiers have both passed, and all that is left are suicidal "joueurs" [players] whom the invention of tanks has reduced to the function of "ramparts" (62). This list of ages recapitulates a progression from individualistic Homeric through civic Roman to modern impersonal and overtly meaningless warfare. But the violent anachronisms of the passage that follow—Iphigeneia shot for abetting a mutiny, Paris disfigured by a grenade (63)—discourage readers from nostalgically privileging the first type of warfare; the collapsing of time draws all warfare throughout literary and factual history into one long continuum of War—war for war's sake.

It is in this undistinguished war setting that Yourcenar's martial hero confronts the corporeality of his friend. Like Homer's Achilles, who in his initial grief "lay stretched all his huge length in the dust" (*Iliad* 18.26–27), Yourcenar's Achilles makes his appearance "nu, couché à même la terre comme s'il s'efforçait d'imiter ce cadavre" [naked, lying on the bare earth as if he were trying to imitate this corpse]. The Homeric verse is commonly read as imaging Achilles' own death, as indicating that he is as good as dead already.[40] Yourcenar gives it a new twist: her supine Achilles "se laissait ronger par la vermine de ses souvenirs" [allows himself to be eaten away by the vermin of his memories] (63). Memories—history, movement through time—invade and waste the "self" just as death wastes the body. Subsequent text reveals that Achilles judges the former destruction as worse than the latter; the fixity of death, in fact, comes to be seen as a heroic corrective to the always potential putrefaction of life.

The product of Achilles' deathlike grief in "Patrocle" is the opposite of the indiscriminate homicidal rage that it engenders in the *Iliad*. Yourcenar's Achilles comes to believe that death is "comme un sacre dont seuls les plus purs sont dignes: beaucoup d'hommes se défont, peu d'hommes meurent" [like a sacrament of which only the most pure are worthy: many men cease to exist, few men die] (63). He creates an arbitrary distinction to fill his empty world with meaning, and with the words "sacre," "pur," and "digne" he gives death—a certain kind of military death—abstract cultural value.[41] The unsettling melange of war/peace nature/culture that opened the story is thus partially corrected.

Homer's Achilles vowed to take vengeance on the man who "having killed Patroklos stripped off his armor" (*Iliad* 18.82–83). Yourcenar's Achilles, on the contrary, envies Hector for being the one to have stripped the veils of life from his friend:

> La haine inavouée qui dort au fond de l'amour prédisposait Achille à la tache de sculpteur: il enviait Hector d'avoir achevé ce chef-d'oeuvre; lui seul aurait dû arracher les derniers voiles que la pensée, le geste, le fait même d'être en vie interposait entre eux, pour découvrir Patrocle dans sa sublime nudité de mort. (64)

> [The unavowed hate that lies at the base of love predisposed Achilles to the sculptor's task: he envied Hector for having completed this masterpiece; he was the one who should have stripped off the last veils that thought, gesture, the very fact of being alive had interposed between them, in order to uncover Patroklos in the sublime nudity of death.]

This metaphor of killer as sculptor resonates with imagery in an earlier passage: Achilles' memories of Patroklos had focused on his *pallor*, his *rigid* shoulders, his *cold* hands, his *stone*like heaviness while he slept—"comme si Patrocle n'avait été vivant qu'une ébauche de cadavre" [as if Patroklos living had been nothing but the sketch for a corpse] (64). The sculptor's work, which displaces warm ruddy flesh in favor of putrefaction-proof cold colorless stone, appears to be this story's analogue to Homeric *kleos*, the immortal glory in epic song that was the goal of Iliadic heroism. But how different these products of warfare—the one, a narrative shaping and re-creation of action, the preservation of *existence* in collective memory; the other, a chiseling down to a hard human *essence* that is proof against the most voracious of personal memories.

The aggression of Yourcenar's Achilles and Hector seems to have a single object: the pursuit of death as the pursuit of individuated human essence. When such essence is achieved in the corpse of his world-replacing friend, Yourcenar's Achilles withdraws from the fighting. No story of Achilles would be complete without this withdrawal: in the *Iliad* it occurs for the sake of heroic "honor"; in the Middle Ages it is motivated by love for an enemy princess; in Yourcenar's strikingly different version, Achilles refuses to kill further "pour ne pas susciter à Patrocle des rivaux d'outre-tombe" [in order not to create rivals for Patroklos beyond the tomb] (64–65). In his desire to maintain the distinctiveness of the dead man, Achilles encloses himself in his death [s'enfermait dans ce mort][42] and loses all consciousness of living beings except as phantoms [les vivants ne se montraient à lui que sous forme de fantômes] (65). He refuses, that is, to acknowledge the flesh of existence.

Fleshly beings eventually challenge Achilles' essentialist reality, force his gaze away from the ideas of purity, distinctiveness, and death that now constitute his world. Yourcenar employs two important Homeric motifs, heroic fire and Achilles' battle with the river, to depict this challenge, opposing the immovable, unchanging essence that is the goal of warfare/masculinity with a flowing, shape-changing existence that is eventually associated with femininity.

As Cedric Whitman has so ably demonstrated, in the *Iliad* fire is associated with "death, sacrifice, the fall of Troy . . . rage, destruction, heroic valor, and heroic honor" (143, 132); it becomes a symbol particularly of Achilles' wrathful prowess.[43] Water, specifically river water, is associated in the River Fight (*Iliad* 21.233–380) with the protection of Troy and, in a rare passage that looks beyond the war to the future Trojan landscape, with the obliteration of the Achaean war camp (*Iliad* 12.15–33). Achilles, in the scene in which he throws Lykaon's body into the river, sees it as a means to deny a dead warrior a funeral (*Iliad* 21.122–27), and so does his retaliating enemy, the river Xanthos, who threatens to "hide Achilles in mud" and "wrap him in sand" so that the Greeks won't be able to find his bones and give him a tomb (*Iliad* 21.318–24). Achilles is saved from drowning in Xanthos's great crest of blood-purple water by Hephaistos, god of Fire, who burns first the corpses on the plain and then the river himself (*Iliad* 21.324–76). The river under control, Achilles continues his rampage against the Trojans and is himself again associated with destructive fire in a simile that compares him to the wrath of the gods burning a city (*Iliad* 21.522–25). Homeric fire, then, images death and the martial heroism that immortalizes one's name in song or tomb; water images both nonheroic life and obliterating change.

Yourcenar transforms the fire-water imagery and the details of this scene, maintaining the fundamental opposition between life and death, obliterating change and immortalizing destruction, but adding a further polarity between feminine and masculine. While Achilles is enclosed in death, there arises from the earth "une humidité traîtresse" [a traitorous dampness] (65). This dampness is first associated with marching feet and loosening earth. Next we read: "les deux camps[44] réconciliés luttaient avec le fleuve s'efforçant de noyer l'homme: Achille pâle entra dans ce soir de fin de monde" [the two camps reconciled struggled against the river that was attempting to harm man: pale Achilles entered into this cataclysmic night] (65). Mysteriously, both Greek and Trojan armies seem to be united in opposition to this manhating river. Achilles' rationale for opposing it is given at length:

> Loin de voir dans les vivants les précaires rescapés d'un raz-de-mort menaçant toujours, c'étaient les morts maintenant qui lui paraissaient submergés par l'immonde déluge des vivants. Contre l'eau mouvante, animée, informe, Achille défendait les pierres et le ciment qui servent à faire des tombes. (65)

> [Far from seeing the living as precarious escapees from an always menacing wave of death, now it was the dead who appeared to him to be overwhelmed by the vile flood of the living. Against the moving, animate shapeless water, Achilles defended the stones and cement that served to make tombs.]

For Achilles, water is exclusively an image of life, nonindividuated and therefore "vile" life. He joins battle against what is "moving, animate, shapeless" on behalf of what is fixed, lifeless, and shaped ["pierres," "ciment," "tombes"]. The voice of Homer in the background suggests further that this water not only lacks shape but deprives of shape, obliterates.

As Achilles joins battle against "l'immonde déluge" of life, he is joined imagistically with fire in a passage that again has its roots in Homer:

> Quand l'incendie descendu des forêts de l'Ida vint jusque dans le port lécher le ventre des navires, Achille prit contre les troncs, les mâts, les voiles insolemment fragiles, le parti du feu qui ne craint pas d'embrasser les morts sur le lit de bois de buchers. (66)
>
> [When the conflagration came down from Ida's forests all the way to the port to lick the belly of the ships, Achilles took the part of fire against the trunks, masts, insolently fragile sails: fire that doesn't fear to embrace the dead on the bed of their wooden biers.]

Achilles' taking "le parti du feu" creates a striking reversal of his behavior in *Iliad* 16, where the sight of fire on the ships makes him anxious "lest there no longer be means of fleeing" (127–29). A reader's consciousness of this reversal highlights the fact that Achilles' heroic fire—which is a constant in both works—is here fighting not other fire but water and the organic matter (trunks, masts, sails) that make survival possible. If, as was suggested earlier, all soldiers are united against this common enemy [le fleuve s'efforçant de noyer l'homme], then we may read this imagery as implying that the true object of war is, simply, the eradication of life.[45] But we must go further than this simple antiwar inference, for, as this passage begins to make clear, "l'homme" that was the object of the river's enmity does not represent generic humanity. The sexual connotations of "embrasser . . . sur le lit" [embrace . . . on the bed] suggest that just as sex had earlier substituted for homicide, now homicide—the fire-embraced corpse—substitutes for sex, and they remind the reader that the warrior has rejected the bisexual bed of love in favor of the monosexual field of war. When the implicitly rejected female emerges from the water in the next passage, the reader may substitute "masculine behavior" for "war" and infer that it is *masculinity* that is fundamentally opposed to life.[46]

The maleficent water takes shape as "alien peoples" pouring "out of Asia like rivers" [D'étranges peuplades débouchaient de l'Asie comme des fleuves] (66). Achilles slaughters the first flowing aliens like animals "sans même y reconnaître des linéaments humains" [without even recognizing their human lineaments] (66). Then come the Amazons, "une inondation de seins" [an inundation of breasts], whose closeness to animality in the soldiers' minds is signified by their exciting "odor of naked fleece" [l'armée frémissait à cette odeur de toisons nues] (66). The men's enemy is unindividuated bodies, fluid and animal and female, whose only distinguishing mark is the breast, the source and symbol of the most basic life-nurturing flow.[47]

Achilles' enmity now becomes quite specifically misogynistic, hinging on a familiar nature/culture dichotomy which is here expressed as (feminine) instinct versus (masculine) choice:

> Toute sa vie, les femmes avaient représenté pour Achille la part instinctive du malheur, celle dont il n'avait pas choisi la forme, qu'il devait subir, ne pouvait accepter. (66)

> [All his life women had represented for Achilles the instinctive part of unhappiness, that whose form he did not choose, which he had to endure but could not accept.]

Women are blamed for inhibition of heroism (Thetis), failure of understanding (Lycomedes' daughters), and the humiliation of love (Briseis, 66–67). Here again, awareness of how Yourcenar is transforming Homer highlights the masculinist workings of her nature/culture dichotomy. In the *Iliad*, Achilles lamented that Thetis did not marry an immortal, but Peleus a mortal, "for you [Thetis] will suffer great grief for your dead son" (*Iliad* 18.86–89). The Homeric passage is ambiguous: we can interpret Achilles' words either as genuine sympathy for the immanent suffering of his mother or as a complaint against the gods who forced her *(émbalon)* to a mortal bed and thereby made him, her son, mortal instead of immortal.[48] Yourcenar's reworking of this lament takes the second interpretation but turns it inside out: Achilles' complaint is against his mother, not the gods, and against being half *immortal*, not half mortal:

> Il reprochait à sa mère d'avoir fait de lui un métis à mi-chemin entre le dieu et l'homme, lui ôtant ainsi la moitié du mérite qu'ont les hommes à se faire dieux. (66–67)

> [He reproached his mother for having made him a half-cast midway between god and man, thereby depriving him of half the merit men get by making themselves gods.]

Thetis has given him [fait de lui] something that is valuable only if self-made [se faire]; her natural gift (divine genes) is negative because it diminishes the scope of culture (that is, men's struggle to surpass their nature). Achilles' second complaint against her is related: she ought not to have bathed him in the Styx, for heroism consists in being vulnerable: "Il lui gardait rancune de l'avoir tout enfant mené aux bains de Styx pour immuniser contre la peur, comme si l'héroisme ne consistait pas à être vulnérable" [He bore a grudge against her for having brought him as an infant to the Stygian baths to immunize him against fear, as if heroism didn't require vulnerability] (67). Her gift of invulnerability deprives him of the possibility of risk and therefore of choice. Heroism, a cultural construct like the godhood that is its goal, involves competing with nature: with the mortality of the body, the instinct to live, the fear of dying. We may note that Thetis's counterheroic baby-bathing fits perfectly into a pattern of oppositional water/fire life/death imagery, as does the pun on *mère* and *mer* that was consciously meant to evoke "le double aspect de Thetis" (preface to *Feux*, 23). Achilles' complaints mark mothering, water, instinct, love, and natural divinity as negative; merit, fear, heroism, vulnerability, humiliation, and achieved divinity as positive.[49]

Yourcenar here shifts from the male battles of the *Iliad* to the male-female battle between Achilles and the Amazons, whose fullest ancient narrations (in Quintus of Smyrna's *Posthomerica* and "Dictys's" *Ephemeris*) are also marked by misogyny.[50] Representatives of everything negative in Achilles' life, Yourcenar's Amazons are attacked and die specifically as women: through with attempting to understand the "mystery of being a woman" ("Achille," 50), Achilles hacks through the unsolvable puzzle of his opponents' female innards [trancha des noeuds gordiens de viscères]; the process of their dying is described as "giving birth" through their newly opened flesh [enfantant la mort par la brèche des blessures]. They end as a heap of "pulpe nue" [naked pulp] (67). There is nothing "pure," nothing "sacramental" about these female deaths. The mushy organic heap at the end of the river is the diametric opposite of the "sculpture" in Achilles' tent.

There is one female who is as hard and inorganic as a hero: Penthesileia, the Amazon queen. She is portrayed as androgynous like the character Misandra in "Achille," who, despite her masculine heart, was entombed in the palace, a prisoner of her breasts (53). Penthesileia is not imprisoned by her breasts, but she is in a sense defined by them: she alone of the Amazons has "consented" to cut one off [Seule d'entre ses compagnes, elle avait consenti à se faire couper le sein] (68).[51] The verb *consentir* provokes the question, who or what proposed/demanded this surgery?[52] We are not given an explicit answer, but one is suggested by Yourcenar's subsequent labeling of the "mutilated" chest as "divine": "mais cette mutilation n'était qu'a peine sensible sur cette gorge de dieu" [but this mutilation was hardly perceptible on her godlike chest] (68). Divinity was associated with butchers (53) and masculinity in "Achille"; here, consistently, divinity makes the "mutilation" of the female body "hardly perceptible"—divinity, that is, provides cover/justification for those who forcefully eradicate the soft feminine part, who suppress the female in order to pursue male ideality.

The metal armor this "Furie minerale" wears has a similar function. "Hard" [dur noyau] (67) like her fellow divinities Misandra and Achilles, Penthesileia conceals her femininity under armor in order to prevent the softening [qu'on ne s'attendrit pas] of her opponents (67). "Masquée d'or" [masked in gold], with hair "d'or" and "de l'or" sounding in her pure voice (68), she is on the outside as metallic as the phallic Patroklos in "Achille." Her armor, however, makes her no more successful at becoming the Other than Achilles' dress had made him. Just as swordlike Patroklos had broken the "charme" of femininity in Lycomedes' palace, Achilles' spear "comme pour rompre un charme" breaks through to the feminine body behind the "pur soldat,"[53] subjecting her to a "viol de fer" [iron rape] (69) that forcefully reimposes her female status and brings the sexual imagery of the two stories full circle.[54]

"Patrocle's" story of this godlike soldierwoman felled by an iron rape adds a further dimension to the connection between masculinity, aggression, and godhood established in "Achille." Both stories associate divinity with domination of the feminine in the self (body or psyche) with domination of the female in society. Here Yourcenar suggests that a woman's identification with masculine ideals can mutilate her femininity but cannot eradicate it. She can therefore achieve only lesser divinity (a Fury) and must eventually fall to the superior force of undiluted masculinity.

It was traditional for Achilles to fall in love with the dead Amazon queen upon seeing the beautiful face under the helmet. In Quintus of Smyrna's version, Penthesileia achieved a kind of equality with Patroklos:

> The son of Peleus grieved greatly as he
> looked on the strong girl's loveliness in the dust;
> wherefore baneful sorrow ate away his heart,
> sorrow as great as before when Patroklos was killed.
> (*Posthomerica* 718–21)

Quintus's equivalency in grief carries no thematic weight; Achilles' instantaneous sorrow is typical of the universal superficiality of the *Posthomerica*'s characters and tends only to trivialize the hero's feeling for Patroklos. Yourcenar adopts Quintus's version to conclude her own story, but rewrites it to produce yet another profoundly pessimistic suggestion about male-female relations.

It is not discovered beauty that provokes sorrow in Yourcenar's Achilles; it is the revelation that the face behind the metal mask has itself become a mask:

> La visière levée découvrit, au lieu d'un visage, un masque aux yeux aveugles que les baisers n'atteignaient plus. Achille sanglotait, soutenait la tête de cette victime digne d'être un ami. C'était le seul être au monde qui ressemblait à Patrocle. (69)

> [The raised visor discovered, instead of a face, a mask with blind eyes that kisses no longer reached. Achilles sobbed, holding the head of this victim worthy of being a friend. It was the only being in the world who resembled Patroklos.]

The head of the woman who died fighting has attained a fixity that associates her both with the "masque blond" of divinely masculinized day in "Achille" and with the sculptured male essence of Patroklos. This implied shift from feminine existence to masculine essence, which is apparently what leads Achilles to accord Penthesileia a measure of recognition, is reinforced by the gendered nouns in the last two sentences: *victime* is naturally and appropriately feminine, but *ami*, which could have been written as feminine to match the sex of the character to which it refers, is masculine. Yourcenar's choice of masculine gender emphasizes a generic rather than personal quality of friendship, a fixed concept rather than a changeable relationship. It also, by contrast with Quintus, whose Achilles felt pain because he had killed her instead of *marrying* her (*Posthomerica* 1.671–72), emphasizes the nonsexual nature of the bond Achilles is acknowledging: the object of desire, as we saw at the end of "Achille," is seen as female; the rival, the partner in competition (Misandra, Patroklos) is seen as male. In the story's last sentence, *être*, which linked the feminine and masculine nouns in the preceding sentence, becomes a masculine substantive, "le seul être," thus making the shift in gender and abstraction permanent. The *femme* behind the armor is no longer available to be raped; she has disappeared for good into the fixed ideality of masculine culture. It is now that "she" can be mourned.

The shift from feminine to masculine, from personal to abstract, in the last paragraph of "Patrocle" occurs also in the naming of the stories between their original publication and their inclusion in *Feux*. Not only do masculine names replace the female ones that subtitled the two halves of "Deux amours d'Achille," but abstract nouns are attached: *le mensonge* and *le destin*.[55] Do these abstractions add anything to our interpretation? Yes: ambiguity. Readers are forced to ask if "lie" applies to the attempt to become the Other or whether it calls into question masculine claims to Apolline categories. Is it "destiny" to recognize the self in the Other only when it is too late? Or is a man "destined" to remake the Other into the self (that is, kill her) before he can love? Yourcenar gives no answers to these questions, but she does suggest that the failure of androgyny, the inability of the male to understand and value the female components of the human psyche and of society, his devaluing of the real in favor of the ideal, is the cause of individual and global tragedy.

Fourteen years after Natalie Clifford Barney declared that "il faut libérer l'homme de l'homme" (*Pensées*, 8), Yourcenar seems in "Achille" and "Patrocle" to ask if it is indeed possible "to liberate man from man." Her narrative, however, shifts the ground ever so slightly from Barney's essentialist formulation. Achilles the biological male who seeks genuinely to participate in femaleness fails for three reasons: first, he becomes too stereotypically feminine to be believed; second, his natural masculine body plus natural tears are rejected in favor of cultural masculinity represented by the metallic overlay on Patroklos's body, an overlay that seems to promise that the enclosed male self will never weep like a woman;[56] third, the women refuse to accept that Achilles' quest to understand femaleness is genuine. This last, at least, seems to be the import of Achilles' complaining that Deidamia and Misandra had failed to recognize that his "travesti" [masquerade] was "le contraire d'un déguisement" [the opposite of a disguise] (67).[57] Although Thetis, the mother, attempts to thwart Achilles' entrance into cultural masculinity by sequestering him in female space and by overendowing him so that he merely *is* and cannot create a story about *becoming* powerful, other women appear to be complicit in forcing *l'homme* upon *l'homme*. The result of this apparent female complicity is not that the reader joins Achilles in blaming women, but a hint that gender is socially constructed at its core: that *masculinité* (with an origin, though not an end, in heterosexuality) is being imposed upon *l'homme* from all sides [Il faut libérer l'homme de la masculinité]. Yourcenar depicts Achilles as creating his adult identity by moving ever more deeply into culture: moving his male body through feminine culture without being enabled to adopt it—functioning only as biological male in female costume—he achieves entry into culture only through the passionate embrace of ultramasculinity, which does not, ultimately, make him happy. Achilles' problem is not, as Poignault believes, that Achilles cannot find a firm identity; the problem is that the only active identity open to him is masculine.

As I said in the beginning, Yourcenar did not set out to write a feminist critique of power relations and cultural ideals. Nonetheless, the critique is there, affirming an involvement with her political and intellectual world that was passionate, discerning, and pessimistic. She focuses on the individual psyche, but the violence she finds there reverberates from and into society. Her concentration on the mental health of the individual (male) human being may thus be seen as an attack on the authoritarian fascism that was beginning to disquiet many in Europe.[58] But her acceptance of the martial bipolar discourse that has dominated psychoanalytic as well as political and cultural theory[59] leads her to impasse, restricts her from imagining any alternatives to the conflictive male-female relations she depicts. In the world of "Achille" and "Patrocle," when the male psyche embraces the female, it cannot help but squeeze it to death. With Yourcenar, as with many other unconsciously feminist women writers, we must content ourselves with the negative vision, with one more agonized "report from the battlefield of sexual politics."[60]

NOTES

This essay is a revised version of "Achilles on the Field of Sexual Politics," *LIT* 2 (1991): 201–20.

1. Written in 1935 and published in 1936. The title of this collection of nine stories and *pensées* was originally the title of the *pensées* published separately in 1935: "Feux," *Revue de France* 4 (1935): 491–98.

2. *Feux* (Paris: Gallimard, 1974), 26. All page references will be to this most recent edition. All translations are my own unless otherwise noted. *Feux* has been translated into English by Dori Katz with the collaboration of Yourcenar (*Fires*, New York: Farrar, Straus and Giroux, 1981), but the reader should be warned that there are places where the English version differs significantly from the French. Let the reader also be warned that I do not intend to do a biographical reading, which Josyane Savigneau's wonderful biography, *Marguerite Yourcenar: L'Invention d'une vie* (Paris: Gallimard, 1990)—*Marguerite Yourcenar: Inventing a Life*, trans. Joan E. Howard (Chicago: University of Chicago Press, 1993), makes possible and tempting to do. Let it suffice to say that with André Fraigneau, the object of her passion, she experienced an intimate encounter with misogyny for perhaps the first time (see Savigneau, *L'Invention*, 112–13—*Inventing*, 102). Those interested in a biographical reading might enjoy Michèle Sarde, *Vous Marguerite Yourcenar. La passion et ses masques* (Paris: Robert Laffont, 1995), 162–85, and E. Real, ed. *M. Yourcenar. Biographie et Autobiographie* (Valencia: Universidad de Valencia, 1988).

3. "The Thieves of Language: Women Poets and Revisionist Mythmaking," *Signs* 8 (1982): 68–90.

4. Marguerite Yourcenar, *Les yeux ouverts. Entretiens avec Matthieu Galey* (Paris: Centurion, 1980), 92–93. Yourcenar, *With Open Eyes*, 67. She intensifies

the sense of eternity she sought by fusing past and present with striking anachronisms: for example, Thetis, Achilles' prescient goddess mother, sees in the eyes of Jupiter a *film* of Achilles' death (42); Paris is disfigured by a *grenade* (63). Colette Gaudin comments that "Le récit mythique, ou plutôt la somme de ses variantes, est pour elle comme un condensé des siècles qui s'échelonnent entre l'antiquité homérique et nous." [The mythical tale, or rather the sum of its variants, represents for her a condensed version of the centuries as they spread themselves out between Homeric antiquity and ourselves.] (*Marguerite Yourcenar à la surface du temps* [Amsterdam: Editions Rodopi BV, 1994], 72). Later she says that "Le mythe permet de parler de différence sexuelle tout autrement que par ce 'petit réalisme psychologique' pour lequel Yourcenar n'a pas que mépris. [Mythe allows one to speak about sexual difference other than by the "diminished psychological realism" for which Yourcenar had only contempt.] (*Th. II*, 103) La mésentente des sexes, leur guerre, ne peut être représentée que par les drames presque sacrés des époux divins ou héroiques" [The misunderstanding between the sexes, their war, can only be represented by the nearly sacred dramas of divine or heroic spouses] (73).

5. Joan Howard has demonstrated through analyses of *Qui n'a pas son Minotaure?* and *Le mystère d'Alceste* that Yourcenar often appropriated exemplary myths "in the service not of revalorization but rather of demythification," that is, to divest them of their power (*From Violence to Vision: Sacrifice in the Works of Marguerite Yourcenar* [Southern Illinois University Press, 1992], chapters 2 and 3, 9–75).

6. "Deux amours d'Achille" was published in *Mercure de France* 263 (1935): 118–27. Aside from the loss of the subtitles (and consequent shift of emphasis in the second part from Penthesileia to Patroklos) there are few major alterations. Changes other than punctuation will be indicated in footnotes.

7. Yourcenar's characters are, as she says in the preface, derived more from other poets, painters, and sculptors from the Epic Cycle to modern times (11) than from Homer. Examples that spring to mind are archaic Greek vase paintings of Achilles killing Penthesileia or carrying her body, and two third-century Roman tombs in the Louvre, one depicting Achilles and Deidamia, the other, Greeks slaughtering Amazons. For a thorough and systematic account of the classical literary sources see Rémy Poignault, *L'Antiquité dans l'oeuvre de Marguerite Yourcenar. Littérature, mythe et histoire* (Brussels: Latomus, Revue d'études Latines, 1995), 29–68, a work published after the original version of this article appeared. An earlier article by Harry C. Rutledge, "Marguerite Yourcenar: The Classicism of *Feux* and *Mémoires d'Hadrien*," *Classical and Modern Literature* 4, no. 2 (winter 1984): 87–99, does little more than note the vitality of the classical tradition and does not back up his problematic assertion that "her characterizations are . . . uncannily 'right' as far as classical myth and history are concerned" (91).

8. 1935 was the year Mussolini invaded Ethiopia. The stories were written before the invasion, but as Yourcenar says in *Les yeux ouverts*, "Le sentiment du danger, accru aussi par la guerre d'Espagne, et par ce que je savais des dessous du fascisme italien, était très fort chez moi en ce temps-là" [In those days I had a very strong feeling of imminent danger, heightened by the war in Spain and by what I knew of the underside of Italian fascism (*With Open Eyes*, 88)] (118). In the preface to *Feux* she says that the balletlike duel between Achilles and Penthesileia in "Patrocle" reflected the "atmosphère de jeux angoissés" of the times (16–17).

9. Recognized as such by Jean Blot, who calls them "les plus beaux" (*Margue-

rite Yourcenar [Paris: Éditions Seghers, 1971], 161) but fails to give them any sort of detailed analysis. Recent years have seen an increasing number of interesting articles on gender issues in Yourcenar, though none focuses on *Feux*. Judith L. Johnston's excellent analysis of *Coup de grâce* in "Marguerite Yourcenar's Sexual Politics in Fiction, 1939," in *Faith of a (Woman) Writer*, ed. A. Kessler-Harris and W. McBrien (New York: Greenwood Press, 1988), 221–28, finds in the 1939 *Coup de grâce* a "connection between sexuality, violence, and entrapment" (227) that is similar to what I find in the more lyrical *Feux*. Linda K. Stillman mines *Feux* for evidence of repressed feminine discourse and figurative matricides, but does not analyze any of the stories as a whole ["Marguerite Yourcenar and the Phallacy of Indifference" *Studies in 20th Century Literature* 9.2 (1985): 261–77].

10. See, for example, Pierre Vidal-Naquet, *The Black Hunter: Forms of Thought and Forms of Society in the Greek World*, trans. A. Szegedy-Maszak (Baltimore: Johns Hopkins University Press, 1986), 163–64; Marie Delcourt, *Hermaphrodite: Mythes et Rites de la bisexualité dans l'antiquité classique* (Paris: Presses Universitaires de France, 1958), 9–10; H. Jeanmaire, *Couroi et Courètes: Essai sur l'éducation spartiate et les rites d'adolescence dans l'Antiquité hellénique* (Lille-Paris: Bibliothèque Universitaire, 1939) and Bernard Sargent, *Homosexuality in Greek Myth*, trans. A. Goldhammer (Boston: Beacon Press, 1986), 253. Vidal-Naquet thinks that antithesis per se rather than specific content is the most important aspect of initiatory ritual. Delcourt believes, building on Jeanmaire's positive interpretation, that cross-sex dressing promoted health and strength in the budding adult by uniting the masculine and feminine principles (22).

11. See K. C. King, *Achilles: Paradigms of the War Hero from Homer to the Middle Ages* (Berkeley and Los Angeles: University of California Press, 1987), 131–33, 181–84.

12. Now is perhaps the time to mention Andreas Embeirikos, who was Yourcenar's traveling companion during the time she was writing *Feux* (Savigneau, *L'invention*, 109–10, *Inventing*, 99–100). A surrealist poet and internationally recognized intellectual, Embeirikos had studied psychoanalysis in Paris in the late 1920s before meeting Yourcenar in Greece. In 1935 he was a practicing psychoanalyst in Athens, and it is difficult to imagine that Freud, Jung, and psychoanalytic theory were not among the topics these two intellectual artists discussed. Artemis Leontis has written a fascinating article about this man's poetic oeuvre in which she demonstrates through his poetry of 1945 how his emancipatory agenda was undermined by essentialist (and ultimately sexist) thinking. She states: "By repeatedly asserting man's power over unruly feminized elements such as water and female functions such as discharge and flow, he represents the controlling element or persona as masculine, and is finally unable to give up the traditional image of the male concerned with mastery and control" ("Surrealist Poetics of Identity and Andreas Embeirikos's Defense of Man," *Modern Greek Studies Yearbook* 6 [1990]: 317). The relevance of Embeirikos's failure to the two stories I am analyzing here will shortly become evident; for now I wish to emphasize that Freud and Jung should be part of the reader's interpretive context.

13. Untranslatable pun: *gorge* = throat, chest, gorge; Katz translates "hard chests."

14. Blot (170) thinks this idea is a logical absurdity since one can never be other than oneself, but it is more fruitful to go beyond the literal "oneself" and to interpret in terms of psychoanalytic or political categories: ego and external world, Self and Other, us and them. Politically, "Self" could consist of a gendered self, or identity, that one could consciously abandon in favor of the Other (gender). In Jungian

terms, which Blot argues penetrate Yourcenar's work (85), being "something other than oneself" would simply mean embracing and bringing to consciousness one's anima/animus.

15. Interestingly, just as modern culture uses martial terms as metaphors for sexual interaction, Homeric Greek used erotic terms as metaphors for one-on-one battle encounters (see Hélène Monsacré, *Les larmes d'Achille: le héros, la femme et la souffrance dans la poésie d'Homère* (Paris: Allein Michel, 1984), 63–77).

16. "Is it not plausible to suppose that this sadism is in fact a death instinct which, under the influence of the narcissistic libido, has been forced away from the ego and has consequently only emerged in relation to the object? It now enters the service of the sexual function . . . it takes on, for the purposes of reproduction, the function of overpowering the sexual object to the extent necessary for carrying out the sexual act." *Beyond the Pleasure Principle*, trans. James Strachey (New York: Liverwright Publishing, 1961), 48. See also *Civilization and Its Discontents*, trans. James Strachey (New York: W. W. Norton, 1962), 66.

17. In Freudian terminology, Achilles' erotic behavior substitutes for indulging the "instinct of destruction," which fulfills the ego's "old wishes for omnipotence" (*Civilization and Its Discontents*, 68).

18. Rémy Poignault interprets somewhat differently, seeing the "petite mort" as *prefiguring* the greater pleasure of "Mort majuscule" (*L'Antiquité dans l'oeuvre de Marguerite Yourcenar*, 38).

19. Achilles and Misandra are both portrayed as androgynous characters: Achilles because of his feminine dress, his attempt to truly enter women's world, and his weeping in frustrated embarassment over Patroklos's rejection later in the story. Misandra possesses several masculine characteristics: muscles (45), large hands (46, 47), hardness (53), and a man's heart (53). Because of the size of her hands, her short hair, and her behavior, it is Misandra rather than Achilles that Yourcenar's Ulysses (as opposed to Statius's) suspects of being a disguised man.

20. It is curious to compare a passage in *Pensées d'une Amazon* (Paris: Émile-Paul Frères, éditeurs, 1921) by lesbian writer Natalie Clifford Barney, Yourcenar's friend, who seems also to feel that men and women relate best to their own gender: "Que tous ceux, purifiés par le feu, s'approchent de nos foyers solitaires: nous serons mieux que l'épouse, la mère ou la soeur d'un homme, nous serons le frère féminin de l'homme" [As for those men who, purified by fire, come singly to our hearths, we will be better than wife, mother, or sister, we will be his female brother] (9). Even though Yourcenar did not attend Barney's salons, she would have read and been influenced by her work. For their friendship, see Savigneau passim and Erin G. Carlston, *Thinking Fascism: Sapphic Modernism and Fascist Modernity* (Stanford: Stanford University Press, 1998), 88.

21. The original text in "Deux amours" reads: "La gloire . . . lui apparaissaient maintenant comme des maitresses dont la possession. . . ." (120).

22. We must remember that tradition made Achilles begin his love affair with Deidamia by violently raping her. Here is the relevant passage in Ovid's *Ars Amatoria* [I.698–700], which puts an unfortunately still prevalent view of the rape victim most succinctly:

> She learned he was a man to her disgrace
> By force indeed was she conquered (thus we must believe);
> She wished, however, to be conquered by force.
> [haec illum stupro comperit esse virum.
> viribus illa quidem victa est (ita credere oportet),
> sed voluit vinci viribus illa tamen.]

23. In addition to the sword imagery discussed below, he is introduced as shaking hands in iron gloves (47) and is later described as clothed in bronze (49). We

might say that Patrocle represents cultural masculinity as opposed to the natural masculinity of life with Cheiron ("forêts," "gorges sauvages," 43) and the cultural femininity of life on the island *(broderie)*.

24. See Cary Nelson's remarks on phallocentric denotative "law" and female connotative "play" in "Envoys of Otherness: Difference and Continuity in Feminist Discourse," *For Alma Mater: Theory and Practice in Feminist Scholarship* (Champaign-Urbana: University of Illinois Press, 1985), 106–7.

25. Today, after Derrida, we would call this kind of conceptualization "logocentric."

26. C. M. T. Wright comments: "The jealous Achille rejects the 'masculine' weapon . . . in favour of 'feminine' strangulation" [no citation of Loraux]. Wright correlates this strangulation with "the female's association with strong repression or *suffocation* of development and freedom of action." " 'Reading Between the Lines': A Study of *Alexis, Dernier du Rêve, Coup de Grâce*, and *Feux* by Marguerite Yourcenar" (Diss., University of Reading, 1987), 215. Wright's dissertation, which I was unable to acquire until after I published the first version of this article, gives a lively and intelligent analysis of *Feux* that outlines the gender antagonism and elucidates especially well its antiwar message.

27. Nicole Loraux, *Façons tragiques de tuer une femme* (Paris: Hachette, 1985)—*Tragic Ways of Killing a Woman*, trans. A. Forster (Cambridge: Harvard University Press, 1987).

28. See C. F. Farrell and E. R. Farrell, "Marguerite Yourcenar's *Feux*," *Kentucky Romance Quarterly, 29* (1982) 27. These two authors have explored the artistic structure of *Feux* and the use of Jungian symbolism in both their article: "Marguerite Yourcenar's *Feux*: Structure and Meaning," *Kentucky Romance Quarterly* 29 (1982): 25–35, and their book: *Marguerite Yourcenar in Counterpoint* (Lanham, MD: University Press of America, 1983).

29. Sigmund Freud, "Question of Lay Analysis," *Standard Edition* 20 (1926): 179–258.

30. Wright interprets Achilles' action and response to killing Deidamia as showing that "the heroic consciousness is emotionally inadequate" (216). Later, Wright coins the phrase "moral asphyxiation" and comments: "Achilles is no momentary madman inspired by jealous fury, but a killer who tightens not loosens his grip" [à mesure qu'il resserrait son étreint] (50) (216). We should note, too, that Yourcenar has purified her masculine-feminine dynamic by eliminating the socially useful child that was traditionally produced by the sexual liaison. Ovid, too, ignored the baby, who was not apt for his professed message that men should lightheartedly take what they want from women even if the latter protest (*Ars Amatoria* I.689–706).

31. Compare discussions of the circle as a symbol of imprisonment in Yourcenar's work by Christiane Papadopoulos, *L'Expression du temps dans l'oeuvre romanesque et autobiographique de Marguerite Yourcenar* (New York: Peter Lang, 1988), 162–68, and Kajsa Andersson, *Le "Don sombre": Le thème de la mort dans quatre romans de Marguerite Yourcenar* (Uppsala: Acta Universitatis Upsaliensis, 1989), 20–22.

32. Wright comments perceptively: "As in *Alexis*, and as often in Gide, the decline of the woman is a prerequisite of the rise of the male. The contrast between the moribundity of the female and the vitality of the male is brought out strikingly: the coffin-like door closing on 'l'ensevelie vivante' is the release-mechanism that releases the caged male." (217)

33. Yourcenar gives her a "rire dur" (52); calls her "la plus dure" of the pair

formed by Achilles and her (53); and declares that not even the most perceptive of gods or butchers would have been able to distinguish Achilles' "coeur d'homme" from her heart (53).

34. In the first version of the story Yourcenar has Achilles subsequently leap into the Greek ship brandishing the mirror like a half-clad Truth: "brandissant son miroir dans le geste d'une Vérité qui ne serait qu'à moitié nue" ("Déidamie," 123).

35. In the first version of the story, he does this because he fears that Misandra's devotion will turn to disgust if she sees him naked ("Déidamie," 122). Yourcenar originally thus strengthened her earlier implication that Misandra and Achilles love only the self in the other.

36. In the first version of the story, Achilles arrives on the ship "pareil en tout à l'image idéale qu'une fille se fait d'un dieu" [identical to a girl's ideal image of a god] ("Déidamie," 123). This creates a parallel with the ironclad Patroklos, who represents the ideal of masculinity to Deidamia. Since the sailors too think Achilles is a god, this earlier version indicates that the ideals of masculinity and divinity are shared by male and female alike, while the ideal of femininity is strictly a male affair.

37. Carl J. Jung, *Psychology of the Unconscious*, trans. B. M. Hinkle (New York: Dodd, Mead, 1961), I.4, 96.

38. This sentiment also recalls Achilles' wish in *Iliad* 16.97–100 that all Greeks and Trojans, that is the whole world, might perish and leave him and Patroklos alone. See Cedric Whitman's interpretation of these lines in *Homer and the Heroic Tradition* (New York: Norton, 1965), 199.

39. Wright nicely teases out the implications of the French phrase for scythe-chariots, "chars à faux." Noting the possible double meaning of " 'faux' + 'à faux' = 'false' while 'une faux' = scythe," she concludes: "The perverse use of tools ideally linked with the bountifulness of Nature and the benefit of mankind is emphasized, as is the misuse of man's energies. This corrupting influence is highlighted by the substitution of 'chars à faux' with its emphasis on distortion and analogy with falsehood and invalidity, for 'chars de combats' (tanks). Time the reaper-warrior, synonymous with death 'already an irony of human existence' is grasped by a gory forelock and accelerated by man himself" (223).

40. *Iliad* 18.71, in which Thetis takes her son's head in her hands as a mother would do at a funeral, reinforces this interpretation. See especially Johannes Kakridis, *Homeric Researches* (Lund: CWK Gleerup, 1949), 72.

41. This creation of abstract meaning in relation to war is reminiscent of a passage in Natalie Barney's *Pensées* in which she compares the role of men and women in war. Women, she says, perform their "heartbreaking tasks" [besognes navrantes] of tending to the wounded and dead with courage equal to that of men. Women's courage, however, goes unseen because it is termed "natural" and is therefore reduced to animal rank, while men differentiate themselves from animality "by fighting for an ideal, for a false value, or for pleasure" [En combattant pour un idéal, pour une fausse valeur, ou pour le plaisir] (33).

42. As Wright notes, Achilles' "isolation here is a form of death akin to life in the female enclave of the tower in *Achille*" (220).

43. See the chapter "Fire and Other Elements" in Whitman, *Homer*, 128–53.

44. The original version has "soldats" instead of "deux camps" (125). The change makes it clear that it is *soldiery* rather than Greek soldiers or Trojan soldiers that opposes water.

45. Additional support for this inference comes from the passage in "Achille" which likens Deidamia's expiring life to water dripping from a vase: "la vie de Déidamie s'échapper de sa gorge comme l'eau du goulot trop étroit d'un vase" (50).

46. This seems also to have been Natalie Barney's position. One of her *pensées* reads: "La guerre, cet accouchement de l'homme. Ils enfantent la mort, comme elles la vie, avec courage, inéluctablement" [War, this childbed of the male. They give birth to death, as females do to life, with courage, inevitability] (6). Another, which I have paraphrased above in footnote, specifies that women's heartrending tasks include "voir blessé ou mort ce qu'elle avait créé vivant" [looking upon wounded or dead that which she created living] (33).

47. We may recall also that in "Achille," Patrocle almost drowned [à demi naufragé] in a wave [houle] of feminine flirtation and laces (49).

48. Greek myth stresses the involuntary nature of Thetis's union with a mortal, forced on her because she was destined to bear a son mightier than his father. Catullus transformed the relationship into a love match (poem 64), and this seems to be the variant Yourcenar is following in *Feux* when she writes that Thetis's only youthful fault was to sleep with Achilles' father "sans prendre la précaution banale de le changer en dieu" [without taking the simple precaution of changing him into a god] (43).

49. Note the absence of father in either list: the male must "se faire."

50. The pseudo Dictys wrote probably in the first century C.E., but aside from a few Greek fragments his work survives only in a fourth-century Latin translation. Quintus wrote in the fourth century, but his Greek continuation of Homer is not influenced by "Dictys." It is interesting that in Quintus, Penthesileia enters battle "like a wave of the thundering sea" (*Posthomerica* 1, 320) and in "Dictys" she ends in a river, dumped there by misogynistic Greeks to punish her for "having dared to cross the natural boundaries of her sex" [quoniam naturae sexusque condicionem superare ausa esset] (*Ephemeris* 4.3).

51. Poignault uncritically judges Penthesileia happier than Misandra, who was trapped by her breasts (63–64). Later Poignault comments, "seule Penthésilée est vraiment Amazone, celle qui a franchi la frontière des sexes: une Misandre qui aurait réussi" [Penthesileia alone is truly an Amazon, she who has crossed over the frontier between the sexes: a Misandra who succeeded] (67). Natalie Barney would not have agreed; as my analysis indicates, it is not that simple for Yourcenar either.

52. The sarcophagus in the Louvre depicts all Amazons with breasts intact, as do all vase paintings and statuary from classical Greece and Rome.

53. In contrast to Patroklos, who *is* a sword, and to Achilles, who wields one, Penthesileia's description nowhere includes this (defining?) weapon.

54. Wright, whose analysis focuses more on war than on gender, comments: "The violation in war of ordinary principles of life and standards of conduct is emphasized by death's connection with rape" (224).

55. All nine of the stories in *Feux* have abstract nouns attached to their titles, but all but one of the other seven bear female names.

56. In other words, Deidamia's rejecting the penis in favor of the phallus precedes Achilles' own choice.

57. Although it is included in a series of complaints that, as Wright points out, "projects inner problems and inadequacy onto women" (221), I read it as narratively true. Biondi interprets "the opposite of disguise" not as "the real" but as "tragedy" (in the sense that tragedy is opposed to game-playing), and she interprets Achilles' tragic destiny in the two stories to be that he is unable to find an identity. It is both much simpler and more politically significant to interpret as Wright and I do.

58. She thus joins the cohort of contemporary women writers Shari Benstock

portrays as universally aware of "the destructive possibilities of a masculine ethic of domination and authoritarianism." *Women of the Left Bank: Paris, 1900-1940* (Austin: University of Texas Press, 1987), 124–25.

59. As Hélène Cixous points out, manhood has paraded "ses métaphores comme des bannières à travers l'histoire. C'est toujours bien sûr de guerre, de combat qu'il s'agit." [his metaphors like banners across history. It's always surely a question of war, of combat.] "Le sexe ou la tête?" *Les Cahiers du GRIF* 13 (1976): 9. This long tradition has forced even feminists like Luce Irigaray to think in oppositional terms: she continues to envision the fluid (real) as feminine, the fixed (ideal) as masculine, but she, unlike Yourcenar, valorizes the former and explicitly names patriarchal culture rather than a masculine principle as the problem. See especially "La 'mécanique' des fluides" in *Ce sexe qui n'en est pas un* (Paris: Editions de Minuit, 1977).

60. So Annis Pratt describes women's fiction, "The New Feminist Criticisms: Exploring the History of the New Space," in *Beyond Intellectual Sexism: A New Woman A New Reality* (New York: David McKay Co., Inc., 1976), 193.

Autobiography and Matricide: Marguerite Yourcenar's *Dear Departed*

Leakthina Chau-Pech Ollier

"Is AUTOBIOGRAPHY SOMEHOW ALWAYS IN THE PROCESS OF SYMBOLICALLY killing the mother off by telling her the lie that we have given birth to ourselves?" (147) asks Barbara Johnson. In her study of contemporary fictions by women, Judith Kegan Gardiner similarly notes:

> With the resurgence of women's fiction in the twentieth century, many autobiographical or confessional novels by women trace the coming to adulthood, that is, to individual identity, of a daughter who must define herself in terms of her mother. In the Oedipus myth, the son murders his father in order to replace him. Contrastingly, in the new woman's myth, the daughter "kills" her mother in order *not to* have to take her place. (146)

In the first volume of the trilogy, *The Labyrinth of the World*, dedicated to her mother Fernande de Crayencour, Marguerite Yourcenar carries this myth to the extreme. Thematically as well as structurally, *Dear Departed*, at least on the text's surface, attests to the voluntary and radical separation of the daughter from the mother. In psychoanalytic terms, the entrance into language, into the Symbolic stage, and thereby into society, is contingent upon the child's separation from the mother. According to Jacques Lacan, "the speaking subject only comes into existence because of the repression of the desire for the lost mother" (Moi, 99). The autobiographical project, with its basic emphasis on self-narration and its underlying or explicit use of the subject pronoun "I," is therefore most representative of the symbolic need to kill the mother so that the child might become a speaking subject. Thus, matricide, which Julia Kristeva defines as "the sine-qua-non of our individuation" (27), constitutes the fundamental and decisive step toward subjectivity and autonomy. In Yourcenar's writing, the necessary act of killing the mother is insistently put into play so that she can be born, thereby affording herself the possibility of becoming the subject of her own discourse.

Yourcenar's autobiographical writing confronts the problematics and ambivalence inherent in the mother-daughter relationship as debated by many psychoanalytic, feminist, and object relation theorists. But to view her autobiographical writing in light of the above mentioned psychoanalytical reading, however tempting it might be, would be an oversimplification. First, it does not account for the question of the mother's absence in a child's life. What happens if the Imaginary Order never took place because the mother was already dead? What happens if, because of this missing stage in a child's life, his/her entrance into the Symbolic Order never materialized and separation and individuation never occurred since there is nothing from which to be separated? Secondly, psychoanalysis also fails to take into consideration what Hélène Rouch, in her interview with Luce Irigaray, for instance, calls the "placental economy." She claims that long before the intervention of the father into the mother-child dyad, before the law-establishing "Name-of-the-Father," there was always already a separation between the mother and the foetus—the placenta—which serves to prevent complete fusion and symbiosis. Thus, this separation precedes the acquisition of language. It has no influence on it and is not contingent upon it (*Je, tu, nous*, 41–42). Third, let us suppose that matricide is successfully achieved in Yourcenar's autobiographical writing, does it then ensue that the author is successful in finally inscribing herself in the text?

Indeed, her insistence on the fact that her mother's death has no bearing on her life and her denial of any "lack" give the appearance of a woman who has succeeded in establishing autonomy and subjectivity. However, her writing, riddled with contradictions, tells another story. *Dear Departed* is rather an attempt at a *continued* separation from the mother, an attempt that has failed and has become symptomatic of Yourcenar's autobiographical writing. Separation is an ongoing process in her writing; it is an unending activity grounded in language and has no clear point of demarcation. Regression to, and separation from the mother constitute the oscillating movements in her discourse. The first step toward disassociating herself from the mother requires an initial return to the maternal body, the maternal voice. At times, Yourcenar's narrative suggests the merging of the mother and the daughter while preserving their separate identities and the fluid boundaries of which Hélène Cixous speaks in *La Jeune née* or "Le Rire de la méduse" and to which Luce Irigaray aspires in *Ce sexe qui n'en est pas un*. At other times, Yourcenar's text reveals a dangerous fusion of her identity with that of the mother. This becomes all the more perilous since she denies her the subjectivity needed in establishing her own, as Irigaray warned in *Et l'une ne bouge pas sans l'autre*. This ambivalence is at the heart of Yourcenar's dialectics—writing her mother as herself or as the (m)other. Separation can only be performed in terms of a radical act.

However, separation means a loss of the origin that might enable the author to speak of her-self, to tell her personal story, if one is to rely on Cixous's and Irigaray's theories. On the other hand, separation and the acknowledgment of loss also result in the formation of one's subjectivity according to theorists such as Lacan and Kristeva. But the advent of subjectivity must coincide with the underlying recognition of a "lack" that Yourcenar so adamantly rejects. Her refusal to admit to any grief that might have been caused by the mother's absence, in addition to her constant need to distance herself from her in her text, only serve to reaffirm in all of its contradiction her ambivalence toward the latter, and the gravity of the impact her untimely death has on her life.

Standing at the limit of the Pre-Symbolic and the Symbolic, the need to commit matricide and the guilt of having already committed it, the return to the body of the mother and separation, Yourcenar's autobiographical discourse translates itself into a discourse of "monstrosity," to borrow Barbara Johnson's term, or a discourse of psychosis. It oscillates between separation and symbiosis, identification and individuation, plenitude and lack, presence and absence, and it is marked by a constant shift in the mother-daughter role. Caught in this unresolved duality, Yourcenar's narrative remains in a state of paralysis, unable to fully progress or regress. Her failed attempts to commit matricide call for the incessant return to the impregnated body of the mother before and during the original crime scene of childbirth. It does not allow her to move beyond this traumatic event. The traces of the maternal blood run through the daughter's writing. But like the Hydra, the mother never dies. After each blow, she comes back to haunt and reclaim the daughter. In the process, the speaking subject never emerges. The "I" that Yourcenar uses is at best the "I" of a commentator, a spectator, and not the "I" of a subject who fully participates in her own life story.

In the tradition of Jean-Jacques Rousseau's *Confessions*, the first chapter of *Dear Departed*, entitled "The Birth," focuses on the short-lived marriage of Yourcenar's parents, Michel and Fernande de Crayencour. Soon after, she proceeds to narrate her own birth and the mother's death of puerperal fever ten days later. Rousseau, however, paints an idyllic picture of his parents and their love for one another. His father, who never recovered from his wife's untimely death, dwells on her memory and does not refrain from talking to his son about the departed. For many of Rousseau's critics, his mother's death is seen as the source of a lifelong feeling of guilt and his writings are often interpreted in light of this pivotal and tragic event. As if she were anticipating similar "misleading" analyses from the critics, Yourcenar immediately and vehemently undermines the validity of such future reading: "I take issue with the assertion, commonly heard, that the premature death of a mother is always a disaster or that a child deprived of its mother feels a lifelong sense of loss and a yearning for the deceased. In my case, at least, things turned out otherwise" (52). Rousseau's lamentation "I cost my mother her life, and my birth was the first of my misfortunes" (6) is not echoed by Yourcenar, although, on one occasion, she mentions that, without this "incident," her mother could have lived another thirty or forty years. This being said however, it is with "open eyes" and without any kind of sentimentality that she envisions what her parents' relationship would have been like had her mother lived. She imagines that her father would either forsake his wife or that they would continue sharing their lives together but in a way that would be unsatisfying for the both of them. As for her own relationship with her mother, she does not delude herself with the thought that it would in any way be harmonious. It would be, like many other mother-daughter relationships, she presumes, marked essentially by a mixture of love perhaps, but certainly by resentment and then indifference. At the end, she adds: "I write this not to be unpleasant but to confront things as they are" (53).

As with some of her fictional characters, Yourcenar contends that the aim of this first volume of her trilogy is an attempt to bring back to life a mother she never knew. In order to do so, she needs to nourish her with her own substance: "She is much like those characters, imaginary or real, that I nourish with my own substance to try to make them live, or live once again" (53). Contrary to the mother in Luce Irigaray's *Et l'une ne bouge pas sans l'autre*, here the daughter is the source of nourishment and representation. As time passes, Yourcenar, at the moment of writing these memoirs, is twice her mother's age when she died. She can therefore perceive her mother as her daughter: "The passage of time has, moreover, inverted our relationship. I am now more than twice as old as she was on June 18, 1903, and look at her as at a daughter whom I am trying my best to understand, without completely succeeding" (53–54). The mother (Fernande) is the one who risks suffocation from an overabundance of nourishment or "substance." The boundaries are blurred and the identities intermingled, for the mother's lack of self-representation leads to the daughter's own lack of self-image, a vicious cycle indeed no matter who does the nourishing and who receives the nourishment.

By the same token, one might wonder also whether it is in fact with her own "substance" or that of her father that she is reconstituting her mother's life. Unlike Rousseau's father, whose mourning and sorrow over the death of his wife is constantly displayed in front of his son, Michel de Crayencour does not dwell on the past. According to the author, he did not even go as far as to show her a picture of the deceased. The term "image" in this context points to the photographs she never saw, at least until her thirties—so she claims—but it could also be read as a global picture of her mother's life to which she never had access. If any memory at all of Fernande reaches her daughter, it is in an anecdotal form, disjointed, and heavily burdened and influenced by the father's viewpoint. Yourcenar's indifference toward her mother seems to reflect her father's nonchalant attitude toward everything in his life, including the death of his wife.

When Matthieu Galey, in *With Open Eyes*, asks her why she felt the need to "resuscitate" a mother she never even thought about until recently, Yourcenar offers a very simple yet perplexing response: "because she existed" (167). As far as her mother is concerned, the conciseness of her answer should not surprise the reader. In *With Open Eyes*, for instance, whereas Michel de Crayencour is given a predominant place in her recollection with an entire chapter dedicated to him, Fernande is mentioned only very briefly twice. One could of course argue that since Yourcenar never knew her mother, there is not much she can possibly say. On the other hand, one might also contend that she did not hesitate to "haunt" her two great uncles, Octave and Rémo Pirmez, whom she never met, and to reinvent their lives in *Dear Departed*. Likewise, she claims that she is regularly "haunted" by some of her fictional characters who became such familiar faces in her daily life that she can say, for instance, that she loves them like a brother (239).

Whether Yourcenar chooses to let herself "haunt" or "be haunted" by her mother is therefore a matter of choice. It has nothing to do with the fact that Fernande just happened to have existed or that she just so happened to be her Mother. Rather, what is at stake here is whether Yourcenar deems her to be worth remembering and her life worth reinventing. In other words, could she be an interesting character in her daughter's literary creation? Irigaray, in her metaphorical tirade in *Le Corps-à-corps avec la mère*, declares: "To bring me into this world is to let me be something other than your production" [Me laisser naître, c'est me laisser être autre chose que ta production] (66, my translation). Likewise, now that the mother and the daughter have traded places, and now that Fernande de Crayencour is born out of her daughter's pen, will she be allowed to become something other than her daughter's production? Is Fernande this daughter that she would seek to understand or to "contain within herself," as the term "comprendre" (to "understand" in French) implies, or will she permit her to be her own autonomous person?

In the chronology to *Oeuvres romanesques* drafted by the author herself, the years 1929 to 1931 were spent between Paris and Belgium "where Marguerite Yourcenar made several trips to recover part of the maternal inheritance" [où Marguerite Yourcenar fait plusieurs séjours pour essayer de récupérer une partie de l'héritage maternel] (XVIII, my translation). Almost half a century later, Yourcenar undertakes the writing of *Dear Departed*, likewise a metaphorical voyage to "recover the maternal inheritance" or "legacy," the "mother tongue." However, this pilgrimage is doomed from the very start. In her enterprise, the author creates a labyrinthine narrative in which Fernande de Crayencour has no chance of coming out alive. She prefigures the sacrificial victim. The daughter, in order to live, must sacrifice the life of her mother; in order to write, she must silence her; and in order to see, she must blind her. If Yourcenar attempts to "resuscitate" her mother in any way, as Matthieu Galey suggested in his interview with the author (214), it is only to simultaneously annihilate her; a murder, tantamount to a purification ritual, which must take place again in the writing. Thus, the reader of *Dear Departed* is given the opportunity to revisit the "scene of the crime" in which Fernande succumbs, not under the forceps of the physician-butcher, but under the pen of her daughter.

There is no doubt that Yourcenar's portrait of her mother pales in comparison to the portrait of Jeanne de Reval in *Quoi? L'Eternité*, a woman who, according to the author, stands as the epitome of perfection. However, it also pales in comparison to her quasi-caricatural depiction of the most hated woman in the author's life, her paternal grandmother Noémi Dufresne. As a character, she embodies the cantankerous woman worthy of any fairy tale's wicked witch. Between veneration and contempt stands the almost insignificant profile of Fernande, a young woman not unlike many of her contemporaries at the turn of the century, who unfortunately did not benefit from any distinctive qualities that would be worth remembering. Like the old photographs upon which Yourcenar partly relies to reconstitute her mother's life, her portrait of her seems faded and lacks contours. There is no definite sense of who Fernande really was, nothing that would distinguish her from other women, no adjectives that would qualify her self and her life. This appears to coincide with Yourcenar's skepticism of the ability to resume the self into one totalizing image.[1] On the other hand, it seems as if she has planned for this portrait to be a perfect match for her father's "praise" on the prayer card—the condescending "She always tried to do her best" (49) for lack of better words.

Contrastingly, Fernande's deathbed constitutes the pivotal event around which the narration of her life story evolves. In her daughter's description, Fernande, even while she was alive, takes on the characteristics of the inert body lying on the deathbed as depicted in the postmortem photograph—mute, eyes shut, and still bearing traces of her pregnancy:

> Her hands, entwined with a rosary, are joined together atop her belly, which is distended by peritonitis; the sheet bulges with the swelling, as if she is still waiting to give birth. She has become what one sees of the dead: an inert, closed mass, insensible to light, warmth, and physical contact, no longer either inhaling or exhaling air and no longer making use of it to form words, no longer taking in nourishment and excreting part of it afterward. (35–36)

By comparison to the general vagueness of her description of Fernande, the portrait of her mother lying on her deathbed is astonishingly vivid, realistic, and rich in details. Ironically, Yourcenar's description of her mother comes alive only when the latter is dead. But the "discovery" or revealing of the mother, as Laurie Lynette Corbin suggests in her reading of Luce Irigaray, is for Yourcenar as treacherous an adventure as that analyzed by Irigaray in *Et l'une ne bouge pas sans l'autre*. For Yourcenar, the process of "discovery" is simultaneous with the process of "covering up" as much as the autobiographical attempt of "uncovering" oneself coincides with the "covering up" of the self. In this picture, Fernande's swollen belly is yet another reminder of her pregnancy, a reminder that the self is still locked in the mother's womb, still waiting to be born.

As in the postmortem photograph, however, the gaze of the mother, so essential in providing the daughter with a self-image and recognition, is mostly absent from the photographed pictures on which Yourcenar was to base her description. On numerous occasions when the author had access to pictures of her mother while she was still alive, she notes that Fernande's eyes and/or face are hidden in the shadow of a large hat or parasol: "Fernande, very pretty and very coquettish, takes shelter from the sun beneath a large parasol" (254). Likewise, several pictures of Fernande's honeymoon trip offer the same consistent image of a woman deprived of her gaze:

> And of course here is Fernande. Fernande leaning toward the fountain at Marienbad, holding in one hand a bouquet of flowers and a parasol, in the other a glass of water, which she sips with a charming expression.... Fernande in city clothes, the *inevitable parasol* in hand, advancing with little steps across a rocky landscape.... Fernande in a white blouse and lightcolored shirt, crowned with one of those *enormous beribboned hats* she was so fond of, strolling with book in hand through some dark Germanic forest, and to judge from appearances, reading a few lines out loud. One of these images seems to testify to a happiness that Michel must have known at least intermittently during those years, the memory of which evidently faded afterward like the photographs themselves. The snapshot shows a room in an inn on Corsica.... A young woman sitting before the mirror inserts a last hairpin in the ornate coils of her chignon. Her upraised arms have let the loose sleeves of her white peignoir slip down to her shoulders. *Her face is a reflection to be guessed at rather than perceived.* (326–27; my emphasis)[2]

The power of specularization is taken away from the mother, echoing her refusal to look at her daughter when the latter was being presented to her after the birth: "The mother, too exhausted to bear yet another strain, turned her head away when the baby was shown to her" (22–23). Here Yourcenar returns the favor: she refuses to recognize the mother because she was not recognized by her and because she failed to give the daughter her autonomy. By avoiding looking at her daughter, she denied her a separate existence and subjectivity. Fernande's face remains a void, the sketch of an unfinished drawing, and Yourcenar makes no attempt to fill in the details, to give her representation. She is the ghostly and evasive mirror without silvering, to borrow Irigaray's use of the play on words between the homonyms "tain" and "teint," "silvering of the mirror," and "complexion of the skin" [*Et l'une ne bouge pas sans l'autre*] (14), that does not reflect and does not offer her daughter the reciprocity of a gaze. She stands as "a mere photographic memory" [*Et l'une ne bouge pas sans l'autre*] (14) on which there is nothing to inscribe and, by extension, does not allow her daughter her own inscription of her self.

On the other hand, the power of the gaze is also often associated with the mythical figure of the Medusa, whose glance is deadly. It petrifies and kills anyone who dares to look at her. Only by looking at her reflection on his shield rather than looking straight at her is Perseus able to approach and kill her. In the same vein, Fernande is only dangerous when she gazes straight on. On the one occasion when Yourcenar is confronted with her mother's eyes, she is swift to point out that, at the time her portrait was drawn, Fernande's life, unbeknownst to her, would only last another fourteen years: "The eyes this time look directly at the viewer. . . . Neither does she know that she has passed the midpoint of her life; fourteen years remain to her" (267–68). Behind her proleptic announcement of her mother's death, Yourcenar is able to shield herself from the deadly glance. In the same movement, the eyes that are presented unveiled and open are immediately closed by the concluding remark. Accompanied by such a statement, the daughter runs less of a risk of being petrified by the mother's gaze. One could even go as far as to say that it is *she* who, with one stroke of the pen, paralyzes Fernande. As Perseus hides the Medusa's head in a cloth after he killed her, Yourcenar "covers up" Fernande in her cloth/narration for she realizes that the danger is ever present, even after the mother's death.

The image of the mother as the potential threat to the child's life and well-being provides for the tragic ending of "The Milk of Death," a short story in *Oriental Tales*. In it, Jules Boutrin relates to his friend, Philip Mild, the tale of a woman whose love for her child defies the boundary of life and death. Chosen as a sacrificial victim according to the superstition of the region, she is walled in alive in a tower so that it will not collapse. Resigned to her fate, the woman's only wish is for her tormentors to leave two open spaces in the wall, for her breasts to feed her child and for her eyes to see him. As the story continues, after a few days, her heart stops beating. Later, her eyes liquify and retract into their hollow orbits: a mask of death. But the breasts remain intact and offer their ever youthful appearance. With the ever-flowing milk the dead mother is able to nourish her child until he no longer needs it and on his own, turns his head away from her.

In this story, the mother epitomizes selflessness and abnegation. Motherhood and motherly love are elevated to the realm of saintliness. But despite its beauty, the story is of course a legend which has nothing to do with reality. In fact, Yourcenar warns the reader: when Philip Mild asks his friend to divert him with a tale, he specifies that he wants to hear "the most beautiful and the least true of all stories imaginable" (37). Reality according to Yourcenar has to do with the rate of infant mortality and the fear of one's own death due to complications during childbirth, which was not uncommon at the turn of the century. Her own mother and grandmother died of the same fate. Reality is what Yourcenar imagines to be the feeling of estrangement that the mother has toward her unborn child, and ultimately the mother's abandonment upon her death:

> Fernande's sisters, who overflowed with advice about diet and with tender exhortations, told her in vain that one loves one's child even before it is born; she did not succeed in establishing a connection between her bouts of nausea, her fainting spells, the weight of that thing which grew within her and would come out of her by the most secret route.... (17)

By contrast to the mother in the legend, Fernande, even if she were to live, would never provide her daughter with the gift of life—her milk. It was unthinkable that a woman of a certain social status should breast-feed her infant. Thus, the little Marguerite was fed with the milk of a cow whose fate and generosity, ironically, is likened to that of the mother in "The Milk of Death."[3] Finally, reality is also reflected in the image of the other mother in "The Milk of Death," the gypsy woman with a child in her arms who comes around begging the two friends for money. The child's eyes are covered with bandages. As the narrator of the tale chases her away, he explains to his companion that the woman has applied filthy plasters to her child's eyes for the last few months in the hope of blinding him so that the passersby would take pity and give them money. The narrator concludes with this dichotomy: "There are mothers ... and then there are mothers" (51). Indeed, the mothers in Yourcenar's conception of reality are the ones who could and would willfully blind their child for their own selfish gain. The mothers with the selfless gift of nourishment and life can only be encountered in myth. Thus, before the monstrous mother can pluck out the child's eyes or turn him/her into stone, an object for her monetary benefit or for any other reason, Yourcenar, in her autobiographical writing, anticipates the tragedy by blinding her mother so she would not do the same to her.

If the gaze could petrify the daughter in her search for autonomy, the mother's voice is no less paralyzing. Through the intermediary of Fernande's old governess, Yourcenar was made aware of her mother's last wish: "If the little one ever wants to become a nun, don't let anyone prevent her" (39). The author's resentment toward her mother's statement can clearly be felt in this thunderous indignation:

> From the age of seven or eight, it seemed to me that this mother of whom I knew almost nothing, whose picture my father had never shown me (Mademoiselle Jeanne did have a photograph of my mother, along with many others, on her piano, but she hardly took the trouble to draw my attention to it), encroached unduly on my life and liberty, trying to push me too obviously in a particular direction. The idea of entering a convent appealed very little to me, but I would doubtless have been just as rebellious if I had known that on her deathbed she had planned my future marriage or named the school I was to attend. Why were all these people interfering? I balked, imperceptibly, resisting like a dog that turns its head when shown a collar. (39–40)

These last words from the mother, perceived as an infringement on her freedom, are constraining in the sense that she viewed her daughter, not as a separate being, but as an extension of herself, wanting her to lead the life she might have chosen for herself. For Yourcenar, these words from the mother, the only ones to which she had access, take on the resonance of an incantation. Despite what she claims to be her complete detachment from her mother, her reaction proves that the maternal "recommendation" does not leave her indifferent since it arouses in her such an outpouring of hostility. She points the accusing finger at "this mother" for her uninvited intrusion in her life and for wanting to shape her destiny when she did not even seize upon the chance to look at, and to acknowledge, her daughter before dying.

To ward off the maternal words that have haunted her since childhood, Yourcenar would proceed through a ceremony of "occultation of relics" (54), a ceremony to free herself of some "pious odds and ends" (57).[4] She got rid of Fernande's notebook that contained fictional writings deemed ridiculous by the daughter. In throwing away her mother's literary attempt, she erases her voice, which remains silent throughout much of *Dear Departed*. Even more prominent is the episode where her mother, before the fatal childbirth, suffered from dental neuralgia. Unable to speak, her only means of communication was to write her thoughts and her requests for her daily needs on a piece of paper:

> Baudouin has already had that. . . .
> . . . .
> Quartermann is intelligent, alert, and kind . . . different from Dr. Dubois yesterday.
> . . . .
> I am just like Trier—wordless. . . .
> . . . .

> With this, it hurts to even suck on a bit of biscuit. . . .
> . . . .
> It's not in the boiling water. . . .
> . . . .
> Ring. . . . Have someone look for a cork. . . . Some wine. . . .
> . . . .
> In the next room, on the fire? (19)

It is ironic that Yourcenar, while trying to get rid of most of her mother's belongings and writing, decided to keep this piece of paper that reflects nothing but a banal conversation. It is as if she attempts to show that even when Fernande was able to speak, she had absolutely nothing intelligent to say. Thus, she doubly silences her. On the other hand, these transcribed words have the merit of being just that—banal. They have no effect on the daughter's life.

The act of killing and distancing herself from the mother by blinding and silencing her is further accentuated by the digression in her narrative. Although the story of her ancestors and two great uncles, which becomes the focus in the two chapters following the chapter on her birth, could be interpreted as the search for her origins and those of her mother, it is nevertheless disconcerting to note that more than half of *Dear Departed* is dedicated to them rather than to the narration of Fernande's life or to the author's own. It appears as though Yourcenar has resumed her usual fascination with history and historical novels, a genre with which she is obviously more at ease. Meanwhile, Fernande has been eclipsed; she could be seen as no more than a support for the representation of her ancestors and the two male characters that follow.

Traveling back in time allows Yourcenar to search for her origins as well as it enables her to distance herself from them, to cut the ties that bind her to her mother. But eventually, she has to move forward and come back to her. Whichever way Yourcenar chooses to go, all roads lead back to the mother. The final chapter of *Dear Departed* resumes the narration of Fernande's life and ends with the image of her, pregnant and lying on a terrace in a chaise longue:

> Like a traveler on the deck of transatlantic liner, she reclines on a chaise longue at the edge of the terrace, from which one sees, or thinks one sees, beyond the pale green expanse of the rolling plain, the distant gray line of the sea. Majestic clouds drift in the open sky, like those once sketched in this same region by painters of seventeenth-century battles. . . . My face begins to take shape on the screen of time. (332)

Yourcenar went full circle with her narration and ends with practically the same scene that is to be found in the first chapter. The analogy made between the threatening clouds in the sky lingering over Fernande and in the depiction of battlefields symbolizes the event that awaits her—the childbirth, which is being compared to a "crime scene" and by extension—a bloody battlefield. But meanwhile, Yourcenar's own birth is only a projection into the future— "My face begins to take shape on the screen of time."

Like the image of Fernande as an immobile traveler on the deck of a cruise ship, Yourcenar's voyage to and from the mother does not lead her anywhere because, in her indecision, she cannot commit herself to moving completely forward or backward. This ambivalence toward her mother, as I have shown, can be detected between what Yourcenar herself asserts and what one is able to read between the lines and in her narrative. In her autobiographical journey toward subjectivity and self-examination, Yourcenar is locked in a womblike labyrinth. The danger of engulfment looms ahead for both the mother and the daughter. Yourcenar's double attempt to give birth to herself and to her mother, by casting her as a character in her autobiographical writing, is aborted. In her unwillingness to provide Fernande with any kind of subjectivity, she keeps her in a state of dependence, killing her with the constant force-feeding of her own "substance." Fernande, as a character in her daughter's creation, never achieves autonomy because the author fails to give her representation and recognition. At the same time, the discourse of her own birth, of realizing herself into the world, is also aborted. The death of the mother does not presuppose the so-called "birth of the self." The discourse of the self, the autobiographical discourse, only emerges in relation to the mother and through the discursive cracks of the narration about the mother. The problem with the mother's murder is that, in the end, the author still cannot see herself being born.

The ultimate irony and tragedy of *Dear Departed* lies in the fact that in sacrificing the mother, in making her the victim, Yourcenar falls victim to her own act. While trying desperately to separate herself from the mother and denying her subjectivity, she unconsciously creates a discourse in which her own subjectivity is lacking. This is reflected, for instance, in the use of the third person feminine pronoun "she" while referring to both herself and Fernande, thus canceling out the distance between them. Likewise, in retelling her parents' life story, it seems as though the author has sometimes let her-self creep into her mother's role in that she has supplanted her mother's life story with her own experience of her life beside her father.[5] Despite her efforts, she fails to safeguard herself against slipping into a fatal symbiosis with the mother. Yourcenar thus retells and relives the same story, that of the mother who has infiltrated her own story and vice versa, prolonging the mother-daughter cycle which can only end with her own adamant refusal to create another life, another daughter who would carry on the same burden. Her repulsion for and refusal of maternity[6] is symbolic of her ultimate acknowledgment that daughters cannot get away from mothers, even by way of matricide. The ghostly image of Fernande's paleness on her deathbed is representative of the blank page on which Yourcenar would inscribe her narration. The pen replaces the metallic forceps in extirpating the child from the mother's womb and in tainting the blank page with traces of blood in an effort to be born. But beneath the page's surface lurks a contradictory discourse of a daughter who is still caught in the mother's all-powerful embrace.

Notes

An earlier version of this article appeared in *Dalhousie French Studies* 48 (fall 1999): 87–89.

1. The impossibility to write about the self is summed up by Yourcenar as follows: "[The] reader . . . is all too likely to rub his nose in the events of the story. Individual life is short, the self is porous; to conjure up an image of the whole from such things smacks of pure illusion" (*With Open Eyes*, XIII). She intends this aphorism to apply not only to her own life writing but to her novels such as *Mémoires d'Hadrien* and *Alexis ou le Traité du Vain Combat*. Both of her characters, Emperor Hadrian and Alexis de Géra, testify to the inability and the vanity of an attempt to recapitulate one's life in a single formula.

2. The English translation of what originally was "un chignon compliqué" to "the ornate coils of her chignon," interestingly enough, reminds us of the image of the Medusa's hair that has been changed into serpents, and the mirror captured in the photograph serves the same purpose as Perseus's shield, which enables him to look at the Medusa's reflection without running the risk of being petrified by her.

3. "The milk calms the little girl's cries. She has quickly learned to draw almost fiercely on the rubber nipple; the feeling of the good liquid flowing within her is doubtless her first pleasure. The rich nourishment comes from a nursing creature, animal symbol of the fertile earth that gives men not only her milk but later, when her udders are finally exhausted, her lean flesh, and last her hide, tendons, and bones, which are made into glue and bone charcoal. Torn from her familiar pastures, she will die a death that is almost always agonizing, after the long, lurching journey in the cattle car that will convey her to the slaughterhouse, often bruised, deprived of water, frightened in any case by those jolts and noises so new to her. Or else she will be herded the whole way under the hot sun, by men who will goad her with their long prods and mistreat her if she is recalcitrant. She will arrive panting at the place of execution, the rope around her neck, sometimes blinded in one eye, delivered into the hands of butchers who have been brutalized by their despicable trade and who perhaps will begin to cut her up before she is completely dead. Even her name, *vache* [cow], which ought to be sacred to the men she nour-

ishes, is a term of ridicule in French, and certain readers of this book will doubtless find this remark and those preceding it equally ridiculous" (25–26). Interestingly, in this accusatory and poignant tirade, Yourcenar is more sympathetic to the fate of cows than that of her own mother, while it seems that Fernande's death at the hand of the physician-butcher is comparable to the tragic death of these "sacred" animals.

4. The French version, "pieux déchets," has a more ironic connotation since the word "déchets" in French also means "waste."

5. "In imagining some of the incidental circumstances of Zeno's or Alexis's childhood, I sometimes made use of my own memories" (*With Open Eyes*, 174), Yourcenar confesses about her narrative strategies. Accordingly, one might as well wonder to what extent she has allowed part of her childhood and her time shared with her father into her descriptive passage concerning, for instance, the intimate evenings her parents spent together. The intimacy, the playfulness, and the idyllic nature of the scene contradicts the very nature of their relationship and the portrait that Yourcenar has given of her mother.

6. In *Marguerite Yourcenar: Inventing a Life*, Josyane Savigneau relates an anecdote in which Yourcenar, during a dinner, was speaking to a woman who was sitting next to her. When she finally realized that the woman was pregnant, she did not attempt to hide her repulsion and immediately stopped the conversation: "She [Yourcenar] had a rather long and very pleasant conversation with Diane. 'At the end of the meal,' recounts Diane de Margerie, 'when we all got up and Marguerite Yourcenar noticed that I was pregnant, I caught her looking at me, full of disgust. She became, in a flash, as cold as ice. And we did not converse together again.'" (248).

Reading Prohibited: The Politics of Yourcenar's Prefaces

Carole Allamand

For a very long time, the prefaces of Yourcenar have had the last word in the critical debate on this author's works. But if her introductions, many notes, comments, and aphorisms no longer rule the interpretation of her fiction, few studies have so far engaged the actual reading of this dense and voluminous paratext.

Yourcenar has often been deemed to write like a man, if not a nineteenth-century man. This essay delineates, in the paratext, the construction of this phallocratic identity. For Yourcenar conceives her books, rather than *delivers them. Beyond the philosophical or ideological discourses that she and her readers have used to explain this distinction, I suggest that we relate the construction of this "neutral" authorial* persona *to the delivery that haunts the paratext, and ultimately refers to the author's tragic birth.*

>   -Are you sure that your readers understand what you're up to?
>   -I'm sure of the contrary.
> —Marguerite Yourcenar, *With Open Eyes: Conversations with Matthieu Galey*

The Guardians of the Meaning

"More than once since the book appeared," Yourcenar writes in her preface to her novel *Coup de Grâce*, "men who had fought in these same Baltic wars have gracefully volunteered to tell me that [this novel] corresponds to their own memories of those years, and no critical article, however favorable, has ever reassured me more as to the substance of one of my books."[1] In 1962, then, Yourcenar felt that literature should mirror the world. And yet this belief is undermined by her practice, and particularly by the writing of numerous and abundant prefaces, which as such contradict the claim of a "natural coincidence" between the text and reality. If *Coup de Grâce* was but a "document" (ix), why not let it speak?

While realism had been muffling the voice of the author for over a century, in particular by erasing the paratext (Genette), Yourcenar left more than three hundred pages of metanarration ranging from prefaces to postfaces or postscriptums, from introductions to forewords and afterwords, and from author's notes to reflections. Not to mention dedications and epigraphs, complex subtitles, and a pseudonym, all of which constitute marks of authorial intervention. She would also quote in Latin or Greek, even though erudite inscriptions, already comical in Dickens, are now practically inseparable from parody. The fact is, Yourcenar is a fanatic of the paratext. Not only did she never allow her novels to be read without careful instructions, she never missed a chance to provide her reader with new prefaces in subsequent editions.

Saturated with reading directions, Yourcenar's introductions have long pleased critics, who waited almost thirty years before daring to question their content.[2] One might wonder why these texts have been taken for so long as a mark of generosity on the part of an author concerned about "better orienting her readers,"[3] even though their brusque tone so often denied such benevolence. If no qualified reader would blindly follow Yourcenar's reading advice today, her compulsive paratext still needs to be explained as such. This article hopes to prove that far from being marginal, these prefaces and postfaces constitute a crucial component of Yourcenar's poetics, in that they further allow the denial of the mother's death.

As a text, the paratext deserves to be read. Its meaning, that is, cannot be restricted to its explicit advisory intent, nor can it be subsumed in the narratives it claims to elucidate. I will thus not only listen to what the prefaces say, but also to the way in which they speak. This leads me to ask, for example, if the courteous visit of these Baltic soldiers only enforced the accuracy claimed for *Coup de Grâce*. For in my opinion their presence in this preface is neither fortuitous nor civil(ian): these soldiers embody the defense that Yourcenar has organized around her fiction. One might ask: in fear of what assailants?

"A Generous Author"

At first sight, Yourcenar's paratext does seem generous. *Anna, soror . . .*'s postface, for instance, is almost half the size of the novella it is supposed to interpret.[4] Similar to the prefaces of *Alexis*, *A Coin in Nine Hands*, or *Coup de Grâce*, this explanation would not seem out of place in Lagarde and Michard. Origins, themes, place in literary history, genesis, stylistic comments, inventory of the corrections, nothing is missing. Nothing, shall we say, but a raison d'être. For *Anna, soror* . . . , as far as intelligibility goes, is perfectly straightforward. Its writing never infringes upon the rules, be they those of the French language or of the realistic novel. The Yourcenarian sentence is as transparent as her narration, it mimics that of the story. *Anna, soror* . . .'s style is so smooth,[5] so predictable that it gets on some critics' nerves.[6]

Then the copiousness of information that characterizes Yourcenar's paratext may sometimes turn against it. The originality of the treatment of incest in *Anna, soror* . . . , discussed with regard to John Ford, Byron, Montesquieu, Chateaubriand, Goethe, Thomas Mann, and Roger Martin du Gard, is likely to escape most readers. In the same way, when she justifies the choice of "an obscure corner of a Baltic country" as the *Coup de Grâce*'s décor, Yourcenar calls on "reasons similar as those which Racine exposed so perfectly in his preface to *Bajazet*" (*Oeuvres*, 79–80), yet neglects to tell us what these reasons were! On the other hand, the detailed bibliographies of the "Notes" following *Memoirs of Hadrian* and *The Abyss* are of no use to anyone without access to a well-stocked university library. (Beside references to the emperor himself, the reader might have little use of studies on numismatics, Trajan's wars and personality, the "affaire des quatre consulaires," or Hadrian's art collection, etc.) The abundance of data found in the "Note" to *The Abyss* raises the same question. Can we believe that this twenty-five-page detailed description of her sources was composed only to "avoid possible confusions in matters of bibliography"?[7] Her portrait of Zeno is for instance bolstered by no less than eleven figures from the Renaissance, whose deeds are examined and then synthesized in the fashion of a philosophy textbook. One would fear, however, that an explanation that mixes scholastics, dynamism, mechanism, hermetism, atheism, empirism, and cabalism would scare off any student of philosophy (363). Yet such zeal raises new questions. What is the point of the veracity of Zeno's character when we know it is fictional? What use are these proofs in the context of a novel?

Yourcenar was not unaware of such a contradiction. "The creation of a fictitious historical character, like Zeno, would seem to require bibliographical evidence even less than would a free reconstruction of a real person" (361). The author repeats here, almost exactly, the apology that opened the *Reflections on the Composition of Memoirs of Hadrian*, "a reconstruction . . . that can dispense with formal statement of evidence."[8] Finally, the reader of the thick preface of *Fires* might be equally surprised to learn that "this book does not require any commentary."[9] Ironically, the only justification for such texts given by Yourcenar is itself another "formal statement of evidence." "En étayant ainsi un ouvrage d'ordre littéraire, on ne fait . . . que se conformer à l'usage de Racine, qui, dans les préfaces de ses tragédies, énumère soigneusement ses sources" [To shore up a literary work in this way, one is simply following Racine, who, in the prefaces to his tragedies, carefully enumerated his sources] (*Oeuvres*, 543).

Such circularity betrays the emptiness of the preface, its uselessness, to which theorists agree. "This is an essential and ludicrous operation," Derrida writes, not only because it confines itself to the discursive effects of an intention-to-mean, but because, in pointing out a single thematic nucleus or a single guiding thesis, it cancels out the textual displacement that is at work "here."[10] But a preface is also futile in that it discusses an object that the reader still ignores.[11] Written "in view of its own self-effacement," introductions are by essence absurd (Derrida, 9). "Anterior and exterior to the development of the content it announces, . . . [p]receding what ought to be able to present itself on its own, the preface falls like an empty husk, a piece of formal refuse, a moment of dryness and loquacity, sometimes both at once" (Derrida, 9). Authors have long been aware of this inanity. Many refrain from writing prefaces, while others exploit their inherent absurdity, such as Zola begging "to be excused by intelligent people who, in order to see clearly, do not need to have a lantern lit for them in broad daylight."[12] If these "préfaces-esquives" have numerous users, Genette urges us not to be fooled by them. Soon these introductions will fall in the very trap they claim to avoid. The awareness of their theoretical impossibility is not enough to prevent writers from writing them. This superb denial, on the part of Yourcenar, tends to prove it:

> No matter how often I say that a collection of love poems does not require commentary (which is true in principle), I know that I seem to be avoiding the issue in dealing at such great length with thematic and stylistic characteristics while keeping quiet about the love experience that inspired the book. (xx–xxi)

Yet the fact that she knows that they are superfluous in no way prevents Yourcenar from writing prefaces. This clearly indicates that the meaning of her prefaces can't be reduced to their content, but has to do with what they perform as such, that is, the *representation* of the author and her intentions, both hovering above the novels, guiding their interpretation. The preface's function is not so much informative as performative, in that it allows their subject to show itself (off) as an "author." No matter the diversity of its topics, her paratext has one goal: to construct her production as an "effect" related to a single, unified "cause." In situating her novels so carefully within the literary canon, as she does with *Alexis* or *Anna, soror . . .*, Yourcenar does nothing but say: "I am an author, and this is my work."

THE HUNT FOR BAD READERS [LA CHASSE AUX MAUVAIS LECTEURS]

The supremacy of the author, for Yourcenar, is gauged in terms of intention. "He alone knows what he wished to do" (*Abyss*, 360), she assures. By the same token, the Yourcenarian author defines himself *against* the reader. Indeed, the paratext tends to polarize these two figures, by endowing the former with that power and knowledge of which the latter is consistently deprived. The postface as such symbolizes the last word that Yourcenar intends to have on the interpretation of the works. "It is for value as a human, and not a political document, that *Coup de Grâce* has been written," Yourcenar insists, "and accordingly must be judged" (ix). Ironically, her need to dominate the interpretation of her works stretches to *An Obscure Man*, whose main character's motivations undergo careful clarification until, she writes, "there is nothing more to say about Nathanaël" (226).

It is, in other words, the reader himself or herself that her Baltic soldiers are supposed to fight off. "Naive," "imbecile," or "rough," her reader is doomed to be wrong.[13] Hence the imperious nature of her prefaces, their tone as *cutting* as the justification of *Anna, soror . . .*'s title: "two words carved on Miguel's tomb at Anna's command, and [which] say everything that matters" (229). When the reader denounces her "preciosity" in *Fires*, "it is because [he or she] cannot follow, all the way through, the idea or emotion that the poet is giving, so that he mistakenly takes it as a forced metaphor or a strained conceit" (xviii). It is because of his or her incompetence, in other words, that Yourcenar has to "underline what should go without saying" (*Oeuvres*, 83). Yet one can never be too careful against stupidity: upon mentioning World War II, Yourcenar felt compelled to add "the one in 1939. . . ." (xii).

To some readers, such didacticism nevertheless constitutes an act of kindness. Hélène Jaccomard observes: "The care [Yourcenar displays] in translating Greek and English inscriptions, as well as in indicating her ... sources, shows a certain tolerance of the pedagogue for the cultural shortcomings her reader might have."[14] No matter how genuine this pedagogical feeling, it already testifies to a superiority complex on the part of Yourcenar, who assumes, for instance, that her reader isn't bilingual, or that he has forgotten his "schooldays' latin," as the preface to *Alexis* insinuates. Yet the author's supremacy isn't merely cultural but also structural ("He alone knows what he wished to do"). Hence Yourcenar's notorious disdain for critics, who "see in my works not what I put, or tried to put, into them but what they want to find" (Galey, 259). If the common reader can still be forgiven—he or she cannot after all know the writer's mind—the professional critic is, according to her, guilty of making a living out of what is necessarily an imposture.[15] Such disdain turns to hate when the critics' "discovery" is of a biographical nature. The long note following *Two Lives and a Dream* was primarily concerned with "[brushing] aside the hypotheses of those simple-minded people who always imagine that every work comes out of some personal experience" (238). To do so, Yourcenar anticipates and dismisses, one by one, the possible parallels between a character such as Anna and young Marguerite de Crayencour. Similarly, her almost stubborn refusal to acknowledge Gide's influence on her first novel *(Alexis)* indicates, indirectly as ever, the same concern:[16] not so much about being cast as marginal as losing the control of her production to a higher, existential reality.

Yourcenar's need for control isn't confined to explicit directives, or a cutting, condescending tone, but rather spreads out to fill all paratextual space. The title of her books, for example, often overdetermine their content. In describing Alexis's venture as a "Vain Struggle," she already encourages a specific interpretation of the novel. In the same way, all of the short stories in *Fires* bear hints in their titles: "Sappho or Suicide," "Achilles or the Lie," and so on. Yourcenar's interpretative diktat also reigned in her relationship with her publisher, Gallimard, who granted her the exceptional privilege of being the author of her own biography in the *Pléiade* edition (she wrote it in the third person). Finally, she also ruled over her works' epitext (Genette), including her correspondence and interviews with journalists. She did not make it easy for Patrick de Rosbo and Matthieu Galey, who remember their stay on Mount Desert Island bitterly. Similarly, Yourcenar would later at least partially repudiate these published conversations. As for some of her letters, she cared enough to have them sealed in a vault for fifty years after her death.

Such a concealment is not uncommon in her prefaces. "I pass as rapidly as possible," the *Reflections* read, "over three years of research, of interest to specialists alone, and over the development of a method akin to controlled delirium, of interest, probably, to none but madmen" (328). Her introduction to *Fires* is careful about not disclosing the nature of the "love crisis" of which these short stories are said to be the "product." Even more obvious are the restrictions in the introduction to *Dreams and Spells*, an astonishing collection of private dreams. As usual, Yourcenar first seeks to inscribe her choice in literary history. But dreams are by nature hard to tame. Ironically, Yourcenar's only literary reference reads like a slip of the tongue. "Dreams are excrements," she says, quoting Novalis. Since the meaning of dreams is impossible to master, Yourcenar resorts to censorship, and awakens and sends forth her (sleeping) Baltic guards with a rather swift bayonet:

> As we can see, I have carefully discarded the physiological dreams, too obviously induced or contributed to by a malfunction of the stomach or the heart; I discard even more carefully those blurred and confused dreams born of an indigestion of memory, and which are nothing but the shapeless residual of small daily tribulations, as unworthy of being dreamt of as lived. . . . Nor do I say anything about the pure sexual or post-sexual fantasies which constitute the mere observation of desire (or pleasure) by a man or a woman asleep. Finally, I discard these grand common dreams, the explanation of which remains uncertain. (*Essais*, 1534)

Censorship, however, is not always so explicit. Even before she sorted out her dreams according to the criteria described here, Yourcenar had already eliminated those she deemed "untellable," using the mythological distinction between the "ivory door" and the "bronze door" (*Essais*, 1539). Her *Reflections* imply a similar restraint: between each comment, a gap, a lack keeps representing authority. "Everything recounted here is thrown out of perspective by what is left unsaid: these notes serve only to mark the lacunae" (324–25).

In addition, these *Reflections* aren't really intended for the reader's use. These seventy notes are in fact addressed to the author of the *Memoirs*. Their casual style indeed evokes the personal notes of a writer. A second layer of comment, this time on the notes themselves, both produces some dialogical depth and ultimately reveals the paratext as a soliloquy.

The Writer's Millstone [Cent fois sur le métier ...]

Yourcenar's compulsive erasing and rewriting of her novels should be interpreted from this perspective. I believe that the prefaces' purpose is to express and justify this peculiar behavior. Indeed, such a statement represents a very important part of her paratext in terms of both quantity and place, since all her prefaces and postfaces start with it. "The idea for this book and the first writing of it, in whole or in part, and in various forms, dates from the period between 1924 and 1929, between my twentieth and twenty-fifth year. All those manuscripts were destroyed, deservedly" (*Reflections*, 319). Similarly, the Author's Note that accompanies *The Abyss* declares immediately that the novel "represents the final development of an isolated fragment, some forty pages originally intended as the first chapter of a vast novel." Yourcenar then nuances this description: "At the most, some dozen pages ... remain" (359–60). These two preambles, obviously, are even less about rewriting than about censorship. Touching up and erasing are one and the same gesture for Yourcenar. Even when she actually addresses the changes that she made over the years in her novels, as she did in *Anna, soror ...*'s postface, it is always after having mentioned the cuts. "*Anna, soror ...* is an early work.... These hundred or so pages originally were part of a vast, shapeless novel, *Crosscurrents* ... (227)." Finally, the introduction to *A Coin in Nine Hands* opens with this reference: "corrections, cuts, and transpositions have left almost no line unchanged" (169).

Such transactions don't always make sense to Yourcenar herself. "The old and the new," she confesses about *A Coin in Nine Hands*, "overlap to such an extent that it is almost impossible, even for the author, to tell where one begins and the other ends" (169). Here the author shares the fate of the reader, and seems excluded from the mysteries of creation. What then of the mastery that so far appeared to be the goal of the prefaces? For Colette Gaudin, this paradox indicates a crucial difference between the Yourcenarien author and the author "killed" by Barthes, or the Father that Derrida catches lost in "narcissistic admiration" before his Son, the Book (Derrida, 52). The prefaces of Yourcenar, Gaudin argues, "question the control of the authorial subject [and] thicken the enigma of origin even though they point to the sources of the works" (Gaudin, 19; my translation).[17] We will indeed see that the subject of the paratext, far from being unified, is gradually disseminated. Nonetheless, as a "thickening" of the "enigma of origin," the prefaces perform a task that is not different from what they usually do. Just like the reprimands addressed to the reader, the careful sorting of the information he or she will be given or denied (such as the mysterious "first versions" of the novels) and the blurring of the authorial subject denies the reader access to the creative process that the paratext was supposed to clarify. Writing, therefore, meets alchemy as another occult form of creation. Alchemy, in addition, differs from modern science in that it precludes the epistemological distinction between subject and object. In a like manner, the paratext of Yourcenar may do more than just put into question the mastery of the creator: it makes it disappear.

My Friend Zeno

According to their author, *Memoirs of Hadrian* should ideally have been written by the emperor himself. The *Reflections* on this novel keep describing the efforts of Yourcenar toward "objectivity," "purity," and "transparence," even though these were precisely the qualities against which the New Novel sought to define itself. The same year, in 1951, Robbe-Grillet published *The Erasers*, and Robert Pinget his first novel. While a "tyrannical Blanchotism" was reigning over French literature,[18] Yourcenar tried hard to "forbid one's own shadow [and] leave the mirror clean of the mist of one's own breath" (331). The writer needs to step aside: to become transparent, to stop breathing. Ultimately, her character has to breathe for her. This is why she claims to "have felt Hadrian's tears running down her face."[19] What she called her "method of delirium" (*Reflections,* 328) points precisely to the deletion of a narcissistic subjectivity in favor of a higher sensorial and imaginative receptivity, an opening to the Other whom she lets "invest" her (Galey, 144–45). Yourcenar isn't so much Zeno's creator as his longtime companion. "How many times," she explains, "unable to sleep, I had the urge to stretch my hand towards Zeno, who lay on the same bed, resting from existence. . . . I know the exact pressure of his hand, its level of warmth . . ."[20]

Yourcenar's "realism" is thus less conventional than one might think. Reading *Coup de Grâce*'s preface, for instance, one realizes that Erick von Lhomond is not considered by Yourcenar to be less real than the Baltic soldiers who congratulated her on the accuracy of his portrait. "Perhaps he had been more in love with Sophie than he says" (vii), the author supposes, just as she would later challenge Hadrian's words. "It has even occurred to me that the emperor was lying. In such cases I had to let him lie, like the rest of us" (340). Yourcenar goes beyond mere rhetorical effect. Her *Reflections* display a firm belief in the existence of the emperor that is not only historical, of course, but also empirical, as if the model she was trying to paint was next to her rather than reconstituted on the basis of documents.[21] This is why, when asked about her choice of the first person, Yourcenar could answer that "surely Hadrian could speak more forcibly and more subtly of his life than could [she]" (329). The readers who told her "Hadrian is you" exasperated her, for they were too blunt [grossier] to realize that she and the emperor were in fact, at this very moment, two different beings. One could wonder if this duality is not precisely what induced Yourcenar to devote long prefaces to her characters, even though they were fictional. From the deep certitude that they were *Other*, Yourcenar draws the desire to treat them as such.

The (over)exhibited belief in the reality of her characters has yet another consequence, which brings us back to the control exerted by the paratext. "Real" beings, endowed with "real" intentions, Yourcenar's characters, instead of the reader, also happen to determine the interpretation of the narratives. The meaning of *Anna, soror* . . . , for instance, is dependent on the complicity of the two children and their mother. Whether Valentine is aware or not of the incest taking place under her roof, the novella participates in a different *genre*. Her knowledge of this fact would compromise a moral parable as such. Also, it would make *Anna, soror* . . . an exception in the genealogy of literary incest established by Yourcenar in the novella's postface. Yourcenar, however, refuses to settle the matter. She takes cover behind Valentine, as if the latter were the only one to know.

> It would appear (and I use this formula of uncertainty because I believe that the motivations of his characters should often remain unclear to the author himself: their liberty is at that price) that from the beginning Valentina perceives the love her two children have for each other. . . . (235)

The reader's freedom, in other words, stops where the characters' begins.

As we can see, the authority of the paratext well exceeds the imperatives articulated by Yourcenar. Ultimately, it is in disappearing as an author that she achieves her ideal of a book shining with an immanent, unambiguous meaning. She will thus allow her characters to "drive the cart," or pretend that her novels have engendered themselves.

"Another's Work"

Without exception, her prefaces begin with statements of which the book is the grammatical subject.[22] Consequently, the author is expressed in the third person, directly or impersonally,[23] or in the form of a circumlocution (a twenty-two, twenty-four-year-old woman . . .). Most of the time, however, the subject of writing vanishes in passive clauses ("changes have been made, chapters have been composed, episodes have been made up," etc.), or in nonsubjective verbal modes (cf. the use of the imperative or the infinitive in the *Reflections on Memoirs of Hadrian*). In the end the reader is made to feel that Yourcenar had not written these novels at all. She herself encourages reading them "as if they were another's work" (*Oeuvres*, 164). And this eventually happened. In the winter of 1948, in her home on Mount Desert Island, Maine, Yourcenar received a trunk that she had left in Switzerland ten years before. She remembers finding a letter inside.

> I came upon four or five typewritten sheets, the paper of which had turned yellow. The salutation told me nothing: "My dear Mark. . . ." Mark. . . . What friend or love, what distant relative was this? I could not recall the name at all. It was several minutes before I remembered that Mark stood here for Marcus Aurelius, and that I had in hand a fragment of the lost manuscript. (326)

The passage is representative of the prefaces' discursive logic: the first person always only designates Yourcenar as a reader.[24] Yet other voices can be heard as well: that of the corrector or of the preface's writer, or even the corrector of the preface's writer, which appear in italics throughout the *Reflections*. No wonder that the author's voice gets lost in this concert. Common sense, of course, would attribute this *detachment* to the many years that took place between the actual writing of the novel and its preface. Yet I think a more productive reading would reverse causality and ask whether this detachment is not precisely the prefaces' aim. Indeed, at times distance becomes part of the story we are told, as in the following tale of *inspiration*.

As she had grown tired of waiting for a train to Canada, Yourcenar rented a hotel room near the station. "The cold and my neuralgia kept me from sleeping," she remembers,

> . . . but for two hours an extraordinary thing happened: I saw pass before my eyes, suddenly issuing out of nowhere in rapid acceleration like the frames of a film, episodes in the life of Nathanaël, whom I hadn't

even thought of for twenty years. (*Two Lives and a Dream*, postface, 222)

Not only profiting from the confusion between an actual person and a fictional character, such a statement treats literary creation as a passive process, which in turn problematizes the status of the author: if the creation of *An Obscure Man* came down to "follow[ing] [Nathanaël's] wanderings from Jamaica to Barbados" (postface, 222), does Yourcenar still deserve to be called a writer? Such a question is already raised by her predilection for the historical novel. Is not History, one might ask, the ultimate author of her works?

By stressing the impersonal aspect of creation, by shifting the text's responsibility from the writer to the scribe, the preface allows Yourcenar to take still tighter control of her works. Between the processes of reading and writing, the prefaces continuously add justifications as well as obstacles to accepting her various stances as scribe/author—which eventually amounts to an extreme polarization of these two roles. On the one hand, reading should be no more than a faithful observance of the advice given by the author in her prefaces. Ideally, Yourcenar's narratives should remain out of the reader's reach, which is to say, unread. In her introduction to *Dreams and Spells*, the author took visible pleasure in the fact that only she could perceive "the secret heat of the talisman [of this text]" (*Oeuvres*, 1541). In dedicating this collection of poems to Hermes, Yourcenar endows *Fires* with an esoteric meaning. If the Baltic soldiers' duty was to repel bad readers, the master of the alchemists stands in the way of just any reader.... "I hope this book will never be read" (3), "This book is dedicated to no one," the *Reflections* (*Oeuvres*, 537) immediately declare, as an overstatement to/of the novel's dedication: "To The Deified August Hadrian." Such a circularity had already prevailed in *Alexis*, which was dedicated "to himself."

To conclude, Yourcenar's paratexts are always composed of two moments. The first is that of *mastery*, which takes the shape of an explanation, or a system, which sheds light on the text by projecting intentions onto it, construing the author and her works in reference to a relationship that is a closed circle. Such a strategy relies on "instructions" rather than "advice." Then comes the moment of *polarization*, of a separation between author and reader so radical that it eventually eliminates them as related to a single process. So diminished is the reader that he or she eventually disappears. Similarly, once declared omnipotent, the author also vanishes, for being everywhere also means being nowhere. Yourcenar's greatest novels have written themselves and should not be read. Or at least not by just anybody. The narrative structure of *Memoirs of Hadrian* best represents the *detachment* that inspires the poetics of Yourcenar, with Hadrian as the author of the book and Marcus Aurelius as its one and only reader. An emperor talking to another emperor: the art of Yourcenar is not democratic.

Rewriting and Repression of the Feminine

This mystification of writing is, in my opinion, yet another manifestation of authorial power in that it locates the text further and further away from its reader. And rewriting is part of that strategy. These "first versions" and other unpublished manuscripts are similar to *le livre* of Mallarmé, which only owes its perfection to its nonexistence, and to the fact that it did not *fall* into the hands of a reader.

Just as the prefaces, rewriting has to do with power, and more precisely with a conflict between two types of writing: on the one hand, the original text, described as impulsive, feverish, inexhaustible,[25] and on the other hand the revised text, a product of "the strict discipline of French narrative" (postfaces, 240). Rewriting, in other words, is above all a matter of constraint: it aims to physically restrain the text to the size of the contemporary novel. As we know it, *Memoirs of Hadrian* constitutes, in Yourcenar's words, "the condensation of a vast work composed for myself alone.... Added all together, these accounts would have afforded material for a volume of several thousand pages" (340). As long as *The Abyss*, one might assume, which was originally to be a "broad fresco extending over several centuries" (359).

Yet rewriting is more than just size reduction. It imposes narrative restrictions as well; *Memoirs of Hadrian*, for instance, was originally a series of dialogues (320). In the name of consistency, other diegetic changes are performed here and there. Lazarus *(A Lovely Morning)* is "sent" to Greenwich in order to make "this child of Amsterdam" more credible in a play by Shakespeare. But stories are more often touched up to match historical "truth." Information gleaned during years of travel or in the pages of a colossal personal library are projected onto a fictional canvas. But if erudition validates fiction, it also ends up erasing the personal experience from which it stems, which Yourcenar scornfully calls the "shavings" *[râclures]* of our own existence (postfaces, 224).

But whatever its particular goal, the discourse of rewriting always stages a shift from chaos to order, from multiplicity to unity, from nature to culture: rewriting is meant to reduce, or, more rightly, channel the flow of this unspeakable source. It is that which tames the original "crosscurrents" into harmless "water that flows."[26] In sum, the role of rewriting is analogous to that of the prefaces. Both aim to channel the text, at the level of its production and reception. In a way, Yourcenar takes over the watch of her Baltic soldiers. And the "writer's idiosyncrasy" she admits to Matthieu Galey sounds indeed like military tactics:

> On the third or fourth draft, pencil in hand, I reread my text, . . . and *eliminate* whatever can be eliminated, whatever seems useless. Each deletion is a *triumph*. At the bottom of every page I write, "crossed out seven words," "crossed out ten words," as the case may be. It gives me great pleasure to get rid of what is futile. (Galey, 183; my emphasis)

I am therefore tempted to argue that rewrites and paratext pertain to a single phenomenon, in this case, a censorship. In other words, revisions and prefaces are but different ways of repressing a unique object, which I will now try to define.

Describing what she erased from the original versions of her novels, Yourcenar often used the word "useless." "I try to eliminate what isn't essential," she explains to Matthieu Galey. "I try not to give in, as I did in my youth, to the temptation to add ornaments" (Galey, 185). In other words she erases the surplus, or the excess (both rendered by the French word *excès*). Interestingly, these two concepts also serve to articulate her "feminism," which is addressed in the collections of interviews with Galey or de Rosbo as well as in her published letters. Surplus and excess, more precisely, represent two facets of femininity that Yourcenar respectively reveres and hates. On the one hand she admits that Sophie's "almost inexhaustible wealth of emotion and feeling is a feminine element that most counts for [her] . . ."[27] while conversely, the "real" modern woman finds no mercy in the eyes of Yourcenar, who almost obsessively blames her for following clothing fashion trends, with their "vulgar commercialism, tyranny and scorn of and for women."[28] But beyond artificiality or ridicule, it is the useless carnage of animals that exasperates Yourcenar the most. "A still worse reproach: fur coats, and, when they were legal, the feathers. The complete and utter indifference of women to the crimes their finest dresses bore."

Under these "bloody furs," "one looks for the woman in vain," Yourcenar sighs (*Lettres à ses amis*, 276). And as a matter of fact, her works are notoriously lacking in female characters. In order to become a published writer, she had to *virilize* her main character. "The initial *Anna* still dated from a period when, struggling with a huge fresco doomed to remain unfinished, I wrote rapidly without any attention to composition or style, drawing directly from whatever springs were within me. It was only later, with *Alexis*, that I set myself to study the strict discipline of French narrative" (240).

The remarkable absence of women in the Yourcenarian fictional universe did not fail to surprise her readers. According to the author, historical imbalance forced her to deal mainly with male characters. "Women's lives, now and in all times, have been too limited in their manifestations," she explains to Patrick de Rosbo (88). Yet this disappearance extends to the narrative level of works that, apart from a few short poems in *Fires*, rely on male voices. When asked about it, Yourcenar usually offered that women's lives were inscrutable. It is for this reason that she gave up her project to write a sequel to *Alexis* in the form of a response from his wife Monique. "Nothing is more secret than a woman's existence" (xiii). In the same fashion, she also considered for a while using Plotine as the narrator of Hadrian's life before abandoning this idea. "It is already hard enough to give some element of truth to the utterances of a man" (*Oeuvres*, 526). This position seems motivated by another opinion, also frequently voiced in the prefaces, that gender does not matter. Recalling the portrayal of Anna and Miguel (*Anna, soror . . .*), Yourcenar describes how she freely crossed from one to the other, "with that indifference to sex which is . . . that of all creators in the presence of their creations" (237). She would later quote Hadrian on this indifference. "A man who reads, thinks, or plans belongs to his species rather than his sex" (De Rosbo, 94–95). Let us notice, however, her slip of the tongue when she cites the emperor to Matthieu Galey, and turns this reader into a writer. "A man who *writes* belongs to his species rather than his sex" (*Yeux ouverts*, 272).

This dismissal of gender is a well-known aspect of Yourcenar's poetics. To my knowledge, however, no one ever dared to flip this statement upside down and wonder whether Yourcenar did not write precisely in order not to be a woman anymore.[29] If rewriting meant for her to erase the text's femininity, then the paratext serves to *authorize* this project. Referring to "the twenty-four-year-old woman" who wrote *Alexis*, Yourcenar distances herself not only from the author of this book, but from the woman who "delivered" it.

The metaphor isn't new, but it is significant. When women were blamed for being writers in the past, it was because they were thought to have subverted their biological destiny. Literary production, as opposed to reproduction, was deemed against nature. But for Yourcenar, such a subversion already represents a moral imperative: writing is for her a means of not adding lives to the "ant-hill" that the planet has become.[30] Born in a social class that entrusts its offspring to nannies and nurses, she rarely missed an occasion to "deconstruct" the maternal instinct, which "is not as compelling as people like to say it is" (*Dear Departed*, 15). Regardless, the purification of the original texts targets femininity and maternity equally. Yourcenar disposes of maternity, for instance, when she touches up *Anna, soror . . .* Or rather she literally displaces it by erasing the story's preamble, a prolepsis which represented an older Anna, a mother herself.

This negation of maternity conforms to the image that Yourcenar gives of her work as a writer in her paratext. Her intensive historical research, the obsessive mapping out of her novels, and the decor of the Yale Library all participate in the staging of an author whose books are *conceived* rather than *born* or *delivered*. The intellectualism displayed in "Notes" that are mere bibliographies and the abstraction that surrounds her literary creation are to be taken literally, as separate from the body. Significantly, she excluded the body from the very place where it *acts* upon the text, namely her collection of *Dreams and Spells*, from which she purged the "physiological dreams." In the same way, if the prefaces so readily prohibit access to the author's sexuality, it is less out of Puritanism than an obsessive fear of the biological. The "purely biographical residues"[31] that she refused to address in the account of her own creative process are the practical, tangible conditions in which she, Marguerite Yourcenar, lies at the origin of her books. The fragmentation of the authorial subject that I observed in all of her prefaces corresponds, I would say, to a desire for dismemberment, or scattering, already figured by the shuffling of letters that transformed Crayencour into Yourcenar. Finally, her paratext serves to annihilate the author's body as a locus of creation. As the French put it, Yourcenar was very concerned that her books did not appear to have come out of her womb (il ne faut pas que ses livres aient l'air de lui *sortir du ventre*).[32]

Yourcenar, Creator

Thus her rewriting of her books ultimately aims to eradicate her maternal ties to them. Under the claim of verbal efficiency or elegance, Yourcenar was in fact conjuring up her own anxiety over motherhood, which is sealed in the oft quoted following denial:

> Je m'inscris en faux contre l'assertion, souvent entendue, que la perte prématurée d'une mère est toujours un désastre, ou qu'un enfant privé de la sienne éprouve toute sa vie le sentiment d'un manque et la nostalgie de l'absente. Dans mon cas, au moins, les choses tournèrent autrement. (*Essais*, 744)

> [I take issue with the assertion, commonly heard, that the premature death of a mother is always a disaster or that a child deprived of its mother feels a lifelong sense of loss and a yearning for the deceased. In my case, at least, things turned out otherwise.] (52)

This analogy, which I believe is crucial, is undoubtedly inscribed in the following passage, in which Yourcenar justifies her need to rewrite her books using not only the same grammatical and syntactic structure, but also the same words.

> Qu'il me soit permis, du moins, de m'inscrire en faux contre l'opinion courante qui veut que se remettre à une œuvre ancienne, la retoucher, à plus forte raison la refaire en partie, est une entreprise inutile ou même néfaste, d'où l'élan et l'ardeur ne peuvent qu'être absents. Bien au contraire.... (*Oeuvres*, 163)

> [Let me at least dispute the validity of the prevalent opinion that taking an older work and retouching or partly rewriting it is a useless or even injurious enterprise because it destroys the original impulse and passion. On the contrary, for me it was both a privilege and an experience to see this substance....] (*Dear Departed*, 171)

The "défaut" of the original text and that of the mother, who died following childbirth, appear interchangeable. Strictly speaking, these first versions are *matrices* (Fr. mold, matrix, and womb), and, as such, they correspond to what Michael Riffaterre has identified at the core of any poetic process. According to him, poetry is the verbal transformation of a *matrice* made of one or more signifiers.[33] Poetry somehow works like a pun, but a neurotic pun, Riffaterre insists, insofar as it aims to repress this *matrice*. It is what the poem speaks of and yet never names.

Reflecting on the stylistic faux pas of her youth, Yourcenar indeed uses a vocabulary that suggests something different and quite probably more serious. When Yourcenar touches up her text, she uses no fine paintbrush. The trowel, even, turned out to be too little to fill up the "faults" in *Death Drives the Cart* (*Oeuvres*, 838), which had to be torn apart and rebuilt from top to bottom in order to become *The Abyss* and *Two Lives and a Dream*. We know how many years this reconstruction cost Yourcenar, and how much effort she put into "grounding" her works.[34] Again, the published novel was grafted on a gap. The word "terrassement," however, leads us to wonder if Yourcenar was not also trying to bury some monster under a heap of soil. When she labors at rewriting every sentence, the author seems to fight her own demons much more than any narrative imperfections. The *"défaut"* she seeks to eliminate ought to be taken in its etymological sense, that is, as both a failure and a lack, which rewriting is meant to cover.

The trauma related to a *mise au monde*, which is always already, for Yourcenar, a *mise à mort*, hovers over these "original works." Their very form ("feverish") as well as their obsession with the ineluctability of death *(Death Drives the Cart)* evoke all too clearly the postpartum fever that took Fernande away ten days after the birth of her only child. The same could be said of the excessive severity with which Yourcenar treats her own literary beginnings, and the guilt that surrounds her birth as a writer. "Sometimes one publishes too soon and in such cases the first version remains, inflicting perpetual remorse on the writer" (De Rosbo, 20).

Before taking on the task of rewriting them, Yourcenar destroyed her original versions and all preparatory work. She thus claims to have burned her notes on Hadrian taken at the Yale library as well as the drafts of the novel (324). "Each morning I would burn the work of the night before. In such fashion I wrote a great number of decidedly abstruse meditations, and several descriptions bordering on the obscene" (340). Yourcenar literally burns what should never have been shown.[35] In its very wording, such an auto-da-fé pertains to repression. But as psychoanalysis has taught us, the repressed is subject to return, and what is repressed here precisely returns (through the chimney) in the preface of *Dreams and Spells*.

> Between the ages of seven and ten I had a recurring nightmare of the most banal variety: I saw a bloodied and mutilated corpse fall into my room through a particularly large and black chimney. Half-asleep, my little girl's reasoning explained this phenomenon as due to the presence of burglars on the floor above whose wrongdoings my nurses read of in the evening's newspaper in front of me; it seemed to me that this was a dream of childbirth, springing from sexual or rather hereditary curiosities in the mind of a young girl who had more than likely frequently

heard whispering allusions to her mother dying while giving birth, and how clamps were used in delivering her.

Its unbearable perspicacity, however, will soon cause this interpretation to be smothered by a footnote.[36] Similarly, the importance of this dream is already denied by the (questionable) assessment of "banality." Finally, Yourcenar's obsession with the slaughter of animals to the dictates of fashion is likely to refer to this original carnage, in that, like the woman wearing a fur coat, she herself owes her life/skin to that of another being.

It is not by chance that the conflict between the obscene and the repressed, between a passionate style and a controlled one, reached a peak with the publication of the short stories collected in *Fires*. In the Yourcenarian symbolic field of matter *[matière]*, *Fires* is hardly at home: from *Crosscurrents* to *Comme l'eau qui coule*, the novels are literally written around surfaces of water. From the ponds of Woroïno to the ocean of Nathanaël, from Miguel's death on a battleship to Antinoüs's suicide, and Zeno's, one might add, which is a bloodbath, the characters seem inevitably drawn to liquidity. What interests me in *Fires*, however, is a less obvious rupture. First, the aphorisms that are printed between the stories represent the last intimate fragment of Yourcenar's paratext. After this, the interventions of the author will take the form of the meticulous exegesis. On the other hand, as I noted before, *Fires* contains the last preface written by Yourcenar, and one might wonder how her strategy benefits from this displacement of the commentary at the other end of the text.

Apparently a postface cannot be as controlling as a preface. It is too late to rectify a bad reading, as Genette has pointed out (239). But at the same time its deferred *[différé]* status contributes to define a certain discursive field, that of the "already-read," from which the question of literary production is excluded per se. As a finished product, the book can take place in an economy of comparison that the writer of epilogues manages as she pleases, while perpetuating the delusion that she is but a reader equally interested in Thomas Mann and in Marguerite Yourcenar. This also presents the book as born ex nihilo, possibly "conceived," but never "delivered."

Her paratext ultimately provides Yourcenar with a form of authorship that functions as a shield against the maternal trauma in Yourcenar's experience. In an all too simplistic fashion, Yourcenar's narrative preferences, that is, her choice of male narrators and characters, have often been reduced to her sexual preferences, which, one readily assumes, entail a desire to be a man. Yet such a statement, apart from being hardly verifiable, leaves out a crucial dimension of Yourcenar's work, even if highly problematic: the family, whose failures dictate the fate of almost all characters. In Yourcenar's fiction, home is a place to run away from, or a set of conditions to transgress. Without family there would be no incest *(Anna, soror . . .)*, without lost fathers, no homosexual desire (Alexis, Hadrien), and without bad mothers, no reason to run away and travel around the world (Zeno, Nathanaël). One should also mention Yourcenar's passion for genealogy, at stake in the historical novel as well as in the huge biography of her own family that she left in lieu of an autobiography. In other words, writing *as a man*, or even *like a man*, isn't about *being a man*, but rather results from the radical refusal of being a mother. If Yourcenar's paratext serves to inscribe this refusal, it promotes by the same token what I would call the *paternity* of her works.

Theory no longer assumes that the *author* is an original entity. It is rather constructed around the notions of unity of meaning and origin: a text is attributed to a single consciousness through a series of signs, such as a signature. Taking this a step further, feminist readers have shown that such a gesture in fact pertains to a male's anxiety toward his offspring. Dorothy Dinnerstein explains that "men's powerful impulse to affirm and tighten by cultural inventions their unsatisfactorily loose mammalian connection with children leads them to value highly cultural inventions of a symbolic nature."[37] After all, Nathanaël is reduced to purchasing his paternity.[38] Likewise, the transmission of the name, the patrilineal succession, as well as the ever anxious control of the woman's body, are ways to make up for the uncertainty of the paternal bond. Fatherhood, in other words, is gained only at the expense of motherhood.

Unsurprisingly, the patriarchal culture has manifested both these fears and the means to fight them in the realm of artistic production. The most eminent of these remedies, biographical criticism, consists of projecting everything that "resembles" the author onto his or her work—and resemblance is all the more cherished in that it represents the only visible feature of paternity. On the part of the writer, the claim of a definite intention plays a similar role, and we have seen how Yourcenar uses her own intention to prescribe legitimate as opposed to illegitimate or, more precisely, *adulterous* readings. As for the anxious control of her production, we shall remember here the tyrannical attitude of Yourcenar over her literary estate, which includes among others such extraordinary measures as the sealing of her letters and personal papers until the year 2037.

Yet what makes Yourcenar's paratext fascinating is that it *verifies* the theoretical connection between authorship and the repression of maternity.

This perspective brings an entirely new light to another important paratextual element, Yourcenar's pseudonym. If anything is repressed in the name "Yourcenar," one would object that it is paternity, rather than maternity, since the anagram has to do with the Name of the Father, Crayencour. When Stendhal parted with "Beyle," one critic has observed, he did so out of a desire to retrieve his maternal genealogy, and, through it, an adored mother whom he lost at an early age.[39] While such an interpretation remains valid and interesting, it should not be applied uncritically to the case of Yourcenar. First, her pseudonym does not constitute a full negation of the father's name, from which it does after all borrow its letters. Then, as she often recalled, Michel de Crayencour took part in the playful creation of the anagram.

In fact, what the name Yourcenar erases here isn't so much the father as ascendancy. In the choice of a pseudonym lies the fantasy to engender oneself. "The egotist," Starobinski noted about the pseudonymous writer, "rises in revolt against the imposition of identity from without: he seeks to achieve sole mastery over the equation that makes him identical to himself."[40] The egotist's dream is thus about absolving oneself from familial bonds, and, ultimately, from the physical dimension of creation. "Yourcenar," then, is another mark of organic discontinuity between the writer and her books, for "Yourcenar" did not come with a body—it is a pure product of the mind, an idea, itself ex nihilo. And what characterizes the Creator is that He has not been created. Such a fantasy of creation ex nihilo is also to be found in Yourcenar's fascination with alchemy. *L'Oeuvre au noir*, if we take this title literally, is not a novel written by her, but a series of magical operations that she merely supervised. In the very same way, the story quoted above of the hallucination of Nathanaël's wanderings eventually hides the more likely *gestation* of this character.

In order to describe the universe of Hadrian, Yourcenar borrowed the famous declaration of Flaubert apropos *Salammbô*. "Just when the gods had ceased to be, and the Christ had not yet come, there was a unique moment in history, between Cicero and Marcus Aurelius, when man stood alone" (319–20). We now better understand the seductive power of the period, which leaves Yourcenar with no one above her. And very likely the fantasy to be "there" herself.

(This article was translated from the French by Peter Glidden in collaboration with the author.)

Notes

1. Marguerite Yourcenar, *Coup de Grâce* (preface), trans. Grace Frick in collaboration with the author (New York: Farrar, Straus and Giroux, 1981), iv. When an English translation was not available, references are made to the definitive edition of Yourcenar's works, published by Gallimard in its prestigious *Pléïade* collection.
2. Colette Gaudin, Linda Stillman, Elaine Marks, and Richard Howard (see our bibliography) were the first to offer critical insight on the prefaces.
3. Patricia De Feyter mentions "the paratextual work with which the author generously enriched her works in order to better orient her readers" (my translation). "Nathanaël ou la désinvolture," *Bulletin de la Société Internationale d'Etudes Yourcenariennes* 13 (1993): 22.
4. The title *Comme l'eau qui coule* has not been translated. The book was published in English under the title of *Two Lives and a Dream*, trans. Walter Kaiser in collaboration with the author (New York: Farrar, Straus and Giroux, 1987).
5. The French "poli" means both "polite" and "polished."
6. The story, Angelo Rinaldi complained, seems "sculpted in a frieze made of Marseille soap with a chisel borrowed from a Prix de Rome of the past century." Angelo Rinaldi, "Montherlant, soror . . . ," *L'Express*, 23 octobre 1981. This nasty crack, however, may not have affected an author who defined her introductory tactics in 1968 with reference to Racine. . . . (*Oeuvres*, 543).
7. Marguerite Yourcenar, "Author's Note," *The Abyss*, trans. Grace Frick in collaboration with the author (New York: Farrar, Straus and Giroux, 1976), 361.
8. Marguerite Yourcenar, *Memoirs of Hadrian, and Reflections on the Composition of Memoirs of Hadrian*, trans. Grace Frick in collaboration with the author (New York: Farrar, Straus and Giroux, 1963), 299. I shall call this text *Reflections*.
9. Marguerite Yourcenar, "Preface," *Fires*, trans. Dori Katz in collaboration with the author (New York: Farrar, Straus and Giroux, 1981), ix.
10. Jacques Derrida, "Outwork," *Dissemination*, trans. Barbara Johnson (Chicago: University of Chicago Press, 1981), 7.
11. Or which he or she is supposed to ignore, given the statistics showing that a preface is in fact most often read *after* the main text.
12. Emile Zola, *Preface to Thérèse Raquin* (Oxford and New York: Oxford University Press, 1992), 6.
13. Those jeers appear, respectively, in the preface of *Coup de Grâce*, in the *Notebooks of the Abyss* (unpublished), quoted by Yvon Bernier in "Genèse et fortune littéraire des *Mémoires d'Hadrien*," *Revue de l'Université de Bruxelles* (1988/3–4), 11, and in *Reflections on the Composition of Memoirs of Hadrian* (*Oeuvres romanesques*, 536).
14. Hélène Jaccomard, *Lecteur et lecture dans l'Autobiographie française contemporaine* (Geneva: Droz, 1993), 203. My translation.
15. In 1977, Yourcenar complained to Lucienne Serrano, who had just sent her an essay on "Sappho or Suicide" and was about to chair a panel on her works at the MLA convention in Chicago: "Let me protest against this sort of dilation of the subject that is constituted by your essay. It is a miracle of art and literature that anyone could draw from a work a whole world of ideas and feelings which were not put there by the author in the first place, yet this kind of exegesis all too often ignores or masks what the author precisely meant to say." *Lettres à ses amis*, 536. My translation.

16. For an analysis of this particular preface, see my article, "Yourcenar et Gide: paternité ou parricide?" *Bulletin de la Société Internationale d'Etudes Yourcenariennes* 18 (December 1997): 19–38.

17. Colette Gaudin's reading stands against the feminist interpretations of Elaine Marks (1990) and Linda Stillman (1985), for whom the paratext serves to repress the feminine, and contributes as such to the construction of the Yourcenarian author.

18. Françoise Gaillard, "La modernité de Marguerite Yourcenar," *Equinoxe* 2 (1989): 13.

19. Béatrice Ness, *Mystification et créativité dans l'oeuvre romanesque de Marguerite Yourcenar. Cinq lectures génétiques* (Chapel Hill: University of North Carolina Press, 1994), 111.

20. "This physical gesture to hold my hand to this invented man, I did it more than once. But let's tell the imbeciles right away: if I have often watched my characters make love (and sometimes with a certain carnal pleasure on my part), I have never fancied sleeping with them." *Carnets de Notes* de *L'Oeuvre au Noir* (inédits), quoted by Yvon Bernier, 11. My translation.

21. Documents, one must add, that are far from being followed, as this paragraph from the *Note* to the *Memoirs of Hadrian* tends to show. "The episode of Mithraic initiation is *invented*; that cult was already in vogue in the army at the time, and it is possible, *but not proved*, that Hadrian desired to be initiated into it.... Turbo, Meles Agrippa, and Castoras are all historical figures, but their participation in the respective initiations is *invented*. Hadrian's meeting with the Gymnosophist *is not given by history*;... All details concerning Attiacus are authentic, except for one or two allusions to his private life, *of which we know nothing*. The chapter on the mistresses has been constructed out of two lines of Spartianus (XI, 7–8). On this subject the effort has been to stay within the most plausible general outlines, *supplementing by invention where it was essential to do so*" (311, my emphasis).

22. "*Alexis* was published in 1929..."; "*Anna, soror*... is an early work"; *Coup de Grâce* was written in Sorrento"; "[*Memoirs of Hadrian*] was conceived, then written, between 1924 and 1929..."; "*The Abyss* represents the final development of an isolated fragment..."

23. "Some of the author's opinions have changed...." (*Alexis*, *Oeuvres romanesques*, 3). Or also, "Never was a novel's creation more directly inspired by the locales in which it is placed" (*Anna, soror*..., postface, 236).

24. We should add: the first person of the plural as well, which sometimes is a "nous académique" ("Occupons-nous pour un temps d'autres travaux!" *Oeuvres romanesques*, 541) and sometimes designates an imaginary group of readers of Yourcenar, including herself. ("We may accept as credible most of the details of the atrocious story, since we have witnessed so many examples of fanaticism and mass hysteria in our own times." *The Abyss*, author's note, 369.)

25. "The 'initial' Anna still dated from a period when, struggling with a huge fresco doomed to remain unfinished, I wrote rapidly without any attention to composition or style, drawing directly from whatever springs were within me" (240).

26. This is an allusion to the titles *Remous* and *Comme l'eau qui coule*.

27. De Rosbo, 89. My translation.

28. *Lettres à ses amis*, 581–82.

29. Twenty years ago, though, while Yourcenarian scholarship still had much to do with hagiography, the French psychoanalyst and literary critic Catherine Clément addressed this symbolic androgyny in a short article which, significantly,

exasperated Yourcenar. "I have to say," she wrote about the collection of articles that the *Magazine littéraire* had just published on her works, "that only the article by Catherine Clément leaves me gaping. It seems that nowadays critics don't know what to do with a chaste character." *Lettres à ses amis et quelques autres* (Paris: Gallimard, 1995), 614–15. The article to which she is referring is: C. Clément, "L'androgynie imaginaire de Marguerite Yourcenar," *Magazine littéraire* 153 (1979): 19–21.

30. *Dear Departed*, trans. M.-L. Ascher (New York: Farrar, Straus and Giroux, 1991), 115.

31. "A deeper analysis of [*Fires*] would probably only yield purely biographical residues" (xv).

32. The French, of course, allows ambiguity between "guts"—as in the expression "coming from the guts"—and womb.

33. Michael Riffaterre, *Sémiotique de la poésie* (Paris: Seuil, 1982).

34. "Les deux romans se sont construits au cours des années par des travaux de terrassement successifs, jusqu'à ce qu'enfin, dans les deux cas, l'ouvrage ait été composé et parachevé d'un seul élan" (*Oeuvres romanesques*, 839). The English translation has erased the word "terrassement," which holds an ambiguity that seems crucial to me. "Terrasser" means "slain," and is used in French to describe St. Michael's vanquishing of the Dragon. "The two novels were constructed over the years in successive layers, as it were, until finally in both cases the last version was composed and completed in a single impulsion" (361).

35. It is the meaning of "obscene" but also of "abstruse," which originally meant "hidden."

36. "I am less convinced now by this Freudian interpretation and believe more in the influence of the horrible current events the nurses recounted with delight. At any rate, if this childhood dream was connected to my own birth, this interpretation does not contradict what I have said elsewhere concerning a young girl's complete indifference towards a mother dead in childbirth of whom one never spoke, but the particular detail of clamps and forceps, recalled more or less in whispers when I was around, couldn't help but interest a child who, like all children, was passionately curious about the physical process of childbirth." *Essais et Mémoires*, original translation by Peter Glidden (Paris: Gallimard "Pléide," 1991).

37. Dorothy Dinnerstein, *The Mermaid and the Minotaur: Sexual Arrangements and Human Malaise* (New York: Harper, 1976), 80.

38. "He gave Lazarus's wet nurse fifty florins for the child in case of extreme necessity. . . . This provision against the future was nothing more than a superstitious gesture, as if a way for Nathanaël to prove his paternity." Marguerite Yourcenar, *An Obscure Man*, in *Two Lives and a Dream*, trans. Walter Kaiser (New York: Farrar, Straus and Giroux, 1987) 49.

39. Such is the function of the pseudonym, according to Maryline Lukacher. "The pseudonym appears as a metaphor for a number of narrative strategies by which modern French writing inscribes its fiction of the maternal." "Pseudonymous Identities," in *Maternal Fictions: Stendhal, Sand, Rachilde, Bataille* (Durham and London: Duke University Press, 1994), 14–15.

40. Jean Starobinski, "Pseudonymous Stendhal," in *The Living Eye* (Cambridge: Harvard University Press, 1989), 82.

Is There No Body on the Scene of Writing? Contemporary Conceptions of Textual Practice in/and Yourcenar's Paratexts

Mieke Taat

Translated by Chantal Rodais

> To take leave of one's senses and no longer know which way to turn—such is perhaps the consequence of dissemination.
> —Jacques Derrida, *La Dissémination*

> Listen from the very heart of your body and understand: the mystery of being a woman is one, a woman, is not alone; the mystery is always that of the body within the body of a woman.
> —Hélène Cixous, *Ou l'art de l'innocence*

YOURCENAR'S INCREASING PRACTICE OF APPENDING PREFACES TO HER works during the last decades of her life surprised the critics all the more because this style was generally disparaged as a relic of the 1960s. There are numerous prefatory texts to consider; the "notes" and "memorandums" connected with *Mémoires d'Hadrien* (1951) and *L'Oeuvre au noir* (1968); the essays devoted to the problems encountered in writing these historical novels in *Sous bénéfice d'inventaire* (1962) and *Le Temps, ce grand sculpteur* (1983); the "prefaces," "postfaces," "reviews," "forewords," "postscripts," and "reports" which were added during the 1960s, 1970s and 1980s to the new editions of plays, short stories, lyric prose, and dream prose that were first edited before 1945; the collections of interviews (conducted by Patrick de Rosbo in 1972 and by Matthieu Galey in 1983). Finally, the recent posthumous publication of *Lettres à ses amis et quelques autres* (1995) was an anthology planned and prepared by the author in order to put her work itself above all personal revelations; as such, the anthology adds bulk and complexity to Marguerite Yourcenar's metadiscursive writings.

It is not the profusion of the author's observations alone that surprises today's readers, but the kinds of clarification that they seem intent on providing. Indeed, at first sight, they appear to perpetuate a decidedly traditional genetic approach that, in the Lansonian sense, "painstakingly trace[s] all sources and influences, as well as pinpoint[s] the stylistic elements in the work."[1] The open disdain of Freudianism appears to some critics to discourage readers from exploring the subconscious or, more generally, the subjective dimension of the prefatory text.[2] The didactic tone of these paratextual works "written in a manner of total supremacy," if not to say in a manner of "defensive strategy," sometimes changing to an "almost offensive" stratagem seems, moreover, to express "[Yourcenar's] unremitting rejection of another, more apprehensive, more overt and more feminine style."[3] One could say that this prefatorial language is alien to the thought and writing in our era of suspicion,[4] even to the point of being "phallaciously" authoritarian.[5]

Considering the wariness these authors' observations engendered, we can be grateful to Colette Gaudin for pointing out their contemporary status.[6] Based on this critic's subtle remarks about the manner in which the Yourcenarian paratext tackles issues of subject and origin, I will endeavor to extract the "gynetic" element from the Yourcenarian genetics, dwelling more particularly on that aspect of the genetics that relates to legetics. Indeed, Yourcenar's prefatory discourse qua induction to writing can hardly be disassociated from the "rules of the game" that govern her induction to reading. Most noteworthy are her remarks about reading when they convey—by means of the underlying womb metaphor—a deconstructive form of questioning and psychoanalytical insights. Most of her critics have ignored this aspect.

Before turning to Yourcenar's paratext that allows itself to be read "in the feminine," I offer a critical rereading of a few celebrated theoretical works of fiction by Roland Barthes, Jacques Derrida, and Gilles Deleuze. In these works, the dismantling of the preface as an authority—in other words the putting to death of the Author, who places himself at the forefront of his work—is connected to a rhetorical mobilization of the "woman," or at least that which our Western culture calls the "feminine."[7] Indeed, it cannot be ruled out that Marguerite Yourcenar's reputation as a "phallacious"[8] writer of prefaces owes much to the impact of the remarks on the topic of *"devenir femme de l'ecriture"* [the "becoming a woman of writing"] from these *maître-penseurs* of modernity.

To Become "A Woman": Without Head-in(g) or Out of In-body?

The misgivings of today's readers when confronted with prefaces are not simply the result of the author's pretense that ideas expressed from a point beyond the work of fiction are Truth. The fact is that notions of the text as a work created by an author have been replaced by a concept of "(inter)text" that is more malleable and polymorphous. It is therefore possible to conceive of writing as being a "movement of difference . . . that cannot be prefaced by any form of identity, unit or innate simplicity whatsoever."[9] This way of thinking about writing offers a space, where, in Foucault's words, access to "a domain in which the writer as a subject never ceases to vanish from sight" so that the text can henceforth be conceived without reference to origin, or, at least—to cite Barthes—"without reference to any other origin than language itself, namely the very element that ceaselessly brings into question all notions of origin."[10] This would appear to be the principal objective of the diverse voices heralding the death of the Author. As Deleuze puts it in *Dialogues* with Claire Parnet: "The drawbacks of the Author are in constituting a point of departure or of origin, in establishing a subject of enunciation upon which depend all utterances that are produced and in gaining recognition and identification in an order of dominant meanings and established powers" (35–36).

Postmodernist deconstructions of concepts of subject and origin are generally portrayed as the symbolic death of the father. It was precisely in these terms that, beginning in 1968, Barthes began to disparage literary history for deferring to authors. In his celebrated essay "La mort de l'auteur," he explains: "The author is reputed to be the father and the owner of his work; literary science thus teaches us to respect the manuscript and the declared intentions of the author" (74). And it is in analogous terms that Derrida holds the pretensions of the auctorial editorial up to ridicule. "As a preface to the book, [the preface] is the word of the father aiding and admiring his writing, answering for his son and gasping in his attempt to support, withhold, idealize, re-interiorize and bridle his seed" (52–53). Of course, to assess the author's commentary and observation poses a problem because it itself equals paternal discourse. It conveys an antidogmatic adoption of a position that has itself gradually frozen into a doxa by nearly completely evading the ambiguity of the underlying metaphors. By way of example, let us reread a statement made by Roland Barthes that stresses the necessity for the "removal," "death," and even "destruction" of the author in terms that, to me, seem far removed from the paternal functions traditionally attributed to the author: "The author is supposed to nourish the book, that is to say that he exists prior to its creation, thinks, suffers and lives for it; he entertains the same relationship of antecedence with his work as a father with his child" (64). First, the metaphors underlying this statement have much less to do with the traditional paternal production of the text than with its conception and the suffering that accompanies its moment of birth. It should further be noted that Barthes transferred the womblike functions associated with the concept of the author from an unmentionable mother to a Father, whose name is (re)mentioned throughout Barthes's theoretical fiction in a gesture full of disparagement and denial, even though it claims to be free from all paternal signs. Viewed against the background of symbolic matricide inscribed in this call for the "destruction" of the author, Barthes's definition of writing does not seem as "neutral" as all that: "Writing is that neutral, that composite, that oblique to which our subject retreats, the black-and-white in which all identity gets lost, beginning with that of the body that is writing" (61). If the text is hereby consigned to being "neutral," is it in order to neutralize that aspect of the writing subject that stems from a phallico-paternal authority? Or is it in order to willy-nilly dispose of that aspect of the imaginary "body" that comes into play when one writes, whose identity Barthes is so eager to conceal, and that belongs more particularly to the womblike realm of the maternal body?

Gilles Deleuze's notion of "becoming a woman" of thinking and writing (particularly in his *Dialogues* with Claire Parnet) raises similar questions. We know that in Deleuzian thinking, "becoming a woman" of the art of thinking is associated with some "minority-revolutionary" becoming, some "becoming with no history, no past and no memory." Writing is thus conceived in terms of a "nomadic movement," tracing out its "lines of escape" on "surfaces" that have neither depth nor interiority, and on "plane" surfaces that are "void of subject." The *Dialogues* further conceptualize writing as lines of "active escape"; once involved in becoming a woman-nomad-minority-revolutionary, writing plays as "putting a system to flight in the same manner as one would burst a pipe."[11] For Deleuze, it is indeed a question of eliminating the whole system of thinking that refers writing to its original source, and to a subjective sphere that is latent with interiority and depth. To him, there is nothing less revolutionary and nothing more "boring" than these so-called "discussions with the author" that recapture the "untainted" progression of writing within a history of genesis and evolution: "It is always possible to tell an author that his first work already contained everything or that, on the contrary, he is constantly renewing and transforming his work. Whatever the case, it comes down to the idea of an embryo that evolves, either from a fully differentiated germ cell or from successive structuring. However, the embryo, evolution are not good things. This is not the way towards progression" (37).

Deleuze's action of making an entire system of concepts related to the notion of subject (author-origin-interiority-embryo) leak or escape raises, at the very least, this question: what kind and genre of "subject" would find itself eliminated "in the same manner as one would burst a pipe"? Are we required to take apart a subject that—cloaked in the phallic attributes of the Author-Genitor-Father—claims to rise up from the center of surfaces ["steppes," "desert"] upon which roams the "nomadic" writing, in order to pin the text "onto the wall of dominant significations"? (57) Undoubtedly. But the fact remains that these *Dialogues* do not simply condemn the connotations of "Executive," "Chairman," or "Father" that relate to the concept of subject.

This is borne out by the following passage in which the subjective sphere finds itself associated with a "black hole"—a term whose astronomical denotation in no way eludes its physiological connotations: ". . . we are always immersed in the black hole of our subjectivity; the black hole of our Ego that is dearer to us than all else. . . . How can we extricate ourselves from the black hole, instead of twirling round at the bottom; which particles should we extract from the black hole?" (Deleuze/Parnet, 57). If Deleuze's nomadic thinking traces lines of "active escape," it is thus not so much in relation to that aspect of the auctorial function which relates to the paternal Phallus as to that aspect of the art of writing and thinking which is likely to reactivate the womb-maternal metaphor. For those who dream, along with Deleuze, of an evolution-without-memory of the process of writing, it would indeed be preferable to associate writing with the overflowing of "weeds" that has no need for genetic preformation and "only exist in the midst of vast, uncultivated expanses, . . . between—amongst the other things."[12] Better, then, to turn toward a centrifugal metaphor of plant "overflowing" than toward that "not good thing" (an object of phobia?) which is claimed to be an embryo twirling round at the bottom of the "black hole of our Ego." Better to activate the "rhizome" in order to evoke the burgeoning and irregular character of a text-tissue whose threads graft upon each other and branch out in all directions upon a surface without depth, than to turn towards the "root" which would arouse unwelcome stories of earth-mother, placental realms, and umbilical cords.

Similarly vague uterofugal impulses punctuate the essay "Hors livre: Préfaces"—Jacques Derrida's introduction to *La Dissémination*. Far from contenting himself with seeing literature emerge from the Book, Derrida appears concerned with reflecting on the movement of writing so that it resists its "semantic enveloping" in the Logos. Indeed, the disseminating role of the text, as perceived by Derrida, does not allow itself to be trapped within the "enclosure" of the "concept" within which the preface—that derisory piece of textual "waste"—claims to recapture it. In Derrida's words: "The Life of the Concept is a necessity which, by including the scattering of the seed and making it work to the advantage of the Idea . . . precludes, by the same token, all loss or random productivity" (56).

How can the unconstrained proliferation of the *semes*-seeds outside of the concept, the dissemination beyond the enclosure after the assassination of the father (in order to conceal the matricidal element), be guaranteed? It appears that we must take the lack of comprehension still further. Like Derrida, we must imagine the "original scene" of writing, the preface of which—as a story of genesis—conveys there is another way, by the representation of a couple of males: "If it were possible, the scene would involve solely the father and the son: auto-insemination, homo-insemination, reinsemination. Narcissism is the rule; it goes hand in hand with it" (53). Yet, it seems inadequate to see the prefatory scene in terms of an original scene steeped in male narcissism in order to convince ourselves that the "dissemination" takes place by way of a process of becoming a woman sheltered from all phallic narcissism. The following remark, held back in the par-ergon of this "Hors livre," leaves room for doubt: "If we turn our attention to it, the dissemination reads like a sort of womb" (57). That the random ejaculation-dispersion of the *semes* be productive without the intercession of a subjective sphere with a womb connotation, even if it means—if necessary—taking up the function, itself, of a "sort of womb." I read this passage as being the desire that engraves itself within the sinuous movement of the Derridian dissemination.

The Cathartic Rites of Modernity

The theoretical works of fiction that are devoted to "the death of the author" and "the decapitation of the text" purify rather than render the text neutral; rather than setting up the becoming "a woman" of writing, they proffer its becoming "properly a woman" (according to the literal sense of the adjective "propre," to be understood as being in opposition to the reputedly inherent stain of the female reproductive organs). In other words, these authors engage in symbolics (some more than others) that are more or less obsessional cathartic rites. The cathartic rites are, in societies that function without the practice of writing, a certain "writing" of reality. Thus, Barthes's stress on the verb "nourish" in order to underline what he considers to be the worst example of an abuse of auctorial power, and Deleuze's rejection of the "embryo—black hole" system by means of "weeds-rhizome," reminds me of the Brahman, who takes his meal according to extremely strict regulations and, in particular, places the pure-vegetable above the impure-animal in order to protect himself as best he can against the "stain" that archaic imagination attributes to the nutritive functions of the maternal in-body. And how can one prevent oneself from making similar analogies upon reading how Derrida, with rhetorical magic, wards off the fundamentally evil enveloping powers that modern thinking attributes to the auctorial realm? Indeed, we are not far from the Bemba who rallies a whole system of rites in order to exorcise the horrific powers that are presumed to emanate from the in-body of women whose menstrual blood affixes the seal of abjection to their power of becoming mothers.[13]

For these reasons, Julia Kristeva's anthropological explanation for the proliferation of the rites of defilement in one society more than in another is relevant. "Fear of the archaic mother," she wrote, "essentially proves to be based on the fear of her creative powers. It is this formidable power that the patrilineal filiation has the task of mastering. It is thus not surprising to witness the proliferation of the rites of defilement in societies where patrilineal power is not securely ensured" (92). It is, indeed, not surprising that the *maîtres-penseurs* of modernity have set up an entire rhetorical war machine in order to combat the disquieting powers of mortifying inclusion and putrid defilement, which their imaginations attribute to the womb. Balzac, for his part, could fearlessly imagine himself becoming a mother when writing. That element in his novels that evokes a fascination with the "creative powers of maternity" is immediately warded off by the parapet [para-hole], constituted by the heading of the *Comédie humaine*. It enables the auctorial Ego to set itself up as the representative of a divine and royal paternity: "I write under the glow of two eternal verities: Religion and Monarchy." Thus, in Balzac's works, the mysteriously internal and singularly disquieting aspect of the creation process is offset by a strong dose of realistic exteriority and by an ultimately most reassuring "All is true."[14] It is, however, quite another matter for the writers and thinkers in our post-Freudian times, who are now without the language of (impossible) objectivity that marked

Balzac's assurance. We try to defend ourselves as best we can against the encounter with the archaic mother, who appears as soon as we address a text that is in the process of being written. And we defend ourselves all the more so today; God-the-Father is numb to the possibility of intervening at the onset of the (pro)creation process in order to take back, under the reassuring dominion of his sole name, the disquieting singularity of the functions of the maternal in-body.

The guiding discourses of (post-)modernity are finally more determined than ever to banish the maternal in-body from the Urscene of writing and turn toward a (re)production by "dissemination" and by "lines of escape" beyond the "enclosure." Naturally, the Mother thus repressed, disavowed, and put to death, has no choice but to come back on stage in the ghostly form of the "Mère Terrible," ready to swallow up everything into her black, visceral aperture. This is a Mother far more terrifying and repulsive than the horde of phallophore shrews that haunt the scene of the final part of the trilogy that Aeschylus dedicated to the theme of the matricidal[15] son.

This—it would seem to me—is the intuition that Marguerite Yourcenar must have had when, in the aftermath of the Second World War, she wrote one of her first forewords, which has, since 1954, accompanied her play *Electre ou la chute des masques*. Here, she made a remarkable statement: "Bereft of the support of the Father as a result of the universal calling into question of laws and dogmas, engulfed into this black, visceral chaos out of which four thousand years of civilization had been striving to wrest him, the modern Orestes gives himself up more than ever to Clytemnestra's Bitches" (*Théâtre II*, 20). Let us leave behind the essentially matricidal violence that marks the becoming "a woman" as it is conjured up by modern Orestes, tormented by the idea of imagining a text being conceived, nourished, and written within the "subjective womb." And let us finally turn to the narratives of genesis with which Marguerite Yourcenar persistently encompassed her works of fiction at the risk of her readers taking it to be nothing other than the "repression of a properly [!] feminine discourse."[16]

TOWARD A DIFFERENTLY "WOMAN" FORM OF GENETICS: THE YOURCENARIAN PARATEXT

Contrary to modern *maîtres-penseurs*, who take a given discourse that refers the text to the writing subject as referring to its origin, Yourcenar offers us a collection of so-called "author's comments" that not only provide her with the opportunity "of saying 'I' in [her] own name" (*Yeux ouverts*, 91), but that evoke in Colette Gaudin's words "the gesture of enclosing [the] text within the narrative of its engenderment."[17] Yet the concept of engenderment requires further elucidation. *Engenderment* refers the text to an act of (pro)creation that presupposes a phallico-patriarchally connoted genitor. However, Colette Gaudin's reading of Yourcenar's prefaces clearly proves that the latter, "whilst adopting an attitude of knowledge, . . . calls the mastery of the creative agent into question, how they deepen the enigma of origin, even though they indicate the starting points of the work."[18] In light of this, it seems important to me that Yourcenar never uses the word "engenderment" in her paratexts, preferring instead to talk in terms of the "genesis" or "birth" of her fictional works.

Indeed, Yourcenar takes the text—and not the writing subject—as the starting point for dealing with the issue of the coming into being of writing. This is evident in the opening remarks to the prefaces and postfaces, which she appended to her so-called "early" fictional works and added over several decades, separating the writing of these paratexts from the appearance of the first edition of the prefaced texts. Gaudin correctly points out that "the emergence of the text as an event" is, on each occasion, "given priority over its subjective source."[19]

On every occasion—that is to say even in the preface of *Feux*—the only one in which the opening lines contain a statement in the first person: "*Feux* is not, strictly speaking, an early book; it was written in 1935; I was thirty-two. The work, published in 1936, was re-edited in 1957 with hardly any modifications being made" (*Oeuvres*, 1043). Writing "I was thirty-two," and not "I wrote this text at the age of thirty-two," positions the writing subject above the emergence of the text. Thus, it stands not in relation to the causal antecedence or intentional layout usually attributed to the author, but rather in relation to what Gaudin defines as "temporal proximity." This relates, in my opinion, to a proximity that is, above all, *spatial*. A passage taken from the preface of *Rendre à César* (a dramatized version of the novel *Denier du rêve*) illustrates my point:

> The author is admittedly not always informed about the intentions that initially guided him; nothing further about decisions taken along the way, which more often than not he does not even notice that he is taking. There is, however, an interval of time—generally very brief—between the moment a work is completed and the moment the author turns to

something else, during which the latter perceives with relative clarity the way in which his work has taken form within him. This is the moment that I would like to take advantage of. (*Théâtre I*, 10)

In other words, by bearing witness to her perceptions of how one text or another was able to more or less successfully "take form" and assume an aspect "that comes about without the author's awareness" (*Yeux ouverts*, 220), Yourcenar does not claim to be the guiding force of the process. It just so happens that she has, literally, given *a place* to the process. It is not *through* her, but *within* her that the work of fiction has taken form and consistence, within the innermost recesses of what Hélène Cixous came to call "the body-place where writing is worked on."[20]

Consequently, Yourcenar prefers a womb metaphor whenever she ventures to discuss the most enigmatic and intimate part of the complex processes of creating a book. Let us reexamine the terms she uses in order to distance herself from the metaphor of virility used by Matthieu Galey when explaining her alleged relationship to the protagonists of her novels and/or with the character Michel de Crayencour:

> M.G. *You are the one who put yourself inside your characters.*
> M.Y. Absolutely not. I am no more Michel than I am Zenon or Hadrian.
> ... One nourishes the character we create with one's own substance; it is somewhat of a gestational phenomenon.
> ... That does not mean that he is us or that we are him. The two remain separate entities. (*Yeux ouverts*, 211)

Far from evoking the gesture of the kind of phallic and narcissistic appropriation that dominant figures of modernity attribute to the auctorial word, Yourcenar's reply not only links the "interior experience" gone through by writing subjectivity to a gestational phenomenon, but also attributes an irreducible *otherness* to these "beings" that are carried "in oneself" in order to let them "nourish" themselves and "evolve."[21] In this work, Yourcenar's conception of writing resembles that of other female writers of our times, whose modernity we are generally far less reluctant to admit. I am thinking here, in particular, of Hélène Cixous, who in her own way takes on the quite relative "position of knowledge" that consists in speaking not as an agent but as a witness of the genesis of "her" works of fiction. In *Three Steps on the Ladder of Writing* (a series of public lectures she recently gave in the United States), Cixous is as open as Yourcenar to the idea that "the whole chronicle of childbearing is in play within the unconscious during the writing period"; she is also just as disposed to conceiving of writing in terms of a "scene of immeasurable separation" (20, 74).

Once again, it is useful to turn to Julia Kristeva, who—in her essay "Le Temps des femmes"—notes that we can no longer simply accept "the Freudian affirmation that motherhood is nothing more than a substitute for phallic and symbolic power," and that we should "listen attentively to the words expressed by modern women on the subject of this experience."

> Pregnancy thus appears to be like a radical test of the cleavage of the subject: the splitting into two of the body, separation and coexistence of the self and another person.... (Kristeva, 18)

Reading Everything

The way in which Marguerite Yourcenar conceives of the role that scholarship plays in the genesis of her works of fiction reveals much about this ordeal of cleavage—experienced, for her as for Hélène Cixous, right from the scene of reading—which ruins the (imaginary) unity and control of the subject. Indeed, where so many readers tend to see only an impressive accumulation of knowledge flaunted by a writer endeavoring to comprehend (to grasp), *la lettre* of the Yourcenarian paratext evokes quite *another* experience: "I think that most people have mistaken ideas about scholarship, about the way in which a writer, who is by definition a "creator"—a stupid term, but it is the one which is employed in the United States; let us rather say poet, like the Germans do, meaning dependent on one's imagination and one's emotions—enters into the world of scholarship.... I did not say to myself: 'I must write about Hadrian and learn about what he thought.' I believe that one never succeeds in such a way. I believe that one must become imbued with a subject until it sprouts up from the earth, like a plant which has been carefully watered" (*Yeux ouverts*, 139–40).

This allusion to a metaphor evoking the processes of "germination" taking place in the depths of the "earth mother" (in the deepest part of the subjective sphere, beyond knowledge and beyond control of the Subject) seems to me to constitute an essential element in Yourcenar's concept of reading. Indeed, although one memorandum (*Oeuvres romanesques*, 528), or another interview page (*Entretiens*, 64–65), may give as the first "rule of the game" involved in the gestation of a book such as *Mémoires d'Hadrien*, the rule of "learning everything," "reading everything," and "informing oneself about everything" which has anything at all to do with Hadrian, this rule is not based on a will to understand in the ordinary sense of the term. Indeed, "pursuing, through thousands of documents, the actuality of the facts," results instead in jeopardizing the very possibility of taking hold of one's subject. Rather, it leads one to watch the "character" of Hadrian, as well as the "world" of the Empire that was under his guard, gradually elude the reassuring hold of the stereotyped constructions of truth and reality such as they are conveyed by the prevailing discourse which, by definition, tends to privilege the known over the unknown and reduce the other to the same (*Entretiens*, 64).

Learning "everything" about Hadrian entails seeing the reassuring cliché of the "great restorer of Roman peace" or the one that is just as familiar, of the "great art lover" become more and more complicated, or even disintegrate into a collection of "unexplained and contradictory, even absurd, elements, as reality so often seems to be" (*Entretiens*, 52). The polylogy of this collection resists all efforts of synthesis; thus the turmoil of this relative structuring, of the repetition of "who . . . who; . . . who . . . and who . . ." reflecting the impossibility of linking together the elements of a phrase which is irremediably disconnected, split up by the disruptive interplay of these interruptions:

> as I drew close to historical facts, such as they come to us scattered throughout a certain number of documents, what I also saw was a man who preferred the rain of Britain to the mosquitoes of Rome, who, irritated by an ignorant secretary, became carried away to the point of hitting him, and poking out his eye, without meaning it, with the stiletto he held in his hand; a man who had bitter quarrels with the philosophers in his entourage; who did not love his wife, but was fond of his mother-in-law, who devoted himself to the insane and poignant endeavor which consisted in trying to immortalize a dead man, ordering statues, medals, coins and poems with such a fervor that we have no other historical examples of the mourning of a lover carried to such lengths; who, when he arrived in Rome, was laughed at because he spoke Latin with a Spanish accent; who told rather dull jokes to his soldiers; and who at the same time had a passion for the most complex, the most difficult poets. (*Entretiens*, 65–66).

In other words, the rule of the game which requires one to "read everything" assumes that the reader applies himself, as diligently as possible, to reading the text "à la lettre"—including all contradictions—even if this means seeing the gradual deconstruction of the monological signified to which the order of "common sense" tends by definition to regain the signifier:

> When two texts, two assertions, two ideas conflict, one should reconcile them rather than cancel out the one with the other: see in them two different facets, two successive states of the same fact. This produces a reality, which is convincing because it is complex and human because it is many-sided. (*Oeuvres*, 528)

"Reading everything" does not only set adrift the simplifying clichés conveyed by the collective imagination. It also sets out to deconstruct the preconceived meanings we tend to project onto the text when we approach it as guardians of professional, specialized reading. Take for example the memorandum of *Mémoires d'Hadrien*, in which Yourcenar refrains from superimposing on this historical text any interpretation or perspective established by our modern theoretical ways of thinking. Rather, she prefers to "let (it) soak in this mother water of contemporary events" (*Oeuvres*, 528). Once again, the use of a womb metaphor suggests that it is indeed a matter of letting the document in question soak in the placental tissue provided by its own intertext. This intertext gives us chaotic inscriptions of contradictory, multifaceted, and changing facts— "facts in crumbs, in dust, which the historian too puts back together, but which he tends to systematize excessively sometimes" (*Entretiens*, 52):

> I am wary of the fact that History systematizes (. . .), that it aggressively advances a theory as a truth, which is itself ephemeral. (The historian) is ruled by theories, sometimes without even being aware of it. (*Yeux ouverts*, 60–61)

She avoids the aggressive projection of a theory taken for a truth onto the text; a theory which, by bending its meaning to our unavowed need for security, is all the more accepted as patently obvious; a theory that exempts us from reading *everything*, and notably from reading everything in the text that questions the theory, displaces it, and deconstructs it.

It is always a curious spectacle to watch the human mind empty an object, dream, or fact of three-quarters of its contents before settling in to study it in the smoky light of a theory or a hypothesis (*Essais*, 1606). The sarcastic tone of this excerpt from *Les songes et les sorts* (the paratext which does not criticize the systematizations of the historian, but those of the "Freudian") serves, in my view, as a clue. This is an essential element in Yourcenarian legetics: its *deconstructive* element. We may ignore this element if we limit Yourcenar's critical reserve only to the contemporary systematizations (and notably regarding the Freudian theories of the unconscious); a reserve that she supposedly does not have for the more "traditional" systematizations which we have inherited from the scholars steeped in the philological tradition and the hermeneutics saturated with Jungian psychological mythology. It must be stated that Yourcenar views these philologists with skepticism, especially because, being governed by theoretical biases, they consider themselves capable of identifying a "style" as belonging exclusively to a given author. According to Yourcenar, they risk ignoring the fact that the author is dependent upon his subject and his characters and that, in addition, "his" style varies with his moods and with the moment (*Yeux ouverts*, 222). Likewise, it is better to reread the review of *Alceste*, in which Yourcenar not only urges us to have a "wise distrust" of the systematizations of the subconscious on which many of today's Freudians rely, but to be just as skeptical toward the systems of archetypological symbols to which we owe the "muddled explanations" of various generations of mythologists—Jungians and others—which the preface writer of the *Mystère d'Alceste* advises us to "leave behind," or even "eliminate": "These scholarly interpretations dating from the distant and the not-so distant past should teach us to have a wise distrust of our contemporary systematizations and of our Freudian or Marxist analysis of the great prehistorical myths" (*Théâtre II*, 85). This does not mean that Yourcenar had a preference for one system of interpretation of "the distant or not-so distant past" over another "contemporary" one; rather, it reveals her distrust of *any* method of reading that seeks only confirmation in the text of a theory, or more generally, of a system of preconceived values and representations: "Instead of imposing on this legend what may not be there, or what may only be there in the form of shapeless residues, we should first look at what is actually there" (*Théâtre II*, 85).

Yourcenar looks at what is unforeseen and unexpected in the text of the legend of Alceste as it is conveyed to us in Euripides' *Alceste* and in other scraps of older texts, so that the experience of reading does not get bogged down in exasperating repetitions of the same. She sees what is contradictory and inextricably polylogical in documents about Hadrian and his time and resists the temptation of monological totalization, so that the *Mémoires d'Hadrien* may be written in the plural like those of ". . . an individual who is unique, as we all are, made up as we all are of fortuitous elements which are assembled rather by chance, and which must be encountered in all their complexity" (*Entretiens*, 66). For Yourcenar, it is indeed a matter of "encountering" a "complexity" (that may remain hidden as long as one contents oneself with applying the order of the prevailing representations to the text). She persists even if this encounter means *implicating herself* in this diffuse and evasive assembly of meaningful elements that are revealed to her through the experience of trying to "read everything." She writes:

> Everything eludes us—even ourselves. The life of my own father is more unknown to me than Hadrian's life. Even my own existence—if I had to write it down—would be reconstituted by myself from the outside, with difficulty, as if it were someone else's existence: I would have to consult the letters and recollections of others, in order to anchor these floating memories. They are never more than just collapsed walls, darkened by shadows. (*Oeuvres*, 257)

Why would this woman writer find it necessary to carry within herself the embryos of her novels and memoirs for long periods of time—sometimes for whole years of her lifetime, from aborted versions to rewritten versions? It was in order to allow them to become—little by little, and more and more—*revealers of otherness*.[22] They become revealers of otherness first of all to the one who nourished them with her "own" substance, with "this blend of visions, memory and acts, of notions and information received during one's lifetime from the spoken word or from books, and of the detritus of our very own lives" (*Oeuvres*, 1036). As Yourcenar explains, "Mornings at the Villa Adriana; countless evenings spent in the little cafes which line the Olympeion; incessant comings and goings on the Greek seas; the roads of Asia Minor. In order for me to be able to use these memories, which are my own, they had to become as distanced from me as the second century" (*Oeuvres*, 520).

The process of distancing oneself from one's ego, which is carried out in the scene of reading-writing, is a slow and difficult one. Indeed, Yourcenar says that in order for memories that make up her "own substance" to dis-connect from her *ego* she must be willing to separate herself from the narcissistic, idealistic, or otherwise simplistic identifications that allow her to objectify herself by objectifying the *other*. This is necessary so that what is *other* may come to be written and read; in other words, to resist reducing the other to no more than a mirror, a projection screen, exclusively at the service of the image which "I" have of "Myself." Nothing could be more threatening to the imaginary unity and autonomy of the Subject than renouncing what Shoshana Felman calls, in the *La folie et la chose littéraire*, "the specular safety of the structure of recognition."[23] It is, indeed, this very safety which Yourcenar sacrifices by adding a second, and equally crucial, rule to the first one of "reading everything." The rule requires "Forbidding oneself shadows; not allowing the mist of one's breath to spread on the silvering of the mirror...." (*Oeuvres*, 528). Reading everything, at least making a serious effort to "learn everything" from the text (or the set of texts) that we have before us, is perhaps the only way to expel from the scene of reading an ego whose shadows confine us to a world without *other*, to these "arid personal deserts" (*Yeux ouverts*, 237) where the mirages of narcissistic complacency govern.

Concerning this point, Yourcenar's view is strikingly similar to contemporary psychoanalytic thinking, which articulates the need to protect analytical listening and thinking from the hold of the Ego. In particular, Lacan, who remarked in his first *Séminaire* (devoted to the technical writings of Freud) that when listening or reading is based on the Ego of the analyst (for Lacan, the Ego is only "the sum of the analyst's prejudices"), it results in "an interpretation of which the foundation and the mechanism cannot in any way be distinguished from those of projection."[24] To be sure, Yourcenar's sharp awareness—one she shares with psychoanalysts such as Lacan—of the "great natural borders which separate, from person to person, from century to century, the infinite variety of beings" (*Oeuvres*, 521)—leads her to characterize the process of allowing oneself to become saturated with what comes from the *other* to be read and written, in terms of a "practically impersonal quest," of a "transition from me to what is more important than me" (*Entretiens*, 171). However, the respect that this genetics-legetics pays to the borders goes beyond this: respecting the borders also involves respecting them as zones of communication, zones of "transition-to-the-other." This explains the equally intense insistence against attaching too much importance "to the merely administrative divisions, to the customs offices or the armed sentry boxes" in Yourcenar's paratext (*Oeuvres*, 521); in other words, the paratext insists on the need to not confine oneself to a type of nihilism which is so radically deconstructive that the relationship to the *other* may only be experienced in terms of absolute difference, of insurmountable resistance, of impossible exchange.

Delirium

As an introduction to the guidelines for the "frontier-crossings," toward which Yourcenar's paratext tends, I will quote a passage from the 1987 interview that Luce Irigaray conducted with Hélène Rouch, a biologist interested in the *in-utero*[25] relationship between mother and child. This relationship (inscribed in nature), which the male imagination tends to picture as fusion, proves to be "astonishingly well-ordered and mutually respectful of life"; leading Irigaray to underline "the virtually ethical nature of the foetal relationship," not only as a bond that brings to light an element of *difference*, but also one of *exchange*:

> The placenta: a tissue formed by the embryo [and which] plays a mediatory role on a dual level. On the one hand, it constitutes a medial space between mother and fetus, which signifies that there is never any fusion between maternal and embryonic tissues. On the other hand, it forms a regulatory system of exchange . . . which transforms, stocks and redistributes the maternal matter for its own good as well as for that of the fetus. (Irigaray, [1990], 46–47)

A similar womb economy fashions the art of reading in Yourcenar's narratives of genesis (i.e., her prefaces). As a matter of fact, whilst the rules of the game oblige us to "read everything," they also involve rules of conduct that are respectful of otherness and difference; the indispensable exchange between these "entities which remain separate" (between the text coming to be read and the subjectivity which gives rise to the process) is brought about thanks to what Yourcenar refers to as her "method of delirium" (*Oeuvres*, 526; *Yeux ouverts*, 143–44).

What is delirium (in the sense of *delire/de-lire*, un-reading) to Yourcenar's work? It means venturing to cross over from the head-in(g) to the in-body, toward which some allusion reaches, to the need to "constantly pay heed to the receptor constituted by the Ego"—that is to say the ego "as a body, feelings and warmth—not as a Person" (*Lettres à ses amis*, 104). This explains Yourcenar's fascination for the physical discipline that the Japanese writer Mishima imposed upon himself in order to surpass "the blind and unhealthy belief in words" that he considered to belong to Western intellectualism in order to gradually attain "a degree of intimacy, with ideas, closer than the one from the mind" (*Essais*, 246–47). In this context, it comes as no surprise to see Yourcenar turn toward a series of meditative techniques that make it possible to "create a vacuum within oneself" and to induce a state of internal receptiveness in herself, open to that aspect of the *other* that comes to reflect itself within the profoundest depths of herself, "in a calm sea" (*Yeux ouverts*, 145). She expresses this notion explicitly in *Oeuvres romanesques*: "[. . .] shaping to one's own purposes Ignace de Loyola's Exercises or the method of the Hindu ascetic who, for years and years, wears himself out trying to visualize a little more precisely the image he creates beneath his closed eyelids" (528).

Thanks to these methods of contemplative meditation and imaginative re-creation that make it possible to confer form, substance, and life to what would otherwise have remained completely ignored, it becomes possible to accomplish that "transition to the other," inherent in the Latin verb *delirare* (to swerve from a groove), and which Yourcenar defines as "that *sympathetic magic* that consists in transferring oneself in thought to within another person" (*Oeuvres*, 526). We are here, indeed, talking of a transition to a point outside the groove of the Ego; a *delirare* which, for Yourcenar, consists in "letting oneself be permeated" by the other (*Yeux ouverts*, 144) to such an extent as to have the sensation—to quote Yourcenar in a hitherto unpublished note taken from her "Journal de *Mémoires d'Hadrien*"—of "feeling Hadrian's tears running down my face."[26] Sympathy—"that fine-sounding word which signifies 'feeling with'" (*Yeux ouverts*, 300), is for Yourcenar synonymous with "compassion"—and is thus not only at the origin of love. It is, indeed, as she tells us in *Les yeux ouverts*, at the origin of intelligence; and sympathy and intelligence are, or should be, interdependent:

> "He who does not indulge in experiments or refuses to let himself be an object of experiments is someone who does not give himself to thought"—is, more or less, the belief held by alchemistic wisdom. Similarly, he who does not *feel deeply* does not give himself to thought. It is almost as though man has indulged in specialization: in the same way as certain insects have transformed their organisms into machine tools, we tend to transform a great part of our sensorial or affective capacities into the computer that we consider our brain to be. We do not stand to gain from this if, by so doing, we lose our quasi-visceral capacity for sympathy. (*Yeux ouverts*, 300–301)

The ability to allow oneself to be both sensorially and affectively permeated by that aspect of the *other* (varius, multiplex, multiformis) is the product of "visceral" intelligence in so very far as it "ushers physiology into the heart of knowledge" (*Essais*, 247).

Thanks to the delirium (thus conceived in terms of a "constant participation—of the utmost perceptiveness—in what is given to be understood of the other"), this indispensable venture beyond the limits of discursive ratiocination and specular objectivization, which shuts the thinking, writing, and reading Subject within the mortifying logic of Same,[27] is accomplished. Thanks to the crossing of frontiers that separate "me" (the "Ego") from the possibility of "feeling with the other" within the intimacy of the subjective sphere, this indispensable umbilical and "visceral" "point of contact" is established. The operation enabled Yourcenar to "replace the customary rigidity of historical documents with the flexibility and warmth of living entities, as well as the fluidity of real life" (*Oeuvres*, 528–29; *Entretiens*, 51–52).

This delirium, remarks Yourcenar, "would only interest the insane" insofar as it is capable of plunging the reading/writing subject into a whirl of emotions and visions similar to the delusion of mystics. Without it, it would be impossible to implement that *vitalizing* transformation and redistribution of "maternal matter" referred to by Luce Irigaray. Truly vitalizing, not only for the text that is in the process of being written or read, but also for the subjectivity that is to be found at the origin of the process. It is clearly a matter of living or abandoning "the other within oneself," as suggested by the thoroughly essential *psychoanalytical*[28] intuition inscribed within this remark in the *Carnets de Mémoires d'Hadrien*: "[. . .] to try to eliminate, not only the distance that separated me from Hadrian, but, above all, that which separated me from myself" (*Oeuvres*, 524).

Prefatorial Exercise and Womb Metaphor

The purpose of the so-called "auctorial" prefaces, postfaces, and other commentaries that have come to encompass Marguerite Yourcenar's fictional works and from which I have gathered those elements that I consider to be the most important, does not, therefore, appear to be the retrieval of the mystery of their genesis under the control of the know-how of an Author who raises himself—by means of headings—to the level of Master-Subject of the process. On the contrary, these paratextual works lead us far away from the patriarchally connoted "phallacy" that a *certain* Modernity (dedicated to "the death of the author") ascribes to the preface. Far, too, from the "powers of horror" that a *certain* Modernity (dedicated to a becoming "a woman" which, ultimately, is rather stubbornly and traditionally matricidal) attributes to the subjective realm, to the extent that it is unconsciously associated with the realm of the womb.

We should remember that these narratives that talk of origin are written by a woman who was acutely aware of owing her life to a mother who died through giving birth to her, opening up, therefore, a *differently* (post)modern angle to the process of reading and writing. As a preface writer, Marguerite Yourcenar does, in fact, appear to want to make today's reader rediscover an awareness of that mysterious internal realm that cultivates otherness and difference in addition to providing visceral points of contact for vital exchange (which "the body that [reads or] writes" can become). Those readers who consent to lend an ear to the polyvalence of the text—instead of stubbornly insisting on evacuating or otherwise neutralizing that element of womb-like in-body that it comprises—will be able to rediscover that mysterious internal realm.

Notes

1. See Gaudin (1990), 18.
2. See Hillenaar (1983), 17–19; Pont (1994), 56–61; Pacaly (1995), 34; Sarde/Brami (1995), 17.
3. Julien (1995), 10; Hillenaar (1983), 27.
4. "[By punctuating] her texts with prefaces, postfaces, postscripts, notes or memorandums . . ., Yourcenar once again positions herself—as she indeed loves to point out—against the current of fashion. Notably, between 1950–70, a period . . . during which most authors—more particularly novelists—delete all trace of their own marks, submitting texts which undertake to advance autonomously and appear to unfold alone. As for Yourcenar, she gives vent to veritable gusts of auctorial frenzy. . . ." (Julien, 1995), 9. See also Delcroix (1995), 43–52.
5. See Clément (1979), 19–21; Stillman (1985), 261–67; Marks (1990), 210–18.
6. Gaudin (1990). See also Gaudin (1994), 30–37.
7. See Barthes (1984), 61–67; Derrida (1972), 8–67; Deleuze/Parnet (1977), passim.
8. Many of today's feminist theoreticians show concern for reflecting not only upon the interest but also the limits of the "semiosis of the woman" conveyed by contemporary French thought (by way of example, see Jardine, 1985, and Braidotti, 1991). It is my intention, over the following pages, to contribute to these present-day theories and criticisms.
9. Derrida (1972), 12.
10. Foucault (1969), 78; Barthes (1984), 64–65.
11. Deleuze/Parnet (1977), 47 and passim.
12. Ibid., 38–39.
13. For the anthropological references that are implied here, see Kristeva (1980), 90–94.
14. Balzac (I: 53) and (II: 217). Regarding the notion of the creative powers of maternity in Balzac's works, see Taat (1981).
15. With regard to this subject, see my essay "Lire *L'Orestie* avec Marguerite Yourcenar" (Taat, 1993).
16. Stillman (1985), 275.
17. Gaudin (1990), 20, and (1994), 35.
18. Gaudin (1990), 19, and (1994), 30 ss.

19. Gaudin (1990), 22. Here are a few examples: "*Alexis ou le Traité du vain combat* appeared in 1929; it is contemporary with a certain period of literature and morals when...." (*Oeuvres romanesques*, 3). "*Le Coup de grâce*, this short novel, situated in the aftermath of the First World War and the Russian revolution, was written in Sorrento in 1938 and published three months before the Second World War...." (79). "An initial, somewhat shorter version of *Denier du rêve* appeared in 1934. The present edition is far more than a simple reprint...." (161). "*Anna, soror*... is an early work, but belongs to that category of work that remains dear and essential to their author right to the very end" (1023).

20. Cixous (1977), 480.

21. These are the terms employed by Yourcenar for her own "Carnets de notes de *L'oeuvre au noir*" (41–42).

22. Expression that I have borrowed from Colette Gaudin (1990), 24.

23. Felman (1978), 153.

24. Lacan (1975), 22, 31, 42. Shoshana Felman, in *Jacques Lacan and the Adventure of Insight* (Cambridge: Harvard University Press, 1987), summarizes the essential points of Lacan's thinking on this subject as follows: "For Lacan the ego is not an autonomous synthetic function of the subject, but only the delusion of such a function. The outcome of a series of narcissistic identifications, the ego is the mirror structure of an imaginary, self-idealising *self-alienation of the subject*. It is a structure of denial: denial of castration (through a unified self-aggrandisement) and denial of subjectivity (through objectification of others and self-objectification). As such, the ego, in Lacan's conception, cannot be the origin of any cure or the reference point for the therapeutic alliance" (Felman 1987), 11.

25. See Irigaray (1990), 45–61, "On the Nature of Women."

26. Yourcenar Collection at Harvard, MS Storage 265. See also Ness (1994), 111, with regard to this subject.

27. Indeed, from the outset, Yourcenar distances herself from both the delirium attached to the narcissistic outbursts of a "romantic" Ego (cf. *Oeuvres romanesques*, 526) and the "interpretational delirium" which involves blindly projecting one system or another of preconceived thought that is raised into the indisputable Truth (cf. *Essais et mémoires*, 1627). The experience of delirium, toward which her prefatorial discourse tends, is the result of an essentially dialogic "slow-moving asceticism" that stems from listening to the other: "one totally suppresses one's own thoughts and listens to a voice: what does this individual have to teach me?" (*Les yeux ouverts*, 224).

28. An adjective which, in this context, is naturally to be understood not as referring to psychoanalysis as a stock of theoretical systemizations on the unconscious, but, primarily, referring to psychoanalysis as an adventurous and dialogic exercise in listening to the other. As regards this subject, see: Lacan (1975) and Felman (1987). See also my first endeavor to delimit the psychoanalytical intuitions inscribed within the Yourcenarian paratext.

Part II
Beyond History: The Politics of Desire

Coup de Grâce as Male Fantasy:
On the Sexual Politics of Fascism

Michael Rothberg

> There is no document of culture [*Kultur*] which is not at the same time a document of barbarism.
> —Walter Benjamin

> Fantasy is on the side of reality.
> —Slavoj Žižek

Documents of Barbarism

WITH THE SIGNIFICANT EXCEPTIONS OF AN IMPORTANT ESSAY BY ELAINE Marks and Saul Friedlander's passing mention of *Coup de Grâce* in his influential *Reflections of Nazism*, Marguerite Yourcenar has rarely been situated in a critical fashion in relation to questions of fascism and anti-Semitism. Indeed, to the contrary, in his 1993 introduction to a special *PMLA* cluster on "Literature and the Idea of Europe," Timothy J. Reiss cites Yourcenar as one of the "writers who foster a spirit that counters the historical and ever-present dark side of economic and political forces" (27). My reading of *Coup de Grâce* (like Elaine Marks's) situates Yourcenar specifically on that "dark side," and I do so by considering her novel in relation to a particular strand of dark Euro-American history "after Auschwitz": the Cold War.[1] As evidence of Yourcenar's alleged contribution to a new "affirmative idea" (25) of Europe that breaks with the traditions of cultural nationalism and totalitarian destruction, Reiss cites a specific text, which he reads as antifascist, and Yourcenar's general sensitivity to the specificities of place and time. In drawing the lesson from Yourcenar that "no future can ignore the past with impunity," Reiss refers to her "scathing 1940 review of Anne Lindbergh's pro-Nazi *Wave of the Future*" (27). Reiss's particular choice demonstrates no particular sensitivity to the lessons of the past since the review in question represents a shockingly ambivalent essay—one that, in any case, was never published until after Yourcenar's death and thus cannot be said to have advanced the antifascist cause one iota no matter how "scathing" it might be. True, Yourcenar calls the Nazis' "barbaric dogmatism" (not their barbarism!) "the most irrefutable appearance of evil." But, on the other hand, she claims that "nobody can contest that there is beauty in the passionate exaltation of the young Nazi," and that Hitler is "in sum a man like any other," and thus must have "some more or less hidden virtues" (*En pèlerin*, 61; my translation). After the *Reichspogromnacht [Kristallnacht]* of November 1938, after the invasion of Poland in 1939, such sentiments are neither "irrefutable" nor open to "affirmation" in the new Europe.

Equally troubling are Reiss's remarks on the "profound respect for and understanding of other cultures" in Yourcenar's portrait of Hadrian in *Memoirs of Hadrian*. Reiss claims Hadrian as one of those "who have begun to grasp the complexity of context and to recognize that cultural artifacts live within a particular contextual complexity," and who may thus use such "generosity of soul" "to think themselves into another's culture, society, and mind" (17, 26). As in Yourcenar's Lindbergh review and, I will argue, in *Coup de Grâce*, the "contextual complexity" Reiss finds in her Hadrian produces its own elisions, whose illumination is fundamental to understanding "Literature and the Idea of Europe." Far from a singularly generous soul, Hadrian was also a conquering power who "forbade the practice of Judaism on pain of death" (Fackenheim, 328). Drawing on Yourcenar's Hadrian as an example of how "one gets a sense of others's histories ... only by dwelling in them" (Reiss, 16) demonstrates not a sensitivity to complexity but rather a blindness to how ideologies that connect "dwelling" to exclusive claims to cultural knowledge tend toward the barbaric. Until the torture, suppression, and murder of Europe's "internal other" are acknowledged as central to European documents of culture (the "idea of Europe"), the opportunity for working through the historical trauma of genocide and opposing contemporary forms of fascism will be missed.

Reiss's portrait of Yourcenar, and indeed the dominant portrait of her, demands complication through a return to the concepts in Benjamin's "Theses on the Philosophy of History." Reversing the terms of Benjamin's thesis, I want to ask if every document of barbarism is also a document of culture. In considering Yourcenar's *Coup de Grâce* (written very shortly before Benjamin's theses) and Klaus Theweleit's *Male Fantasies*, I want to draw attention to the risks involved in the task of documenting barbarism, risks that persist and take on new forms "after Auschwitz."[2] Theweleit's literary historical project takes seriously the fictions and fantasies of the men of the *Freikorps*—proto-Nazi bands of German soldiers for whom World War I never really ended—in order to demonstrate in frightening detail how barbaric desire resides "on the side of reality." Yourcenar's novel recounts the sordid adventures of one fictional *Freikorps* soldier during the unrest following the end of the First World War and the Russian Revolution. Yourcenar provides the kind of subjective "document" that Theweleit demands that we comprehend in order to understand and combat the reality of fascism as it lives on beyond the interwar period of its germination.

Yet after a generation or more of poststructuralism we know that no documentation (just as no documentary) can document any historical or psychological situation innocently. Such questions are immediately mediated, which is to say, ideological. To document barbarism is to risk the purity of one's own position as the speaking subject of "culture." My initial question about culture and barbarism thus becomes: What are the politics of documenting fascism? And—given the specificity of the texts at issue here—what are the *sexual* politics of fascism and its critique?[3] I will explore these questions by reading Yourcenar's and Theweleit's texts together and historically situating them in their sites of production in order to glimpse the politics of their representation (or lack of representation) of politics.

My study, which proposes to look back at the immediate aftermath of World War I in Europe through the lens of a work of fiction, arises out of contemporary concerns about this "return of the repressed," and out of questions about the historical genealogy of those contemporary concerns. The era that both *Coup de Grâce* and *Male Fantasies* document mirrors our own, serving as an imaginary double through and against which we in the contemporary West might attempt to define ourselves. The recently concluded First World War had done more to unsettle European politics than to grant closure to the struggles of its various nations and ethnic groups. Arno Mayer has described this moment following the Versailles Peace Conference as "reflect[ing] the intersection of the ending of a gigantic military conflict with the opening of a universal international civil war" (vii). The two works I am considering here take us inside the experience of this terrible historical moment. The landscape that Yourcenar's (anti)hero, Erick von Lhomond, and Theweleit's *Freikorps* occupy seems to consist solely of roving bands of soldiers torturing, killing, and slogging their way through mud and snow. But, as historian Claudia Koonz suggests about Weimar Germany, we must consider this culture dialectically, identifying its possibilities as well as its ominous tendencies; she suggests writing the history of the era with "a retrospective double vision that encompasses both the prospect of emancipation and progress . . . and the etiology of a disreputable and insignificant movement which spread, undetected, through the body politic and was diagnosed only after it could not be halted" (21). I will argue that, for all their perspicacity, the stories which both Yourcenar and Theweleit construct retroactively about their subjects show us predominantly the latter side of this dialectic between emancipation and terror. While this surprising univocality might derive from the polemical nature of these texts within their original, intended contexts, by shifting the terrain and exploring the linguistic and spatiotemporal translations of these texts, we begin to grasp their politics at a deeper level—a politics that is all the more troubling given the persistence of fascism "after Auschwitz."

THE POWERS OF DESIRE

Klaus Theweleit's two-volume study of the novels and memoirs of the fascist and proto-Nazi *Freikorps* soldiers was originally published in Germany in 1977, but translated into English only in 1987 and 1989. In its original context, Theweleit's work challenged German citizens' pre-1960 refusal to accept responsibility for their role in the recent Nazi past, and it grew out of a movement of students obsessed with their parents' guilt and with the psychology of fascism and authoritarianism. *Male Fantasies* also responded to what Theweleit understood as a shortcoming in the dominant Marxist models of fascism provided by the Frankfurt School: an inability to acknowledge the reality of fascist fantasy and to understand the attraction of fascist violence.[4] Although *Male Fantasies* was written with the belief that the authoritarian structures of contemporary German society carried with them the possibility of fascist renewal, there was no explicit Nazi mobilization during the era in which Theweleit wrote.

Male Fantasies appeared in English, however, on the cusp of the neonationalist era, during a rebirth of fascist street violence and amid a series of scandals that caused cultural workers to confront the politically suspect pasts of some of their intellectual forebears. In 1987, Victor Farias published *Heidegger and Nazism* in France (it was translated into English two years later), causing a furor among latter-day Heideggerians and deconstructionists with his claims that the German philosopher was significantly more implicated in fascism than had previously been popularly believed. Also in 1987, scholars discovered that Yale literary critic Paul de Man had written a number of articles for a collaborationist newspaper in Nazi-occupied Belgium during World War II.[5] My concern here is neither to defend nor to indict Heidegger, de Man, or the philosophies with which they are associated, but rather to outline the conjuncture in which Theweleit's study of fascist subjectivity was introduced into American discourse. The Heidegger and de Man cases testify not only to a "crisis in witnessing" brought about by the experience of fascism and genocide, as Shoshana Felman has argued about de Man (Felman and Laub, 120–64), but also bear witness to a crisis of nationalism that irrupted on the world stage shortly after their unearthing in the late 1980s. Theweleit's work (and its translation into English at the same moment as the Heidegger and de Man cases attained public attention) also anticipated the political upheavals of national and ethnic violence with which the world continues to struggle.

While crises in ethnic and national identity obviously constitute part of Theweleit's landscape, upheaval in the realms of gender and sexual identities have also invigorated his intellectual project. Thus, we ought to situate Theweleit's endeavor in specifically feminist contexts. Although not explicitly acknowledged in the text, Theweleit wrote *Male Fantasies* during a decade of intensive feminist activism in West Germany. Starting with the founding of the Action Council for Women's Liberation in 1968 and the first national women's conference (of the new movement) in March 1971, and continuing through the establishment of women's centers and battered women's shelters during the rest of the decade, the issues of violence, gender, and sexuality addressed by Theweleit were brought into public discourse and consciousness by the Autonomous Women's Movement. From the mid-1970s, theoretical work from France also began to influence German feminists, along with the theoretical-stylistics of Irigaray's and Cixous's *écriture feminine*, which Theweleit's "flowing" style often seems to be approximating.[6] In Alice Kaplan's words, "The authority he substitutes for the fascist one is female" ("Theweleit," 160).[7] Given this context, it is not surprising that Theweleit would be welcomed by many feminists upon his text's translation into English. Both volumes of his work, for instance, were prefaced with essays by prominent feminists (Barbara Ehrenreich, for the first volume, and Jessica Benjamin, with Anson Rabinbach, for the second). At the same moment, the issue of "men in feminism" was also coming to attention in the English-speaking world, and Theweleit's text, I will argue, illustrates some of the benefits and many of the pitfalls of that troubled subject-position.[8]

We can best arrive at an understanding of Theweleit's problematic relationship to feminism if we first understand his explicit debt to a certain version of psychoanalysis. His approach to the subjectivity of the soldier males derives not from Freud or Lacan, but from Deleuze and Guattari's heterodox *Anti-Oedipus*, published in the early 1970s. According to Deleuze and Guattari, the Oedipal structure is not a human universal, as Freud and some anthropologists have attempted to demonstrate, but rather a determinate social relation enforced from above (Theweleit I, 210). In the anti-Oedipal model, the concept of unlimited desire displaces Oedipus as the universal upon which the theorists found their model. The anti-Oedipal model privileges neither the father nor the phallus (II, 175), but rather the subject's relation to its own desiring-production.

Theweleit understands drives within the body to produce revolutionary streams of desire. The soldier represses not the specific desires themselves, but the fact that he produces them: "he subjects the unconscious itself . . . to repression" (II, 6). According to Margaret Mahler's research on psychotic children (another model upon which Theweleit draws), this repression effects a "progressive displacement of libido . . . from inside the body . . . to the periphery of the body" (II, 216). The communists, workers, women, and Jews who haunt the soldier male threaten the boundaries of his body because they embody the liberation of the very desiring-production which he has repressed (II, 7). Julia Kristeva's writings on the "abject" emphasize this same anxiety over the boundaries of the body which she also finds in both "borderline" psychotic patients and in fascist writing, such as that of Céline.

But if we can always rely on Kristeva to find *"jouissance"* in the experience of limits, Theweleit's warrior is in fact an ascetic subject, and what he produces is not bliss, but death (I, 216). The *Freikorps* sees itself engaging in "a battle against everything that constitutes enjoyment and pleasure" (II, 7). Theweleit understands anti-Semitism as deriving not primarily from anticapitalist sentiments about Jews as exploiters, but "instead [from] a coupling of 'Jewishness' with a 'contagious' desire for a better life" (8–9). Given the micropolitics of his theory of fascism, Theweleit probably would not want to admit it, yet this unveiling of asceticism does not differ enormously from Adorno's analysis of anti-Semitism.[9] Adorno implicitly links anti-Semitism to the workings of the capitalist Culture Industry by explaining both phenomena as (in Fredric Jameson's words) "negative embodiments of the deeper *ressentiment* generated by class society itself" toward the "promise of social and personal happiness" which both Jews and art represent (*Late Marxism*, 154). The most significant difference is that Adorno's analysis explains asceticism as a social fact, while for Theweleit it derives from psychological structures.

According to this psychoanalytic model, the very tenuousness of the soldier male's ego, the fact that he is "not yet fully born" (II, 213), requires him to establish "maintenance mechanisms" as a prop to identity. The soldier male's ego comes not from identification with the father, as in the Oedipal model, but, rather, through punishment. The fascist "must acquire an enveloping 'ego' from the outside," but his only experience of the outside comes through acts of violence, first perpetrated against himself, and later against others. As Theweleit paraphrases Freud, "Where pain is, there 'I' shall be" (II, 164). In military drills and beatings, the soldier's body submits to "the pain principle," which reorganizes his fragmented drives and organs into a bodily whole bounded by skin which is quite literally becoming thick beneath the blows of the whip (II, 150, 144). Such a process of ego constitution guarantees that, in the face of the ostensibly liberated and threatening other, this subject will only be able to ensure "his own survival, his self-preservation and self-regeneration" through "the act of killing" or other expressions of violence.

In Theweleit's account, the threatening Other is almost always female, and fascism in fact derives from the relations between the sexes established by a transhistorical patriarchy. His methodology seeks to "trace a straight line from the witch to the seductive Jewish woman" (I, 79). Fascism represents, then, not a break with traditional gender relations, but an extreme example of the norm, "the tip of the patriarchal iceberg" (I, 171). When killing women, or fantasizing about killing them, the soldier male also expresses hatred of his own self as patriarchy has formed it. He must "dam up" the feminized, interior drives of his body: "When a fascist male went into combat against erotic, 'flowing,' nonsubjugated women, he was also fighting his own unconscious, his own desiring-production" (I, 434). The soldier's permanent state of war against communists, women, and Jews tenuously props up his ego, just as the permanent war economy enables the survival of capitalism, although at the cost of deferring the liberation of desire.

Since the ego of the fascist is not a given, but an external imposition, it best fixes itself in external structures, such as the army or youth organization. In Germany these institutions in part derived significance from historical circumstances. With the nationalist hysteria of the beginning of World War I (also documented by Modris Eksteins [55–64]), "the soldierly core of the army . . . became nation, and leader of the people" (II, 81). With the mortifying defeat of 1918, and the truly external imposition of Weimar democracy (see Koonz, chapter 2), "the key to [the nation's] rebirth was the arming of the *Freikorps* against the Republic" (II, 81). The true Nation, a roving band of assassins, saw itself as shaping the People out of an amorphous mass, all in the name of the Führer. But at the same time, "the army, high culture, race, nation, Germany—all of these appear to function as a second, tightly armored body enveloping [the soldier male's] own body armor" (II, 84). For Theweleit, the social and the psychological mutually constitute each other, although, in the last instance, the process starts with the attempt to establish the borders of the body.

Taking off from Deleuze and Guattari, Theweleit derives two basic social structures that he defines as fascist and revolutionary, respectively: the molar mass and the molecular masses (II, 3, 75). According to Theweleit, Deleuze and Guattari define the molecular as a fluid, always changing multiplicity, while the molar mass channels the flow of desiring production into rigid organizational structures overseen by a Führer or leader. These two structures probably coexist under "normal" circumstances; for "the soldier male, however, the two appear strictly antithetical. . . . [H]is bodily interior (the molecular ordering of the unconscious) is incarcerated by an incarcerating body armor (the molar arrangement of domination), and the two are irreconcilably opposed, one subject to the other" (II, 75). In fact, Deleuze's and Guattari's elaboration of the molar/molecular model is considerably more subtle than Theweleit's appropriation, and does not privilege the molecular over the molar in absolute terms. They claim, for example, that "every politics is simultaneously a *macropolitics* and a *micropolitics*," and that fascism, in particular, "is inseparable from a proliferation of molecular focuses in interaction, which skip from point to point, *before* beginning to resonate together in the National Socialist State" (*Plateaus*, 213–14).[10] Theweleit's celebration of the molecular and his allergy to the molar ultimately hinder his ability to propose concrete alternatives to the fascist social organization.

But, despite such theoretical simplifications, Theweleit's critique of the left's attempts to understand fascism, which follows from this distinction between the molar and the molecular, puts forward theses that are valuable in a local context. According to his argument, the old left inevitably reproduced the same "molar" organizational structures as did the fascists, therefore blocking and channeling the potentially revolutionary flows of desire. By calling the language of the fascists whom Theweleit reads "irrational, insane, lacking in substance," leftists missed the point of such discourse: that "what the texts [of the soldier males] have most clearly demonstrated is a refusal by fascism to relinquish desire—desire in the form of the demand that 'blood must flow,' desire in its most profound distortion" (II, 188–89). The refusal to relinquish desire (also the source of Lacan's ethics) does not constitute fascism—on the contrary, the source of fascism's violence comes from the coexistence of overflowing desire with structures of containment. Fascism reterritorializes desire's revolutionary power by repressing the subject's own production and projecting it onto the Other. If the left continues to ignore the power of emotions and cannot learn "that there might be pleasure in liberation, pleasure in new connections, pleasure in the unleashing of new streams" (189), fascism will continue to grip the masses.

Fascism recognizes the powers of desire, and redirects them from serving the purposes of liberation to serving those of domination. Fascism interpellates the People in the name of desire, and then channels this force into hatred and nation-building. The truly revolutionary subject—the schizo—in the truly revolutionary molecular mass, will never cede its desire, and will never have desire constrained by a hierarchical social organization, such as the totalitarian state. Because of the contradictions of fascism (its ultimate reterritorialization of the desire it unleashes), it produces a psychotic and paranoid subject. This "persecuted persecutor" can today be found among supporters of white supremacy, armed militias, and "family values" in the United States, and among anti-Semites in European countries without Jews.

Fascist Confessions

The psychotic subject that Theweleit derives from the writings of *Freikorps* soldiers and other proto-Nazis finds a remarkable expression in Yourcenar's *Coup de Grâce*. Her depiction of Erick von Lhomond foreshadows many of the theoretical precepts that Theweleit develops in coming to terms with fascism forty years later. Von Lhomond represents an almost pure example of the warrior-male as it developed during the epoch of the *Freikorpsman*. The narrator who frames Erick's story describes him as "one of those men who were too young to have done more than brush with danger, but who were transformed into soldiers of fortune by Europe's post-war disorders, and by their incapacity for satisfaction or resignation, either one" (4). Although a soldier of fortune ought in principle to be less "ideological" than the nationalist groups of *Male Fantasies*, in fact Erick signs on only with reactionary causes: fighting the Bolsheviks in the Russian civil war and siding with Franco in Spain.

As with the soldier-males, Erick can give form to the social and psychological "disorders" of his era only by joining with the repressive state apparatus as, in one or another of its forms, it wages permanent war against "the enemy." Erick describes his first military experience—the defeat of 1918—as a losing battle with bodily and political boundaries:

> the time came when I had to slip over the border to report for military training.... I took my first drill under sergeants weakened from dysentery and hunger.... Some of my drillmates were agreeable enough, and were already launched upon the wild freedom of the postwar era to come. Two months more and I should have been used to stop the gap which the Allied artillery had made in our ranks, and should at this very moment, perhaps, be peacefully amalgamated to French soil. (15)

Although Erick preserves his own life, the defeat confronts him with "a totally empty future" (16). Erick's military training follows from a desire, a movement across a border, which should be reterritorialized by his "first drill" [mon entraînement] (144). However, since the sergeants cannot control the boundaries of their own bodies, they have "dysentery" [les maux de ventre], they cannot tame "the wild freedom" [le grand chahut] (145) which will therefore reign during the years of Weimar emancipation. Since Erick has not been used to "stop the gap" [remplir une brèche] (145), and the gap has not been stopped, his first experience with the military does not fully accomplish his disciplining and subjection. Even though he appears to laud his drillmates' freedom, he cannot acknowledge the desiring production within his body—the way it wants to "slip over the border" [faufiler à travers la frontière] (144)—rather, he winds up feeling "hollow" and "empty."

Only in the Russian civil war does Erick find his place and develop what Theweleit calls a "body-armor" which is full, but contained: "The fullest ten months of my life were passed in a command in that godforsaken district where even the names ... meant nothing" (7–8). Erick's position in the army comforts him by inserting him in a rigid hierarchical machine; although he commands, he is in turn commanded: "Once swept into the Baltic imbroglio I tried only to be a useful wheel in the whole machine, and to play as rarely as possible the role of crushed finger" (10) [d'y jouer le plus souvent le rôle de la roue de métal, et le moins possible celui du doigt écrasé] (140). This odd, bodily metaphor follows close on the heels of a description of torture, which, although projected onto the "Mongol traditions" of "the Reds" [les bourreaux rousses] (139), divulges what is at stake in Erick's self-construction. (Theweleit includes images of Soviets "orientalized" by Nazi propaganda: cf. II, 270.) Coyly taking pleasure in his description of the "Chinese Hand" [le supplice de la main chinoise] (139), Erick recounts that the unfortunate "victim was slapped with the skin of his own hand stripped from him while he was alive" (8–9). He reminds us that such stories "harden the auditor that much more" [durcir chez l'auditeur quelques fibres de plus] (139), clearly revealing the connections between torture, the military machine, the armored soldier, and the experience of the body's boundaries.

If Erick takes a certain "idle excitement" in the telling of such details and in his soldiering experiences generally, these would seem to be the only pleasures in his life. Like the *Freikorps* adherents, Erick ascetically denies his own desire, instead projecting it onto the female Other and hinting at, but ultimately repressing, a homosexual subplot. Beneath the triangular, if not strictly Oedipal structure that Erick applies to the characters' relations, we sense that the flow of desire between Erick, Sophie, and Conrad is polymorphous and fluid. In order to take himself out of the flow of sexual drives, the narrator uses two strategies: he attempts to turn all interpersonal relations into family ones, and he repeatedly insists on his own utter lack of desire in the face of the Other's overflowing want.

When Erick brings his command back to Kratovitsy for the first time, he is greeted by Sophie: "In the first excitement of our return she had kissed me warmly [à pleines lèvres], and I could not help thinking, with a shade of melancholy, that that was my first kiss from a young girl, and that I had never had a sister [et que mon père ne m'avait pas donné de soeur]. So of course, insofar as was possible, I made a sister of Sophie [j'adoptai Sophie] (152)" (24). The surprising insincerity of the "of course" [bien entendu] gives it away; faced with the unfamiliarity of desire evoked by Sophie's passionate kiss, Erick can do nothing but transcode his emotion to an ostensibly safe arena, the family. (He also refers to her boyishness, asserting that she could be "a brother to her brother" [30].) In a moment of particularly twisted logic, he attempts to explain Sophie's alleged desire by way of the family:

> I seemed just made to fulfill the aspirations of an immature girl confined, up to that time, to the company of a few dull brutes of no consequence and the most seductive of brothers; nor had Nature seemed to endow her with the slightest inclination towards incest. But perhaps even incest figured here, for memory's magic transformed me, in her eyes, into an elder brother. (33)

The breathtaking contradictions of this passage demonstrate that Erick will go to any length to avoid what would appear the most obvious explanations of desire. Perhaps desire is not normalizable in *Coup de Grâce*; just beneath the surface it flows indiscriminately without respect for social categories such as gender or kinship, but overtly it must be denied. Like Theweleit's soldiers, Erick "familializes" the erotic and eroticizes the family (I, 152).

Erick also goes out of his way to emphasize the fraternal nature of his eroticized relationship with that "most seductive of brothers," Conrad. Not only did they leave "identical footprints on the sand" (12) during their youthful frolics, but their "physical make-up" was similar right down to the requisite "shade of blue in [their] eyes" (14).[11] Naturally, "the country folk took [them] for brothers, a simple solution for those who have no conception of ardent friendship" (14); although the precise name of this ardent friendship remains unspoken, Erick is pleased at the familial alibi provided by their homologous physiques. Such insinuations add erotic resonance to Erick's assertion that although "there was no lack of girls" during their youth, he "treated all such fancies [engouements] with scorn" (13).

Homoeroticism, according to Theweleit, served certain purposes among the Nazis: it was "simultaneously prohibited and commanded," punished and held as a reward for initiation into the power elite (II, 339). Before the purge of the openly homosexual SA commander, Ernst Röhm, in 1934, a homosexual tendency existed within Nazism, and can be seen in the writings of Hans Bluher, author of *The Role of Eroticism in Male Society* (II, 138—volume I refers to Bluher as Ernst). Since Conrad drops out of focus almost entirely after the first few pages of the novel, we could read Erick's relationship with Conrad as mimicking the tendential repression of homosexuality during the course of German fascism's rise and fall. But, regardless of the historical parallel in Nazi Germany (the full examination of which would take us beyond the scope of this article), *Coup de Grâce* bears out Craig Owens' more general assertion that a common "apparatus" produces both homophobia and misogyny (219).[12]

The novel suggests that this commonality finds its most obvious expression in antisex ideology. In turning away from homoeroticism, Erick certainly does not turn toward heterosexuality. Like the rest of the soldier males, he experiences either a "lack of inclination" or "disgust" and "aversion" (54) vis-à-vis sexuality. Almost the only sympathy evinced by Erick for Sophie comes when he senses a "lack of inclination" on her side: "Here before me was a Sonia indignant [une enfant outragée (154)—another familial metaphor] at the slightest suspicion of desire, and everything in me which differentiates me from mere women-chasers, for whom any girl is a windfall, could not but approve her despair" (27). Immediately afterward he learns of her rape by a Lithuanian sergeant: "now that she was sullied, her experience bordered on my own [souillée, son expérience avoisinait la mienne], and the episode of the sergeant made a queer parallel [équilibrait bizarrement] (155) with my unique and revolting visit to a brothel in Brussels" (28). In Erick's "queer" logic, the "parallel" equates not the prostitute's experience, but Erick's voluntary visit with Sophie's involuntary violation. In an attempt to repress his own "queer parallel" with Conrad through a trip to the brothel, Erick also belittles female sexual exploitation and re- presses female sexual agency.[13]

As the novel progresses, and the idealistic homosocial world recedes behind the more realistic homosocial world of war, Erick's misogyny overflows across the page. To describe the horrors of Sophie and other women, Erick draws on classical images of threatening women, also found in *Freikorps* discourse (cf. II, 4–6). Sophie's hair in curlers "made her look like Medusa, serpent-crowned" [une Méduse coiffée de serpents] (173), and the "humble cafe singer" he picks up in Riga ends up clinging to him "with the tenacity of an octopus" [une tenacité de poulpe] (175) (52, 55). In the former case, the simple evocation of femininity (the curlers) threatens, and in the latter, the equation of femininity with insatiable desire provokes a similar dread. Later, the one time Erick kisses Sophie on the lips, he finds that his "ecstasy changed into horror" almost immediately, and he remembers a starfish [cette étoile de mer] that his mother had forced into his hand, "almost provoking convulsions in [him]" (76–77).[14] If these confrontations with the tentacles of the feminine evoke something beyond "hatred or terror" in Erick, they also form the basis of his self-conception. As Freud describes it, "The sight of the Medusa's head makes the spectator stiff with terror," but this bodily erection ultimately offers him "consolation," for it reminds him that he, at least, has a penis (SE 28:273). The fascist subject similarly uses the revolting female to remind him of his hard, military body. But both Freud and the soldier males may, according to Theweleit, be producing a similar repression in their confrontation with the Medusa's head. What Theweleit finds significant in this symbol is not the woman's castration, emphasized by Freud as the antinomy of male "stiffness," but *her ability to castrate*: "It is in no sense, as Freud thinks, the castrated genitals of the mother that she displays as a deterrent; it is the symbol ... of man's fear of her uncastrated, horrifying sexual potency" (I, 201). In Theweleit's view, then, the hardness of the male body is always much more tenuous than either Freud or the soldiers would want to admit; hence the need to expel Sophie from the scene.[15]

Indeed, only when Sophie has left Kratovitsy can Erick regain the imaginary fusion of his early days of homosociality: "Our ever diminishing group was returning to the great traditions of austerity and manly courage [courage viril]; Kratovitsy was becoming again what it had been in times supposedly gone by, an outpost of the Teutonic Order, a frontier fortress of the Livonian Brothers of the Sword [un poste de l'Ordre Teutonique, une citadelle avancée de Chevaliers Porte-Glaives] (226)." This "ideal of happiness" reminds him of his childhood (123–24). The casting out of the "Red woman," the communist sympathizer, turns the men's bodies into a fortress, an outpost, a borderline experience of ascetic and racial purity. In what Theweleit calls the "troop-machine," "new body-totalities are formed," as the parts of individual soldiers re-fuse into "other totality formations between men, such as the 'nation'" (II, 154–55). Since the reestablishment of the Teutonic nation is constructed on the absence and demonization of Sophie, *Coup de Grâce* confirms in this specific instance Theweleit's overly general (and thus problematic) assertion that "racism must be seen as patriarchal domination in its most intense form" (II, 77).

But the absent woman, projected from out of the flood of their own desiring production, continually threatens to expose the frailty of these soldiers "clad in armor" [à l'intérieure d'une armure] (227). Only the tenuous totality of the troop-machine protects them from being "lionized by women" [livrées ... aux femmes] and "subject to certain insidious dissolution, like the loathsome decay of iris ... [which] die miserably in their own sticky secretion [la gluante agonie], in marked contrast to the slow, heroic drying of the rose [le dessèchement héroïques des roses] (227)" (125). But, since the troop-machine "*is* the front," a permanent war-machine, it must continually transgress and reterritorialize its borders (II, 155). The attempt to keep his mechanized body dry leads the fascist to wade in blood, the "sticky secretion" of the enemy; only by killing, by actually moving through corpses that serve as so many Medusa's heads, can the fascist confirm the "hardness" and dryness [dessèchement] of his own body.

In the end, Erick's hatred of women, of communism, of everything that threatens property and his proper body, must culminate in a slaughter. Erick rediscovers Sophie "in the middle of flooded land" [en plein terrain inondé] (234), where several soldiers had already drowned (136). For the soldier-males, communism and the sexuality of women both seem "to be a kind of ocean that surges onward in waves, inundating and engulfing" (I, 229). It is ironic then, and perhaps ultimately troubling to Erick's narrative strategy, that his murder of Sophie turns his own past into pure flow, cut off from solid ground: "The disappearance of Conrad's sister would at least liquidate [liquiderait] my youth for good, and would cut the last bridge between that country and me" (147, translation modified; see French version, 243). Sophie, a reminder of his own internal drives, creates "a kind of sickening fury in the pit of [his] stomach that made [him] say 'all the better' for her death" (146). But before he actually kills her, Erick literally de-faces her: "The first shot did no more than tear open the face" (150). As Paul de Man has provocatively argued, one of the primary structures of language may concern the trope of prosopopoeia, a "giving face" to subjects which also "de-faces" them by subjecting them to the impersonal machine of language ("Autobiography," 930). De Man discusses de-facement as an attribute of autobiography, and indeed de-facement figures importantly in the ways de Man's own life has come to be understood; here, however, the narrator, Erick, de-faces the narrative's object, Sophie. Thus, the narrative shifts the uncertainty at the heart of its own enunciation (its own potential de-facement) onto the scapegoated woman, who now becomes a repository for fears not only about femininity and communism, but about the slippage of language itself. But language, in any post-Lacanian context, immediately entails questions of desire. It becomes clear that in killing Sophie, Erick is killing more than just "woman." As he approaches her with his gun, he "clung to the thought that [he] had wanted to put an end to Conrad [j'avais désiré achever Conrad] (245), and that this was the same thing" (150). In killing Conrad and Sophie simultaneously, he kills desiring-production itself, the whole tangled web of drives that unconsciously saturates all of the social relations represented in the novel.

But Erick cannot simply kill desire once; it demands constant vigilance, hence his own retelling of the story—"the interminable confession which he was making, in reality, to no one but himself" (5).

Instead of coming to consciousness of his polymorphous drives, he attempts to fix them through one final projection onto Sophie: "One is always trapped, somehow, in dealing with women" (151). For Erick, however, being trapped is the condition of his paranoid subjectivity; the real "disorder" lies in the repression of the entire unconscious. This repression amounts, in Theweleit's terms, to the fascist mode of production, an "antiproduction" whose goal is "the transformation of life into death" (I, 216).

Naive Readers and Amateur Anti-Semites

The above reading derives from an application of the theoretical apparatus provided by Theweleit to the text of Yourcenar's novel. *Coup de Grâce* lends itself to such a reading, given Erick's resemblance to the *Freikorps* warriors. Since Yourcenar initially published the novel in France in 1939, just before the beginning of World War II, and just before she left Europe for the United States, it would have been hard for contemporary readers not to understand it as a novelistic indictment of fascism, even if, according to Friedlander, it also obviously displays a disturbing fascination with the "kitsch and death" of fascist iconography. When we consider the prefatory material the author appends to her American editions of the novel, an entirely different reading emerges—one inflected by the conditions of post-Holocaust politics but not by the ethical demands of Adorno's formulations. Although the gloss that Yourcenar gives to her novel in and after 1957 initially appears diametrically opposed to Theweleit's critique of fascism, I will show that they actually share certain precepts.

In 1957, Yourcenar published the novel in English, translating it "in Collaboration" with her companion Grace Frick (to cite the title page). At this time, she affixes a curious foreword to the story, which, in a later edition, expands into an even more curious preface dated 1962.[16] The preface attempts to forestall any reading that does not accept Erick as the "clear sighted" "hero" of the novel. She claims that the narrative depicts not a sadist, as "a naive reader might make . . . of Erick," but rather "a human being . . . looking squarely upon his own life." In claiming to depict what Derrida would call a subject self-consciously present to himself, Yourcenar attempts to solidify her own authority to dictate the terms of her text at a moment in literary history when the author is, if not dead, at least withering away.

But the stakes are not strictly literary, as Yourcenar's own language reveals. Her preface demands "strict collaboration from the reader" [la collaboration du lecteur] (130); we must not "mistake [Erick] for a professional anti-Semite" [un anti-Semite professionnel] (131). The reader must collaborate in wiping out the traces of fascist collaboration. Yourcenar's plea for a vigilant forgetting, for the power that comes with ignorance, occurs just around the moment when the "Holocaust" first comes into public consciousness (but not with that specific name until later in the 1960s); that is, when the "professional anti-Semites" have regained their amateur status, which they will secretly cherish until the late 1980s when they will once again "go professional."

1957 is also the year when, in France, Céline publishes *D'un château l'autre*, his novelistic attempt to produce collaborationist-readers who will help erase his guilt. In a manner similar to Yourcenar, Céline both rewrites the past and, in a radio interview from that same year, claims that his work has only aesthetic, and not political, significance: he is merely "a stylist."[17] If Yourcenar's novel can so easily be read as a critique of fascism, why, outside of personal predilection, would Yourcenar want to use the same strategy as Céline, whose anti-Semitism could never be "mistaken" by even a "naive" reader? As Elaine Marks argues in an extremely perceptive consideration of the relations between the preface and the novel, Yourcenar "naturalizes" anti-Semitism and links it to the sadistic and sexist acts that the text details (212, 217). Marks also places the novel in the context of Céline's 1937 anti-Semitic pamphlet, *Bagatelles pour un massacre*, claiming that "it is impossible ... not to implicate the author" of *Coup de Grâce* in anti-Semitism (212).

While I am in complete agreement with Marks, I would also claim that Yourcenar's collaborationist strategy has another agenda, particular to the postwar era. The late 1950s and early 1960s in Yourcenar's adopted home, the United States, were a time of fierce ideological containment characterized in part by the polarity of the Cold War and by claims that, in fact, we had reached "the end of ideology." Consonant with the antipolitical politics of the time, Yourcenar stresses that in telling Erick's story she has "tried to show that particular intimacy or affinity which is stronger than either conflicts of political allegiances or physical passions [la passion charnelle] (133)." She explicitly represses desire, which, for Theweleit, would include precisely what this formulation precludes—passion and politics. Instead of reading politics or passion into the novel, we should look to its value as a "psychological" or "human ... document" [un document humain] (134). Thus, according to this authority, "*Coup de Grâce* does not aim at exalting or discrediting any one group or class, any country or party" (French version, 134).

But why not discredit fascism? The answer, again, slips out of the otherwise rigidly controlled language. In the 1957 cloth edition, Yourcenar phrases her apologia this way: "In the present state of the world, and in view of the conflicting attitudes of our day, the author wishes to stress the fact that this account is not intended to defend or discredit any particular group or party." Underneath this seemingly balanced sentence lurks the problem. If we were to discredit Erick and fascism, we would have to accept Sophie and thus communism as the only textually available heroines of the antifascist struggle. Given "the present state of the world" and "the conflicting attitudes" of Cold War politics, given rabid anticommunism in other words, such an option becomes untenable for Yourcenar. In the two decades after its initial publication, *Coup de Grâce* took on new meanings its author could not control. Her depoliticizing reassertion of authority amounts to a retrospective undermining of what once had been a potentially liberating text.

As is almost always the case, appeals to "human" meaning tend to exclude women. Ironically, this happens in *Coup de Grâce* at the very moment when a woman enters the text: in the establishment of a pact between the female author and reader. In her preface, Yourcenar repeats what Ingeborg Majer O'Sickey has found to be Erick's relation to Sophie. Both author and "hero" "retrieve [themselves] from exile," and establish their authority, by "ingesting" Sophie (382). Yourcenar manages this by first portraying Sophie only through Erick's narrative, and then, more seriously, by portraying this portrait as the product of a "clear-sighted" narrator, not the sadist we sophisticated readers know him to be.

More Male Fantasies

If Yourcenar opposes human psychology to politics, and in so doing exiles women from the social realm, Theweleit unifies psychology and politics, claiming that desiring-production and material production are one (I, 323). But, despite his obvious intentions, Theweleit also banishes women and, ultimately, the social itself from his study. Although he succeeds in conveying the intimate thoughts of his subjects, Theweleit fares less well in establishing the context of their literary output. Theweleit's very considerable contribution to the understanding of fascism—that it is a form of reality production, that we must "feel" its utopian pull—ends by limiting his discussion. Just as does *Coup de Grâce*, Theweleit constantly evokes women, but he never takes them seriously as anything but effects of male fantasies.

If, as he claims, "a specific male-female (patriarchal) relation might belong at the center of our examination of fascism," not much can be gained by understanding these relations as simply expressing the "sexuality of the oppressor and the oppressed" (I, 227, 221). Women have no place in Theweleit's history (which he attempts to extend to all of Western history), except as either victims or possessors of some vague, emancipatory "nature." The "male-female" relationship that Theweleit promises to unpack turns out to be simply a "male-male" relationship in which women are "malleable" and passive. In this, he proves himself no different from most historians, who "have not defined women's support for Nazi Germany as a historical problem" (Koonz, 4), and have thus reinforced the appearance of the lack of female agency throughout history. Despite the misogyny of the *Freikorps* and later the Nazis, women supported them out of "conviction, opportunism, and active choice. Far from being helpless or even innocent, women made possible a murderous state in the name of concerns they defined as motherly" (Koonz, 4–5). One of Theweleit's great acomplishments lies in his demonstration that the soldier-males were neither insane nor irrational; yet, because he does not discuss how and why women helped create, as well as resist, the culture that produced fascism, he seems to relegate women to that very realm of irrationality.

What *Male Fantasies* lacks is not a consideration of the "reality" of women's agency, where reality would be opposed to the fantasies of the soldier-males, but rather an analysis of the discursive context in which the soldiers announced and acted upon their desires—a context that also included the writings and actions of women. Women did produce texts during this period, and a real counter-discourse would consider these female fantasies alongside more traditional, male documents. The few places where Theweleit promises to reveal "the actual behavior of those women" (I, 138) whom the soldiers depict end in yet more male fantasies. Take, for example, the "Aside on Proletarian Reality, Proletarian Woman and Man of the Left" (138–71). Although Theweleit cites one or two primary sources by women, practically the only ones in either volume, he ends up using these pages to discredit Marxism by revealing that proletarian men and communist theorists were almost as misogynistic as the *Freikorps* troops. Similarly, after asserting that the oppressive male ego could not evolve "without the (admittedly enforced) cooperation of women themselves" (I, 301), Theweleit launches a 150-page history of the world that is unorthodox in everything except its refusal to acknowledge women as political agents or subjects of their own desires.

Although Theweleit wields a politicized psychoanalysis as his subjects wield a bayonet, his analysis falls more on the side of the psyche than the political. He understands the fascists' permanent state of war as "a function of the body of these men" (I, 192) and as "the ultimate form of male sexuality at odds with itself" (II, 84). Since his view of social formations—any social formation—derives from his study of the partriarchal male body, he reproduces the *Freikorps* dystopia of a society without women. Like Yourcenar, he ingests possible female subjectivities in order to armor his own theoretical construction of men as the sole social agents. He cannot conceive that even under patriarchy both men and women actively construct society, although not to their equal satisfaction.[18] He cannot see, therefore, that to take society apart will entail not an asocial explosion of desiring-production, but a dismantling from within received identities and positions.

Although I would not in any way claim that Theweleit, like Yourcenar, collaborates with fascism and patriarchy, his figurations of women are idealized—"Female chauvinism is a contradiction in terms" (II, 87)—and his only solutions remain utopian: "The pathway to a nonfascist life is marked out a little further by every act of lovemaking in which the participants touch neither as images nor as bearers of *names* defined by the social" (II, 104). This may sound like the early 1970s love-in that it is. But such an equation between fascism and the symbolic and social orders suggests an untenable notion of sexuality and a dangerous paucity of political options. The idea that "participants" could confront each other without bearing names derived from the social order not only ignores the last century of humanities and social scientific thinking, it misses the subversiveness built into acts of naming. According to some contemporary feminists, sexuality that foregrounds social roles and names erodes the foundations of patriarchy much more effectively than appeals to some natural, extradiscursive realm.[19] Furthermore, as Theweleit himself writes elsewhere, it is precisely men, such as the soldier-males, with fragmented ego-structures who seek to transcend the social realm and "want a contact with the opposite sex—or perhaps simply access to sexuality itself—which cannot be *named*" (I, 205; see also 284). This contradiction in Theweleit's text results from the privileging of desiring-production as a ubiquitous and quasinatural force.

But desire is culturally specific and neither organic nor natural. It is produced by social formations, by the very barriers that Theweleit would exile from his utopian model. We who today are facing a renewal of nationalism and fascism need to be very careful about understanding the social formations that produce such structures of desire; only by acknowledging the materiality of desire can we begin to construct alternative social formations that will oppose fascism and patriarchy. Since, in the end, all such barriers to the free flow of desire are equally oppressive in Theweleit's model, he cannot distinguish between capitalism, fascism, and communism, and he cannot propose an alternative.

While all existing hegemonic social formations may be the same in upholding patriarchal relations, patriarchy cannot be said uniquely to determine fascism, even if it provides its ground. According to Maria-Antonietta Macciocchi, fascism builds on a particular religious articulation of patriarchy: "The seizure of power by fascism and nazism uses as levers the martyred, baneful, and necrophiliac femininity of the widows and mothers of men killed in the first world war, and the femininity of Woman as Reproducer of the Species" (68). Macciocchi also makes clear that we cannot explain patriarchy without acknowledging women's agency in simultaneously upholding it and resisting the establishment of its barriers. Both Theweleit and Yourcenar (despite herself) have succeeded in documenting barbarism; but they will not be able to explain it until they break with psychologizing models that eliminate the interplay of phantasmic bodies with social formations. For bodies and fantasies are social formations, but social formations are not bodies, and they are definitely not fantasies. The personal is political, but the political is always more than personal.

Antipolitical posturing—whether in the name of humanism and aesthetics or anarchy—constitutes the common deep structure from which Yourcenar's and Theweleit's superficially different projects unfold. Their interrogation of fascist sexuality and their cross-gender identifications (a woman speaking as/for a soldier; a man writing like a feminist) are not ultimately subversive, but they lead us to further questions about theory and methodology. Perhaps one of the tasks for the critique of fascism in this era of resurgent nationalisms and proliferating sexualities remains the search for methodologies that understand history not as simply "incoherent" and "unstable," but—to paraphrase Benjamin—as a present-day struggle over the future with forces from the past. As long as misogyny and homophobia meet only a depoliticized and antisexual resistance, a fascist return-of-the-repressed will continue to inhabit all male fantasies.[20]

NOTES

An earlier version of this essay, "Documenting Barbarism: Yourcenar's Male Fantasies, Theweleit's Coup," was published in *Cultural Critique* 29 (winter 1994–95).

1. For the significance of Theodor Adorno's concept "after Auschwitz" for the consideration of post-Holocaust culture, see Rothberg, "After Adorno" and *After the "Final Solution."*
2. Unless otherwise noted, all citations from the novel given in the text in English will be from the English translation. The novel was originally translated into English in 1957. When I refer to the French version I will be quoting from a later edition of Yourcenar's novel: *Alexis ou le traité du vain combat* suivi de *Le Coup de grâce*. This edition contains the 1962 preface, reprinted in the English edition and crucial to my reading of the novel. Throughout, I will intersperse sections of the French text whenever the language differs significantly from the English or when I am paying particular attention to specific word use. As I hope my reading demonstrates, I am less interested in establishing an "authentic" text than in revealing the specificities of the different versions and editions of *Le Coup de grâce*. Theweleit's work was originally published in Germany in 1977 and 1978.
3. The work of Maria-Antonietta Macciocchi remains among the most provocative on this topic.
4. See Anson Rabinbach and Jessica Benjamin's foreword to volume II for a discussion of Theweleit and the Frankfurt School (xii).
5. For documents pertaining to the de Man case, see Paul de Man, *Wartime Journalism*, and Hamacher, *Responses*.
6. This history of German feminism is taken from Altbach. Besides this helpful introductory essay, her volume also contains ample documentation from the movement.
7. Kaplan also situates her reading of Theweleit within the context of the de Man and Heidegger "scandals." Her suggestive analysis considers *Male Fantasies* alongside Art Spiegelman's *Maus* and Duras and Renais's *Hiroshima mon amour*.
8. For documents from this debate, see Jardine and Smith. Theweleit's work is cited as an example of "engendered male criticism" in the bibliography of Boone and Cadden.
9. See the final two chapters of Horkheimer and Adorno's *Dialectic of Enlightenment* for an analysis of the capitalist culture industry and of anti-Semitism, which links these two phenomena on the basis of a critique of instrumental reason.
10. To be fair, this text entitled "1933: Micropolitics and Segmentarity" was published in 1980, after Theweleit had completed his work, but the complexity expressed here by Deleuze and Guattari typifies their work—if not always that of their followers.
11. The French is less specific here. Their eyes do not share the marker of Aryan identity; they simply have *"la même nuance d'yeux"* (143).
12. Owens also explicitly refutes Macciocchi's assertion that "the Nazi commu-

nity is made by homosexual brothers who exclude the woman and valorize the brother" (223).

13. Clearly, the notion of the "queer parallel" upon which I am playing here is specific to the English text, but as a choice for translation, it remains significant. The translators are, after all, two women living and working together during a period when "queer" and not "gay" or "lesbian" was probably the dominant term of self-identification for homosexuals. See Delany's memoir of this period for a discussion of these identity issues.

14. Elaine Marks also draws attention to the connections between these passages. I will return to her important essay.

15. See Hertz for a more developed consideration of how "questions of sexual difference, of perception and of politics are rapidly brought into relation" (27) around the figure of the Medusa's head.

16. I have not been able to locate the 1957 foreword in French, but the 1962 preface is, as I noted above, affixed to the 1971 French edition. Contradictions exist between these two documents, neither of which (in the English versions) are given page numbers: she claims to have written the novel in 1939; in the second she says 1938; she claims to have heard the story directly from "Erick"; in the second she says it came from one of his friends.

17. The radio interview is with Albert Zbinden and was broadcast July 25, 1957, on Radio-Lausanne. I am grateful to Alice Y. Kaplan for supplying me with a tape of this interview.

18. For the contradictory forms of female subjectivity and agency in the Germany of this era, see the essays collected in Bridenthal, et al.

19. I am thinking for example of Judith Butler's discussion of butch-femme sexuality (122–24).

20. I would like to thank Jane Marcus and Ingeborg Majer O'Sickey for their help on this essay. I am also grateful to Nancy K. Miller for her reading of this piece in the context of the larger project from which it was originally taken.

Questions of *genre*: History and the Self in Marguerite Yourcenar's *Mémoires d'Hadrien*

Ksenya Kiebuzinski

INTRODUCTION

MARGUERITE YOURCENAR'S 1951 NOVEL *MÉMOIRES D'HADRIEN* RECOUNTS the life of a second-century Roman emperor. Hadrian narrates his story in the form of an autobiographical letter addressed to his adopted grandson, Marcus Aurelius. Hadrian's lengthy monologue is just as much a self-contained meditation on the meaning of existence as it is a sort of manual for princes. If it is understood as a memoir, Yourcenar weaves the sometimes convergent, sometimes divergent perceptions that Hadrian has of his own personal history: what he believed himself to be, what he wished to be, and what he actually was ("Carnets de notes," 342). If, on the other hand, it is taken as a manual for princes, Yourcenar shows how Hadrian strives to maintain a balance between competing elements of both private and public knowledge in order to rule more benevolently and to prepare his empire for a peaceful near future.

Identifying the manner in which Yourcenar's novel relies on history and goes beyond the essay, Christian Murciaux surmises that "Cet art de vivre d'Hadrien fait de ce livre un 'Manuel'" [Hadrien's 'art of living' turns this book into a 'Manual'] (146–48).[1] Janet Whatley also argues that the novel should be read as a "manual" in the tradition of the "mirror of princes" since it explores the disparate qualities that a prince must have or keep in check. In addition, Whatley aptly categorizes *Mémoires d'Hadrien* as at once a meditation on history and an invented narrative. As a meditation on history the novel focuses on a political power's ability to adapt to periods of peace and upheaval, while as a work of fiction it deals imaginatively with human experience which is "something other than the discursive voice of an essayist author" (Whatley, 221). This interplay between instruction and history versus fiction and subjectivity raises complex questions about *genre*, signifying here both "form" and "gender," since the novel does so much more than elucidate the emperor's personal account of ancient Graeco-Roman times.[2]

Whether one considers the *Mémoires* a fictional autobiography, a catalog of ancient culture, a meditation on history, or a manual for princes, the twofold generic problem of this work lies in its trying at once to recreate Roman history and to invent a self. Yourcenar's work resembles a meditation on history, especially on the art of writing history. It also corresponds to a philosophical memoir, which in looking for the meaning of existence seeks to transcend external reality in order to reach one of a more intimate nature. The author presents us with a hero who not only acts and expresses himself in situations of historical importance—such as the stabilization of the Roman Empire—but of personal importance as well—his love for Antinoüs, his daily routines (sleeping and eating), his own death. The blurring of the lines that demarcate private and public spheres causes the emperor's life to commingle with that of his empire. He thus comes to resemble what one reviewer labeled as "un humaniste couronné, le type en somme du bon tyran et de l'honnête homme" [a royal humanist, a mix, in other words, of a beneficent ruler and a civilized man] (Henriot). Ultimately, Hadrian's desire to unite "human knowledge and consciousness and imperial knowledge and consciousness" (Horn, 33) is a quest to incorporate the different truths and archetypes within his empire into an all-encompassing worldview that will endure, a sort of "cosmos harmonieux" [cosmic harmony] (Tournier, 76).

Yourcenar, using Hadrian's narrative voice as a masquerade, proposes to her readers a system of human knowledge that will help achieve this end. This system is based on the erotic union with another's body and spirit: "un système de connaissance humaine basé sur l'érotique, une théorie du contact, où le mystère et la dignité d'autrui consisteraient précisément à offrir au Moi ce point d'appui d'un autre monde" [a system of human knowledge based in the erotic, a theory of contact, whereby the mystery and dignity of a fellow being would consist precisely in his or her offer to serve as a place of support and comfort] (*Mémoires*, 22). Such a system, a theory of contact, represents a paradigmatic and epistemological shift away from a purely imperial viewpoint to one that includes an understanding of both the world of emperor and citizen, whether the citizen be an old female petitioner or an injured male soldier (22). Yourcenar's theory of contact also mitigates the binary construction that posits mind over body, culturally associated with the hierarchy of dominant masculinity and subjugated femininity, and offers instead an intermingling of the set of terms through an erasure of boundaries distinguishing one from the other.

(A)Historical Novel?

In her "Carnets de Notes de *Mémoires d'Hadrien*" ["Notebook on *Memoirs of Hadrian*"], which serve as epilogue to the novel, Yourcenar clearly defines the objectives of the work as historical in nature: "De notre temps, le roman historique, ou ce que, par commodité, on consent à nommer tel, ne peut être que plongé dans un temps retrouvé, prise de possession d'un monde intérieur" [In our era, the historical novel (or, for convenience's sake, what passes as such) can only emerge from time that is rediscovered, the product of an individual conscience] (331). Restated in another way, she inverts nineteenth-century archaeological work—reconstructing history from within (327). In order to portray this inner reality, Yourcenar chose to write the novel in the form of a monologue, thus providing Hadrian a dignified form of speech (oratio togata [or style of the toga]), a style suitable for a man of his stature during antiquity and one that allows him to address directly—beyond Marcus Aurelius—"un interlocuteur idéal, à cet *homme en soi* . . . donc à nous" [an ideal listener, the inner man . . . thus all men] (*Le Temps*, 37). Despite her historical objectives, the choice of the treatise-monologue as the literary genre for *Mémoires* allows the author to put into doubt the category of the historical novel that she claims to hold in little esteem.[3]

Even though she had such little regard for the historical novel as genre, she had great respect for history per se. Yourcenar found her protagonist's voice only after extensive research on and respect for the details about the Hadrianic era, whether they were to be found in the few remaining personal and official documents written by the emperor, or in writings by contemporaries. Besides written works, she also examined art and artifacts relating to Hadrian, including archaeological sites, monuments, inscriptions, statues, reliefs, and coins. This material often provided factual details lacking in the ancient documents. Yourcenar's research proceeded in much the same manner as in her essay *Le Temps, ce grand sculpteur [Time, that great sculptor]*, where she describes how the passage of time causes ancient statues to erode into bits: "Le jour où une statue est terminée, sa vie, en un sens, commence. La première étape est franchie, qui, par les soins du sculpteur, l'a menée du bloc à la forme humaine; une seconde étape, au cours des siècles . . . le ramènera peu à peu à l'état de minéral informe auquel l'avait soustrait son sculpteur" [The day when a statue is finished, its life, in a sense, begins. The first stage is complete: the sculptor's hand has transformed it from block to human form; a second stage . . . will lead it bit by bit back to the original unformed mineral state in which its sculptor found it] (*Le Temps*, 61). In *Mémoires d'Hadrien*, she set out to reconstitute from the past the bits of voice—several lines of Hadrian's memoirs, a few intimate letters, and the rare quoted words of the chronicles—that make up his entire tone "comme d'autres avec des éclats de marbre reconstituent un buste brisé" [as others with bits of marble repair a broken bust] (*Le Temps*, 39). Contrary to Rousseau, who in his preface to "On the Origin of Inequality," speaks of history as a disfiguring force that corrupts the primitive state of Glaucus's statue, Yourcenar sees historical time as cyclical and natural.

Applying the metaphor of the statue—which in its lifetime has form, loses form, and undergoes restoration—to Yourcenar's text, one can see that she acknowledges how she has reconstructed and reanimated Hadrian's life through her writing. Nevertheless, she claims that the memoirs continue to express Hadrian himself, or rather his inner reality, since she has eliminated any intervening points of view and used "only real stones" ("Carnets de notes," 342).[4] She writes in a letter to the German writer Joseph Breitbach that in composing the *Mémoires*, facts prevailed over form and interpretation; yet she also admits history's indebtedness to human memory (*Lettres*, 84–85). But, as in the case of any writer who attempts to combine history and invention in order to represent the human condition of a particular era, Yourcenar must draw upon her own interpretations of history to create a narrative that will conform both to the laws of history and of poetry.

But are not the materials of history and the forms of poetry irreconcilable? Alessandro Manzoni points out in his nineteenth-century essay *On the Historical Novel* that "the principal subject of the historical novel is completely the author's, completely poetic, because merely verisimilar" (125). This statement is borne out in the detailed, lengthy bibliographical note included with Yourcenar's novel where she concedes that the narrative follows the laws of poetry to render a more accurate portrayal of Hadrian's life. She admits to certain historical distortions in his portrayal, such as rearrangements, simplifications, modifications, and filling in of information, but claims that these changes were necessary to make Hadrian appear as much as possible as he was and as his contemporaries saw him. Despite the apparent contradictions inherent in a project that desires to combine historical facts with a first-person narrator, the author contends that within certain limits inaccuracy may improve the authenticity of the intended meaning (*Le Temps*, 40–41). She does not wish to imply, however, that this uncertainty prevents the attainment of historical truth. On the contrary, the ambiguities present in any reading of history most probably were present in life itself so that truth, historical or other, hinges upon the interpretation of uncertain memories: one is more or less mistaken ("Carnet de notes," 331).

Yourcenar strongly insisted that unlike Flaubert, who claimed he was Emma, she is not Hadrian but rather became Hadrian (Savigneau, 231). If we accept her assertion, then it follows that any liberties that she took in establishing a coherent tone and language for her novel from imperfect and partial facts coupled with her character's ambiguous relationship to the past, only further reflect the inexactitude of her historical project. She acknowledges the merits of poetry as a unifying factor for her historical findings, but remains nonetheless preoccupied with factual knowledge. When openly criticized in the journal *Revue Archéologique* by Charles Picard for inaccurate details, specious historical sources, and, sarcastically, for a lack of a feminine point of view (no pictures of the handsome Hadrian or Antinoüs) (85), Yourcenar, instead of giving a nod to invention, indicates in a letter to her Italian translator Lidia Storoni Mazzolani that she responded to this historical authority and revised certain passages following the chapter "Animula." She explains to Mazzolani that: "Les chapitres qui suivent contiennent, eux des révisions légères, mais assez nombreuses, fautes d'impression dans les noms propres ou ailleurs enfin corrigées, phrases ajoutées çà et là pour clarifier un point ou pour répondre aux objections d'un archéologue" [The chapters which follow contain slight but rather numerous revisions, typographical errors finally corrected, sentences added here and there to clarify a point or respond to an archaeologist's objections] (*Lettres*, 148).[5]

In writing the *Mémoires*, Yourcenar speaks of erring more or less, and, despite her attention to historical "truth," perhaps the reader should conclude that the emphasis is on more. Echoes of this same approach to truth are found in her narrator's meditations on the documentation of his own life:

> Les trois quarts de ma vie échappent d'ailleurs à cette définition par les actes: la masse de mes velléités, de mes désirs, de mes projets même, demeure aussi nébuleuse et aussi fuyante qu'un fantôme. Le reste, la partie palpable, plus ou moins authentifiée par les faits, est à peine plus

distincte, et la séquence des événements aussi confuse que celle des songes. (34)

[Three-quarters of my life cannot be explained by my acts: the mass of half-formed ideas, my desires, even actual projects remain as nebulous and fleeting as a ghost. The rest, the accessible part, more or less authenticated by the facts, is hardly more distinct, and the sequence of actual events is as confused in my mind as are my dreams.]

Yourcenar's Hadrian essentially undertakes to convey to his reader the three-quarters of his life that official chronicles cannot but fail to comprehend. He wishes to recount not only a summary of facts about his life, but also to evoke a lifetime of wishes and desires. The task of integrating the facts and desires of his life requires diametrical procedures, a movement into and outside of oneself (32). Hadrian cannot escape from what "he" perceives himself to be and from what the public sees his life to be, nor can he deny that the actions by which his citizens judge him bear some resemblance to his person. The lucidity of Hadrian's narrative, then, must lie in his acknowledgment that since no one single character trait can explain him, he will recall his life the way he wishes to remember it. He thus favors consciousness over action.

Choosing to privilege one individual's consciousness rather than describing a universal Roman experience, Yourcenar's work differentiates itself from other works of historical fiction according to the general criteria of the genre. Her main character particularly departs from Walter Scott's and Lukács's notion of typicality that heralds "the mediocre, prosaic hero" as central to this type of narrative (Lukács, 34). Yourcenar's use of a noble character such as Hadrian seems to run counter to Lukács's idealization of the classical form of the historical novel so aptly followed by Walter Scott's middling heroes, who never side with either faction during crises of historical life and who represent the collective aspects of the social orders in conflict. Instead of following Scott's model, whose heroes are usually decent and average rather than sophisticated and eminent, Yourcenar chose to look to the world-historical model of imperial authority to locate an imitable model for the future.

In the years following the Second World War, the author still believed that it was possible to find, or to hope for, a man capable of "stabilizing the earth," someone who could influence and guide society through difficult times with some likelihood of success (*Les yeux ouverts*, 158–61) *[With Open Eyes]*. While the question has been raised of whether such a search for a model tyrant is advisable considering "who could more closely resemble a Hitler or a Mussolini than an ancient Roman despot" (Howard, 185), Yourcenar was convinced that a more discerning person—in her own words "one more skillful at navigating in difficult straits"—could rule both authoritatively and sublimely (*Les yeux ouverts*, 158–59). Her reliance upon Hadrian's imperial perspective would seem to deny a totalizing view of life, one that would encompass points of view from below as well as above. The transcendent quality of her character, however, permits him to be measured as a complete man of his time. He is, according to the praise of French academician Emile Henriot, complete in "action and thought, creation and work, at times a soldier, builder, poet, or philosopher; an idealist and realist, believing in things over words; enjoying to be in command in order to serve; in short voluptuous in every way and taking interest in ideas even to imagine those of tomorrow." Unlike the Lukácsian minor character, who represents popular life from the viewpoint of average consciousness, Hadrian emerges as a world-historical figure with pacifist and humanist tendencies who is both citizen and ruler, human and god.

Although not poised immediately between conflicting social forces nor on the verge of a great historical crisis, Hadrian does to some degree come into contact with enemy camps, but often through his own provocation as anything but an impartial hero. Nevertheless, these conflicts are not extreme and do not threaten the immediate future of the empire. His fortune lies in having inherited a world in need of reorganization and not resuscitation. It is a period when the future looks unstable and uncertain, yet also a period of time that appears steady enough to last for some time to come (*Les yeux ouverts*, 63). As in other historical fiction, Yourcenar's character negotiates the conflicts of his time by putting aside his role as statesman to take up alternately the position of an aesthete, art lover, poet, musician, traveler, general, economist, master builder, and political scientist (Horn, 32) as well as the more virile roles of debaucher, hunter, warrior, and tyrant. His multiple roles, which he sees as "les différentes professions dont se compose le métier d'empereur" [the various professions that the role of emperor comprises] (138), allow Hadrian to enter into human contact with diverse social forces, or in Lukács's words, different "warring camps" (37). In these interactions the emperor strives to locate that diversity in unity that would serve as a standard for the empire as a whole (134). Seeing his various roles as a divine continuation of the work of great Greek and Roman innovators and rulers helps him lead the citizens and institutions of his empire toward reforms based on pluralism:

> Je m'imaginais secondant celui-ci [le divin] dans son effort d'informer et d'ordonner un monde, d'en développer et d'en multiplier les circonvolutions, les ramifications, les détours. J'étais l'un des segments de la roue, l'un des aspects de cette force unique engagée dans la multiplicité des choses, aigle et taureau, homme et cygne, phallus et cerveau tout ensemble, Protée qui est en même temps Jupiter (159).

> [I imagined myself seconding this last one (the divine) in his efforts to inform and order a world, to develop and multiply its ripple effect, its ramifications, its detours. I was one spoke of the wheel, one small part of that unique force engaged in the multiplicity of things, eagle and bull, man and swan, phallus and brain combined, Proteus and at the same time Jupiter.]

Hadrian does not, however, take the middle road when he seeks to impose Greek culture on all human endeavors and Roman administration on all imperial projects. Averring that wherever he travels he feels himself to be "a Roman away from Rome" shows in many ways how little the emperor adapts himself to the diversity of his universe. He prefers to identify Rome with half the globe, "Rome n'est plus dans Rome" [Rome is no longer in Rome] (124). Furthermore, as a colonialist he fails to understand that not all nations will consider the apparent civilizing achievements of Graeco-Roman culture as essential or even practical. His blindness will cause the near annihilation and dispersal of any surviving Jews after a brutal war waged by the emperor's forces against Judaea. This weakness, though, should not necessarily be understood as completely atypical of the historical hero who may be portrayed simultaneously as virtuous and immoral. As Lukács described, the hero may be someone who lives "himself out to the full as a human being," and who exhibits "freely all of his splendid and petty human qualities" (45). In fact, the barbarous Judaean campaign, as well as the unemotional execution of his brother-in-law, Servianus, and his sister's grandson, Fuscus, serve precisely as reminders to Hadrian that he is but human and not capable of godlike control over elements opposed to his rule. This self-awareness of his limited power to maintain peace leads to a dim but still hopeful outlook for the world's future: "Les catastrophes et les ruines viendront; le désordre triomphera, mais de temps en temps l'ordre aussi . . . les mots de liberté, d'humanité, de justice retrouveront çà et là le sens que nous avons tenté de leur donner" [The catastrophes and decay will come;

disorder will triumph, but now and again order will triumph as well ... words of freedom, humanity and justice will here and there take on the meaning we have attempted to ascribe to them] (314). Here, in uttering the words humanity, liberty, and justice, Hadrian speaks to the heirs of his Roman ideals.

Hadrian's anachronistic political lucidity and prophetic voice in the above citation raise an interesting question regarding genre and gender in *Mémoires d'Hadrien*. How does Hadrian's prescience distinguish itself from Yourcenar's hindsight? In other words, is the "I" or "Je" of the narrator actually the semiautobiographical voice of the author hidden behind the traits of the Roman emperor? In his article "Une oeuvre à la première personne" ["A Work in the First Person"], Christophe Carlier asks "Qui parle?" ["Who speaks?"] in the *Mémoires*. He accounts for four voices in the work: the real Hadrian, who is the author of the epigraph; the fictional Hadrian, who addresses Marcus Aurelius in his letter; the novelist Marguerite Yourcenar, who records the gestation of the work in her "Carnets de notes"; and the historian Marguerite Yourcenar, who documents her research in the bibliographical "Note" (Carlier, 98). This progression of perspectives in the novel slowly destroys the illusion that Hadrian is the author of his "memoirs." While the apocryphal nature of the memoirs would seem to call for them to be read as a work of historical fiction, the overt presence of the author makes them more like Yourcenar's personal meditation on love and politics. Rather than an autobiography of a Roman emperor, the work presents itself as a sort of treatise written from a post-Hitlerian and late French colonial perspective. Furthermore, in what Lorna Milne argues as the author's impersonation of the masculine in this work, Yourcenar gets to explore rigorously another world of "ce qui n'est pas elle" [that which is not her] (217). Yourcenar insisted that Hadrian could speak more skillfully about his life than she, and acknowledged that at times she allowed him to deceive her (330). However, the inclusion of her bibliographical note and reflections on the writing of the novel certainly raise doubts about the author's ability to extricate herself fully from what she called "a symbiotic relationship" with her character, which began as early as 1924 and ended only upon publication of the *Mémoires* in 1951 (*Les yeux ouverts*, 155).[6]

(A)SEXUAL SELF?

While Yourcenar admitted to having cocreated Hadrian's "history," many readers, particularly feminists, remain dissatisfied with the level of her avowed involvement. Those readers who expect women writers to create feminist texts find that Yourcenar does not speak forcefully enough for her sex in this novel, as well as in her other works of fiction. Yourcenar has been frequently criticized for emphasizing the masculine experience, a male worldview, and for recreating a male consciousness. In 1952, Denise Bourdet spoke of Yourcenar's "firmness of style" and "virility of thought" as cloaked in a reassuring feminine exterior (Bourdet, 128–29). Twenty years later, Jean Blot, who wrote the first booklength study on the author, found that Yourcenar put more of her own personality into her male heroes than into her flat, empty, female characters (Blot, 94). Similar approbations continued into the late 1980s and were reiterated by Georgia Hooks Shurr in her reader's guide to Yourcenar. Shurr stated that "those characteristics which generally identify a female sensibility or the literary style of a woman writer are particularly absent in her novels" (Shurr, 89–90).

There is no question that Yourcenar overwhelmingly uses male narrators in her fiction—Hadrian is just one example. These male narrators, however, are often depicted as sexually ambivalent. Such ambivalence may be read as a rejection of the heterosexual dyads male/female and masculine/feminine. One might also argue that her male characters are in search of a multiplicity of possible physical and spiritual relationships that extend beyond sexual identity. Yourcenar's artistic self-consciousness and her rejection of feminism (as well as of any other kind of label—national, religious, or even human as opposed to animal) cannot be easily disengaged from Hadrian's desire to rise intellectually above his sex. The author finds that Hadrian's narrative advantage lies in his complete impersonality, which is a trait she rarely finds in women (*Les yeux ouverts*, 291).

Yourcenar apparently refers to impersonality as the ability to transcend specifically personal identifications. She thinks women have a lesser tendency toward breaking with sexual particularism and a greater tendency toward conforming with the existing order. Could it be that she feels that women are more compelled toward experiencing gender as a unified experience of sex, identity, and performance? In her analysis of feminism and the subversion of identity, Judith Butler calls this unified experience a "stylized repetition of acts" and a "regulatory fiction of heterosexual coherence" in which gendered bodies take up "styles of the flesh," for instance, "as *a corporeal style*, an 'act,' as it were, which is both intentional and performative, where *'performative'* suggests a dramatic and contingent construction of meaning" (137–39). While the reader cannot know the true authorial intention behind the representations of Yourcenar's female characters, the author takes the trouble in her "Carnets" to note the impossibility of making a woman central to her narratives. She deems women's lives to be either "too limited, or too secret," as well as no longer truly feminine once they tell their own story (329). It would appear then that Hadrian's created voice intermingles with Yourcenar's own. Both narrator and author, as well as the main character, believe that a thinking man who can transcend his maleness and his masculinity "belongs to his species" and can rise "even above human," while a thinking woman, with rare exceptions, continuously acts out her femaleness. Nonetheless, the author's appended comments in her "Carnets" are included not only to echo Hadrian's beliefs but also to reaffirm the validity of his voice to the reader, and thereby, hers too.

Hadrian's differing opinions with regard to men and women should be recognized as biased, for Yourcenar presents him as a literate and reasoning man who escapes his gender and, in a Beauvoirian sense, takes up identity in the category of "body-transcendent universal personhood" (Butler, 9). Hadrian for the most part describes femininity as a cultural performance, and accuses women of putting on their passion as simply as if they were applying rouge, adorning themselves, or weeping like actresses onstage. Despite recognizing the performative aspect of femininity, he does not believe that women have an identity outside of their gender, and goes so far as to say that the patriarchal institution of marriage represents their one great venture in life (130). Still, he does understand that heterosexual male desire seems to demand of women a masquerade of femininity, "l'esprit du jeu exigeait ces perpétuels déguisements" [the spirit of the game required these continual masquerades]. Furthermore, he recognizes that the excessively disguised image is reinforced by those men who, "passionnés des femmes s'attachent au temple et aux accessoires du culte au moins autant qu'à leur déesse elle-même" [so in love with women, attach themselves as much to the cult of femininity and its accessories as to their chosen goddess] (74).

In rare instances, Yourcenar's protagonist reveals a fondness for a particular mistress, but only if she exhibits qualities beyond her "femininity." The mistress in question either exactingly sounds out her physical and spiritual desires—"parmi ces maîtresses, il en est une au moins que j'ai délicieusement aimée. . . . J'aimais sa fureur et son détachement dans le plaisir, son goût difficile, et sa rage de se déchirer l'âme" [among these mistresses, there was one whom I loved deliciously. . . . I loved her fury and detachment in taking her pleasure, her exacting taste, her rage as she rent her very soul] (77)—or she stands above her sex—"je me découvris un faible pour les danseuses aux crotales. . . . J'aimais ce bruit sec, ces bras levés, ce déferlement ou cet enroulement de voiles, cette danseuse qui cesse d'être une femme pour devenir tantôt nuage et tantôt oiseau, tantôt vague et tantôt trirème" [I discovered in myself a weakness for belly dancers. I loved the dry sound, the raised arms, the flinging out or rolling in of veils in the dancer who ceases to be woman in order to become now a cloud now a bird, now a wave and now a trireme] (247). Yourcenar shows that in most of Hadrian's relationships with women, however, he cannot make contact with their spiritual nature which he so desires to unmask: "J'aurais voulu davantage: la créature humaine dépouillée. . . . Il devait y avoir autre chose . . . j'épiais avec curiosité les rumeurs d'un intérieur inconnu, le son particulier des bavardages de femmes, l'éclat d'une colère ou d'un rire, les murmures d'une intimité, tout ce qui cessait dès qu'on me savait là" [I would have liked more: the human being laid bare. . . . There has to be something else there . . . I listened with curiosity to rumors of a secret inner life, to the particular sound of women's conversations, to bursts of anger or laughter, to intimate murmurings, to everything that ceased as soon as they gleaned my presence] (75). His friendship with the empress Plotina stands as the unique exception to this case. He has solely a spiritual relationship with her—an intimate contact of two minds—based on a mutual passion "d'orner, puis de dépouiller notre âme" [to illuminate, then to bare our soul] (95). Out of this convergence between two like minds comes a shared esteem for one another that on the part of Hadrian endures even after Plotina's death, "l'impératrice restait ce qu'elle avait toujours été pour moi: un esprit, une pensée à laquelle s'était mariée la mienne" [the Empress remained what she had always been for me: a spirit, a thought to which my own was married] (182). Only his love for Antinoüs can surpass this union between similar minds.

Prior to his discovering the higher form of love and beauty as personified by Antinoüs, Yourcenar recounts Hadrian's life from the perspective of physical appetites, quests, and conquests. This lust for life characterizes his past sexual predilections and his political ambitions, although in these pursuits he had always been able to find some level of nonphysical satisfaction; for example, the bloody initiation rite of the Mithra cult induces Hadrian to believe in a state of being beyond his human condition, "Chacun de nous croyait échapper aux étroites limites de sa condition d'homme, se sentait à la fois lui-même et l'adversaire" [Each one of us felt he had escaped the rigid limits of his person, feeling as if he were at the same time both himself and his adversary] (64). In speaking of other sensual experiences, Hadrian writes of the pleasure to be found in the presence of an Other who can animate one's own passions simply by being individually distinct and unknown. This same mystery that attracted yet separated him from his lovers, patterns his career as sovereign. His career begins when the prophetic stars reveal to him in childhood that one day he shall rule the world; and it comes to fruition with the mysterious realization of his "full self" as emperor in the concise, two-lined will written in Plotina's steady but feminine hand (104). Hadrian's successes, whether amorous or political, are all tinged with uncertainty as to whether they came about through sincere or duplicitous means. Until Antinoüs enters his life, love and political destiny reach Hadrian with divine fortuity. These two realms will take on an even deeper significance after the Bithynian youth's suicide.

Yourcenar describes how Hadrian, during his relationship with Antinoüs, ably unites pleasures of the body with those of the mind. This invasion of the flesh by the spirit, or the hinge where destiny meets the supple response of will, eventually becomes the guiding principle not only of Hadrian's private life but also his politics. At first, through physical contact with the living Antinoüs—"Ma main glissait sur sa nuque, sous ses cheveux" [I slid my hand over his neck, under his hair]—Hadrian feels a direct connection with earthly nature: "j'avais ainsi le sentiment de rester en contact avec les grands objets naturels" [Thus I had the feeling of remaining in touch with the great natural objects] (213). He cannot, however, sustain a spiritual contact with his lover, a meeting of souls so to speak—"Mais aucune caresse ne va jusqu'à l'âme" [But no caress goes as deep as the soul]—until Antinoüs sacrifices himself. This suicidal act is the only means by which Antinoüs can free himself from what he perceives to be a purely sexual love (one based on his jealous obsession with and servile relationship to Hadrian), and advance to a divine state of love. His sacrifice also helps Hadrian discover the perpetuity of love and entrust his own faith in its immortality. It is as if the hidden tomb in which Antinoüs has been interred will, by preserving his body unchanged through time, be a marker of eternal life rather than death since it will store the physical fact that he had once existed. The young man—body and soul—comes to be commemorated both materially and spiritually. Upon the death of Antinoüs, Hadrian returns to Athens and then to Rome, determined to transpose his own spiritual awakening into bettering himself and the state. This period of time is marked by intensive reading, writing, religious devotion, and philosophical conversations. In addition, Hadrian restructures the administration of Athens and Rome, constructs monuments and other cultural edifices, and contemplates the transfer of his imperial heritage. The latter action becomes especially important for Hadrian since he recognizes that not only is he becoming physically too vulnerable, but so is the legacy of the state. He discerns, despite an apparent renaissance in building and the arts, a general decline in civilization. Both his body and that of the empire are weakened and in need of regeneration. This regeneration needs to be guided by a pure heart wedded to a supreme authority as engendered by the future emperor Marcus Aurelius, who embodies the corporeal and spiritual virtues favored by Hadrian.

The relationship between rider and horse—a metaphor that Yourcenar repeats during the course of the novel—reflects the emperor's own constant desire to enter this permeable boundary between body and mind, self and Other, private and public. Hadrian writes he would have chosen the centaur as a condition of his life. Such a choice would have allowed him to embrace Yourcenar's philosophy of life in its totality, a theory of contact that espouses an equal union between the mind and body: "La vie m'était un cheval dont on épouse les mouvements, mais après l'avoir, de son mieux, dressé. Tout en somme étant une décision de l'esprit, mais lente, mais insensible, et qui entraîne aussi l'adhésion du corps, je m'efforçais d'atteindre par degré cet état de liberté, ou de soumission, presque pur" [To me life was a horse to which I married my movements, but only after having done my utmost to constrain it. All in all a decision of the mind, slow and imperceptible, but bringing with it the body—thus I forced myself by degrees to attain a nearly pure state of freedom, or of submission] (52). Much in the same manner as in speaking about a rider's acquiescence to a horse's motion, Hadrian outlines a political philosophy of state-building that centers around the idea that Rome is a living organism that will change with time regardless of his contributions: "Mais toute création humaine qui prétend à l'éternité doit s'adapter au rythme changeant des grands objets naturels, s'accorder au temps des astres" [But all human creation that pretends to eternity must adapt itself to the changing rhythm of natural objects, tune itself to astral timing] (125). Yet, despite these metamorphoses, his conceptualization of Rome, "State, citizenry, and republic," will continue to exist because of the superimposition of his principles and laws guiding human conduct, similar to the way a well-trained mount accedes to its master: "Aux corps physiques des nations et des races . . . nous aurions à jamais superposé, mais sans rien détruire, l'unité d'une conduite humaine, l'empirisme d'une expérience sage" [To the bodies of nations and races . . . we will have forever superimposed, but without destroying anything, the unifying principle of humane conduct, the rationalism of wise experience] (125).

In order to instill in his successors some meaning of his political philosophy as well as a sense of heritage, Hadrian chooses his direct heir in accordance with the Roman rule for imperial accession. After making the near disastrous mistake of following his youthful inclinations—that is, keeping his promise to the flamboyant Lucius that he would wear the imperial purple—Hadrian has a second opportunity to bequeath to the "world" a virtuous ruler and thus sidestep the maxim "one fool per century." He selects the honest and kind Antoninus as his heir, and the stoic Marcus Aurelius as the second in line. Hadrian's adoption of these two men as his heirs, along with Lucius's son, creates a type of spiritual genealogy. This genealogy resembles the Platonic idea of spiritual pregnancy as developed in the banquet eulogies of the *Symposium*, in which the aim of procreation is immortality. Hadrian's immortality will be achieved, though, not by biological children, but rather by children of spirit or intellect. In other words, ideas must be generated and bestowed upon successive generations in order to perpetuate them. Hadrian's adopted heirs are in some ways the offspring of the once erotic and now divine union between the kindred souls of Hadrian and Antinoüs. Without the latter's sacrifice, the emperor might not have discovered the potential of supreme devotion in love. He can now spend his remaining days on earth instructing Antoninus and Marcus Aurelius in the values of intelligence and virtue. In addition, since Marcus Aurelius is the addressee of the narrative (as are the readers of the *Mémoires*), he will be the realizer of Plato's dream. In his fictional memoirs, Hadrian explains why he favors adopted over biological children when he states:

> Je n'ai pas d'enfants, et ne le regrette pas. . . . je me suis parfois reproché de n'avoir pas pris la peine d'engendrer un fils, qui m'eût continué. Mais ce regret si vain repose sur deux hypothèses également douteuses: celle qu'un fils nécessairement nous prolonge, et celle que cet étrange amas de bien et de mal, cette masse de particularités infimes et bizarres qui constitue une personne, mérite d'être prolongé. . . . Ce n'est point par le sang que s'établit d'ailleurs la véritable continuité humaine (273).
>
> [I have no children and do not regret it. . . . I have at times reproached myself for taking no pains to beget an heir, a continuation of myself. But such a vain regret rests upon two equally dubious hypotheses: that a

son necessarily carries one into the future, and that this strange mix of good and evil, this lowly mass of bizarre quirks that makes up an individual is actually worth projecting into the future. . . . Furthermore, it is not by blood that the true human chain is forged.]

While such a bypassing of biological descent devalues the offspring of a heterosexual union as well as the female experience of childbirth, spiritual progeny may not be exclusively a product of masculine desire. Yourcenar's Hadrian shows little respect for the institution of the family and bemoans the inherent hatred that it excites among its members. For this reason, he abolishes marriage against women's consent. He himself scarcely considers his marriage valid and ends up having no children of his own. Notwithstanding, he distinguishes Plotina as a spiritual lover, someone with whom he has a loving, harmonious relation, "L'intimité des corps, qui n'exista jamais entre nous, a été compensée par ce contact de deux esprits étroitement mêlés l'un à l'autre" [Bodily intimacy, which we never shared, was compensated for by the connection of two like minds tightly intertwined] (96). She could even be considered his spiritual mother in that Hadrian's accession as emperor is largely due to her foresightedness, which enables him to become heir to a revitalized empire. Nevertheless, their intimate relationship limits itself to a meeting of minds. In contrast, Hadrian's homosexual experiences express both loving and erotic desire. The privileged position of homoeroticism in the memorial narrative indicates his preference for alliances between men. Ultimately, however, the supreme mode of erotic union turns out to be the spiritual form of beauty configured by Antinoüs's self-sacrifice. Thus it would appear that Hadrian abandons the body, male or female, in favor of divine contact with the spiritual world. Yet as his own body fails him, he also casts off his soul as he tells of its entombed future in harsh and barren places (295). His last thoughts indicate that even in death the body and mind, flesh and will, need to coexist.

Conclusion

Yourcenar, in writing the *Mémoires d'Hadrien*, blended oppositional constructions to create a treatise-monologue that espouses a theory of contact. Besides questioning the concepts of femininity and masculinity, her work combines history with autobiography, fact with fiction, and politics with spirituality, in order to communicate a different model of reality. Hadrian is at once represented as a public, historical figure owned by his citizens, "the Olympian Zeus, Master of All, Savior of the World," as well as a private individual who goes from being a god to simply being a gray-haired man mourning openly for the loss of a loved one (216). His memoirs, as penned by Yourcenar, blur the lines that separate the emperor's two spheres of life, allowing his personal self to merge with his imperial person. Yourcenar narrates the emperor's life from both his subject position as well as the object position, since much of what he knows about himself comes from public perception. In the same manner, Hadrian's individual self also blends exteriority (the body) with interiority (the mind). This intermingling of notions of identity leads to a mode of self-awareness that allows for a multiplicity of physical and spiritual relationships based on the sensuousness of bodies and the beauty of minds. Although the depicted erotic unions show contempt for heterosexual relations, they also establish a point of view that displaces a hierarchical construction of masculinity over femininity as the two gendered qualities are integrated into the psychology of each individual. While Yourcenar positions the "portrait" of Hadrian's voice as masculinist, she also strives to combine it with complementary virtues that are both masculine and feminine to indicate a transcendence of a unified gendered experience at a moment in historical time. This historical moment extends from the second century A.D. to the 1940s and beyond through the association of Hadrian's Rome with Yourcenar's present and that of her readers. This association between narrator and author unites Hadrian's voice with that of Yourcenar, thus allowing her to transcend gender and take up the subject position of the Roman emperor. Historical continuity also transforms the novel into a humanist treatise about the relationship between power and moral knowledge from a twentieth-century perspective.

Notes

1. All translations from the French in this article have been done by the editor, J. H. Sarnecki.

2. For an informative discussion about the difficulties in identifying the literary form of the *Mémoires*, see also: Pauline A. H. Hörmann, *La Biographie comme genre littéraire:* Mémoires d'Hadrien *de Marguerite Yourcenar* (Amsterdam: Rodopi, 1996), and Alain Trouvé, *Lécon littéraire sur* Mémoires d'Hadrien *de Marguerite Yourcenar* (Paris: Presses Universitaires de France, 1996).

3. In an interview with Shusha Guppy on April 11, 1987, Yourcenar states that, "I have never written a historical novel in my life. I dislike most historical novels. I wrote a monologue about Hadrian's life, as it could have been seen by himself."

The interview was published in "The Art of Fiction," *Paris Review* 106 (spring 1988): 228–49.

4. In an interesting article entitled "Scholarship and Vision in Marguerite Yourcenar's *Mémoires d'Hadrien*" published in *Classical and Modern Literature* 13, no. 3 (spring 1993): 203–15, Charlotte Hogsett compares Yourcenar's work on the novel to that of a sculptor who uses an incomplete set of stones and arranges them in her own way, "cementing them with her own mortar into a monument of her own making."

5. Yourcenar's preoccupation with historical accuracy did earn her respect by certain historians. G. W. Bowersock's bibliographical note to his entry on Hadrian in the *Encyclopaedia Britannica* 15th ed. includes the following: "Bernard W. Henderson, *The Life and Principate of the Emperor Hadrian, A.D. 76-138* (1923, reissued 1968); and Stewart Perowne, *Hadrian* (1960, reprinted 1976), are not wholly reliable. The fictional evocation, Marguerite Yourcenar, *Memoirs of Hadrian* (1954, reissued 1974; originally published in French, 1951), is, however, remarkably successful."

6. The "Carnets de notes" were included beginning with the second edition of the *Mémoires* published in 1953. They were first published separately in *Mercure de France* in November 1952.

The Essays of Marguerite Yourcenar: Analogy and Eternity

Henk Hillenaar

Translated by Gervais E. Reed

THE ESSAY IS AN OPEN, EXPERIMENTAL GENRE; IT IS NOT CONSTRAINED BY tradition, has no rhetoric, is not guided by a poetics. More perhaps than other genres, it possesses two "faces" that require a reader's attention. The first is the subject treated that, in order to avoid ambiguity, I will call "object," i.e., the question or the reality that the author "essays," puts to the test, walking around it and looking at it from all possible angles. Take in Marguerite Yourcenar's case, for example, the *Historia Augusta*, Chenonceaux, Mishima, or the life of her parents. Next, and more explicitly than in other genres, we deal with a writing subject, i.e., personal thought influenced by personal emotions—for Yourcenar people have even talked about "wisdom"—that "essays" or tests itself, shows its principles and the unity of these principles with each new object that the author is led to study.

These two approaches—the material studied and the author—have, of course, a mutual influence. The distinction that we propose here is, as in the case of so many other distinctions, of a character that is less relevant for judging the texts than useful for analyzing and understanding them. It can nonetheless help us reflect on these texts, some of which are among the most beautiful that Yourcenar wrote, and formulate questions about them.

So let us turn first to the content and the presentation of the essays. We shall limit our discussion to a single essential point. It seems to us that a fundamental trait of all the texts is to be found in Yourcenar's unwavering concern for tying each event and especially each character that she presents to analogous events and characters. Concern for analogy lies at the center of all her essays. At first glance such a method or attitude has nothing special about it. It is understandable that speaking of executions at the stake in the fifteenth or sixteenth century, the author is thinking about pogroms against the Jews, even about Buchenwald and Hiroshima, and it is just as understandable that the image of the Saint Bartholomew's Day Massacre might recall the executions of the "Communards" in 1871 or the Revolution's scaffolds (*Sous bénéfice d'inventaire,* 58; Howard, 40). Metaphor and metonymy are not simple figures of speech, as we know, but forms of thought and writing. Authors frequently proceed in this way. What is specific to Yourcenar's essays is the frequency of the process, especially in the case of proper nouns. Each name mentioned carries with it a veritable constellation of other names, which has the effect of widening the text indefinitely.

Thus in the essay devoted to Agrippa d'Aubigné we meet one by one—and here I omit the names from the subject's immediate entourage—Victor Hugo, Virgil, Heliogabalus, Jeroboam, Shakespeare, Titian, Goya, Bosch, Brueghel, Elizabeth I, and a list of a dozen Englishmen burned or strangled, Tintoretto, Caravaggio, Dante, Milton, Aristotle, Plato, Lucretius, Signorelli, Corneille, Ronsard, Mallarmé, Valéry, Vigny. Comparing these famous personages, Yourcenar shows what differentiates them from d'Aubigné and especially what links them to him. This manner of writing ensures an extension of the text, for each new name expands, becoming a center that attracts stories, thoughts, and images or from which they extend. The interstices of every sort that exist among these often radically different personages are filled by four registers of writing, the same in which Yourcenar registers the history of her family: formal written histories, lesser history of everyday life (more than once recreated from personal memory), cultural history of the Europe of yesteryear, and the expectation of disasters that will strike the Europe of today.

As a search for the "self within differences," analogy also assures more fundamentally the unity of the text. In her way—her secularized way, it may be said—Yourcenar returns to traditional religious thought that antedates modern science and that had connection as its principal objective, finding the one in the many (*Le Temps, ce grand sculpteur,* 128), entering the universal (*Sous bénéfice,* 292), always discovering the same man (*Quoi? L'Eternité*), connecting despite their differences human beings from all times.

Let us add right now that having thus found unity, as satisfying as that may be, does not, however, reveal its final secret. In Yourcenar's universe we are dealing perhaps with a hidden God and in any case with a lost center. Writing confronts us, Yourcenar states, "like the threads of a tapestry, and we fail to grasp the whole"

(*Sous bénéfice,* 201). The world created by her sometimes strangely resembles the world of Piranesi as she understood it, "a world deprived of a center that is at the same time perpetually expandable. Behind those dungeons with their barred windows we suspect that there are other, similar dungeons that we have inferred or that remain to be inferred in all imaginable directions" (155).

There is, nevertheless, a very real danger that in proceeding this way, i.e., in seeking while expanding, Yourcenar does not always go deeper. Thus it is in her presentation of the works of Constantin Cavafy; more than once his work risks disappearance in the constellation of stars in which the critic Yourcenar places him: Anatole France, Gide, Browning, T. S. Eliot, Musset, Forster, Ungaretti, Utrillo, Van Gogh, Petronius, Chénier, Mantegna, Plutarch, Shakespeare, Omar Khayyám, Fitzgerald, Callimachus, Straton, Proust, Pirandello, Rilke, Parmenides, Heraclitus, Dante, Hadrian, Marcus Aurelius, Mallarmé. Many names that figure in that "turba magna" are mentioned only in passing, others at length or several times over. Certainly there seem to be too many of them. Two or three comparisons of this sort clarify, ten or twelve dazzle, twenty risk losing readers and leave them wondering where they are.

Yourcenar not only creates links between visible beings. Working continually outward from the particular to the general or universal, she also creates links between the visible world and the invisible world of idea and values. She writes like Selma Lagerlöf, "the only one among the authors of her time who constantly rises to the level of the epic or of myth" (*Sous bénéfice,* 177), or like d'Aubigné who, despite his partisan anger, remains no less obsessed by the appalling problem of man's inhumanity to man" (51).

More than once these generalizations take on a sententious tone as, for example, when speaking of Lagerlöf's work, she states that "in all great serious art carnal love is expressed not in physiological detail but symbolically" (*Sous bénéfice,* 187). Maxims, indeed the sententious tone for which Yourcenar has sometimess been criticized, seldom occur in the collections of essays. Contrary to what one might believe, the genre lends itself less well to maxims than do the interview perhaps or the novel where the author is free to let fictional characters speak. But in Yourcenar and Galey the fault certainly lies with Matthieu Galey.

If these beautiful texts have a fault, a lack, one ought to think of a sin of omission. Readers will need to face a more or less conscious yet constant refusal to answer questions about what is irreducible—unique—about historical or fictional characters. Yourcenar observes, describes, associates, unites, reconciles; she seldom analyzes or interprets. Why beings and things behave as they do, i.e., the scientific method that has never been absent from literature and that has enjoyed an increasing dominance since the seventeenth century, seems to be forgotten or neglected. While others are not content to let "a man be what he is"—an expression dear to Yourcenar—but try to extricate often secret motives in each human being and define his uniqueness, Yourcenar treats psychology as a poor relation. "These analysts are like all of us," she says, "they refuse to face the dismal emptiness that every life contains more or less" (*Archives du nord*, 224). She thinks that she has a soul mate in Thomas Mann, who is, however, a good psychologist. "The taste for biological reality, on the one hand," she notes, "and, on the other, an obsession with the metaphysical kept him from a pure psychologism" (*Sous bénéfice,* 302). Common sense and confidence—qualities that Yourcenar eminently possesses—allow her to scorn the secrets and torments of the human soul. Her gaze turns outward, toward the infinite riches of a world that offers itself to her curiosity. Rejecting "the delirium of interpretation to which post-Freudian times accustom us" (242), she does not limit herself to defining the individual but devotes herself to the "more sacred definition of the person" (279).

As for her own intentional method of sequencing names or events as the web of an essay, she declares: "What continues to make us dream is the number and intensity of obscure nudges that have pushed us towards one name, fact, or personage rather than towards another. There we get into a forest without paths" (*Temps,* 102).

Thus Yourcenar lends weight to prescientific explanations—setting up an order by means of analogy—about cause and effect that are the means of thought and even of poetry in our time. For example, Yourcenar speaks about her mother's family, in which there was an unusually large number of sickly and feebleminded people; this cannot fail to make us think of her grandparents, who were first cousins. She does not stop at such a probable hypothesis but resorts to metaphor, i.e., to a solution by analogy: "Mathilde's fertility," she writes, "makes one think of the luxuriant flowering of fruit trees attacked by rust or by invisible parasites or undernourished by a depleted soil." Then comes one of those generalizations so characteristic of her: "Perhaps the same metaphor may be applied to the unwarranted population explosion today" (*Souvenirs pieux,* 158).

Her favorite field—history—is treated no better. In Yourcenar's work, the image of immobile time that she takes from Parmenides always ends up replacing Heraclitus's image "of the river eroding its own banks, drowning at the same time the person who contemplates and the object that is contemplated" (*Sous bénéfice,* 245). That is why "the modern reader is at home" in the history of Rome as well as in the Renaissance or in all periods following Chenonceaux. The mythical point of view, she states, leads us further than historical perspective. It is the wise person's point of view, for the secret of each human being lies not in a personal past but in the mythical past of all humanity.

As for personal or social problems that we have to resolve during our lifetimes, Yourcenar intentionally takes them back to a single original or eternal problem; according to her, we always come back to "the struggle between good and evil" (Yourcenar and Galey). She opts for this kind of distant but certain solution rather than seeking more immediate causes or proposing more uncertain hypotheses. She has an affinity for Carl Gustave Jung's symbols and has little appreciation for Freudian explanations. In fact, if we go back far enough, she seems closer to Romantic impulses than to Voltairean questions. To Voltaire's clarity she prefers the fire and sorrow of the Romantic soul, which is no easy feat at a time when irony and intellectual games reign supreme.

That remark leads us to the second panel of our diptych, the personal world of Marguerite Yourcenar, her thoughts and feelings that come into play in her essays. It must be made clear that this world does not in any way encourage turning back on the self but is organized around a certain number of recurring images or themes, the same ones that we encounter in Yourcenar's novels and other writings. Without wanting to reduce her work to these themes and images, it seems to us nonetheless that they form its nourishment; without them none of the essays or even the novels could have been written.

No one will be surprised if we cite among Yourcenar's major preoccupations in the essays the recurring theme of death. That has been iterated and reiterated about all of her work and remains true in approaching the essays. *Sous bénéfice d'inventaire*; *Le Temps, ce grand sculpteur*; *Le Labyrinthe du monde*; *Mishima*: death haunts all of these works on almost every page. In these texts Yourcenar continually seeks not to flee death but to tame it or, to use an eloquent turn of phrase from *Ah. mon beau château* she "draws from death its poetry, splendor, and intimation of eternity" (*Sous bénéfice,* 195). Whether dealing with the *Historia Augusta* in which all of Hadrian's lackluster successors do no more than live out the end that awaits them, with the château of Chenonceaux as a residence for Widows, with "the dark brain of Piranesi" (Howard, 88) in which lurk torture and death, with Michelangelo's dead young friends, or with the tombs of *Le Temps, ce grand sculpteur*, death is the theme of each essay from beginning to end.

The three autobiographical collections need no commentary on this point, but even in texts that seem at first glance "neutral," Yourcenar sets aside a place for her continual obsession. For example, Cavafy is presented as the aged poet who, like the aged emperor Hadrian, knows that he is going to die and remembers. Lagerlöf, the weaver of Marbacka, ends up as the woman "whose work death comes to interrupt" (*Sous bénéfice*, 208). But in this last essay as in *L'Andalousie ou les Hespérides*—the country of the sunset—death, tamed by Yourcenar, seems transformed into eternity. We leave history, we see no more than "historical and legendary figures" who multiply in the land of the auto-da-fé, it too having died young, and so it has always been (*Temps*, 178). Everything else—themes, images, structure, and even the time in which she places these tales—emanates from this central, governing obsession.

Death seems to close any perspective on the future to such an extent that the future does not exist in the essays. We find only one future here, and that is the future in the past. Almost all of Yourcenar's work carries with it the mark of that tense—the past future, the future in the past—the only tense that allows death to determine the narrative and to keep life from playing itself out. The real future—hers, ours—is absent from Yourcenar's books. If it is to be found, which is rare, it expresses an expectation of nothing, disappointment, a lament, especially the expression of sorrow that confirms death surrounding us, death in mother earth.

It might be said that, for Yourcenar, history is a long degeneration with now and again a renewal of life or vitality in man who nonetheless remains the same eternal Man. About today's world—in which there is already enough to disturb modern readers—Yourcenar consistently refrains from saying anything that is even slightly positive or optimistic. To encourage us she offers only the smoke and mirrors of historical heroes who reflect our eternal image. And she expresses doubt about even those illusions and will-o'-the-wisps: "What remains," she concludes, "is infinite pity for our insignificance" (*Souvenirs*, 157).

Even in the enormous love that Yourcenar expresses for the animal world we would be inclined to see an extension of her obsession with death. In order to explain the presence of animals almost everywhere in her books, she deliberately resorts to a theological vocabulary: animals belong "to a purer, more divine world than the one in which human beings inflict suffering on other human beings" (*Archives,* 19). "Even the wild and cunning beast is prelapsarian," she states (*Sous bénéfice,* 191), thus ante-Death. So animals are often presented as victims of human barbarity and thus as warranting our sympathy. Animals share that characteristic with all of the marginal beings that populate Yourcenar's tales, a characteristic in which she seems also to find traces of primeval innocence. Matter also participates in this world of original innocence. On the occasion of her entering the French Academy, Yourcenar pleaded for the word "matter," a word, according to her, scorned by the French intelligentsia and yet a word that does not fail to represent the universe in its original form—earth, air, fire, water—the only form that undergoes death without dying.

We must not forget that Yourcenar sees the human body as animal and, in its way, as matter par excellence. Hence the importance that she grants to it and the pleasure that she takes in quoting Cavafy's "Corps, souviens-toi" (*Sous bénéfice,* 243), a distant echo of life before the Fall, before sin. Sin might be said to be in the last analysis the sin of the human mind, source of all evil in the world. But if Yourcenar's thought turns in this direction, toward this dualism, she will never say it just that way.

We come now to the well-known prominence that Yourcenar lends in all of her writing to male characters. Obviously, she almost always identifies with the male and not with the female character who usually plays only a minor role. As we have tried to show elsewhere, Yourcenar closely associates women with death either as its victim or as its instrument. Rather than assuming the hazardous role, Yourcenar prefers to identify with male characters who seem at least to be free to master their own life and death. The men that she creates or studies, we hasten to add, all belong to the category of those who do not fear the feminine element that they carry within themselves.

Be that as it may, in Yourcenar's essays as in her other works, men have the best part, whereas the few women who appear are the women in mourning at the château of Chenonceaux and Selma Lagerlöf who, as Yourcenar herself says, "with a smile," "has been placed more often than not in her books to reflect men" (*Sous bénéfice,* 185). Writing about Thomas Mann, she points to an analogous transfer of "masculine feeling within a feminine physiology." The problem obviously interests her, but she refuses to go further on this slippery slope. She notes only that "life is like that" and that "tradition until now has scarcely permitted woman to look freely at life" (176).

We do not want to dwell on this question but prefer to move on to a final theme concerning death, a theme that allows us to come closer to the source that nourishes Yourcenar's work. This is her fascination with human sacrifice. Once more the essays echo the novels. After the sacrifice of Antinoüs that, one might say, holds a place of honor in Yourcenar's work, after the sacrifice of Zeno, who refuses to flee to England or Holland, or after the sacrifice of Nathanaël that is less voluntary yet freely consented to comes first the character Mishima, whose suicide will be the subject of a long essay, subsequently "the sinister ease of dying" shown by the children of Lille who throw themselves into flames, then Uncle Remo, the hero of *Souvenirs pieux* who puts a bullet through his head. Elsewhere Yourcenar treats at some length Saint-Just's heroic attachment—going as far as death—for the person of Robespierre and his cause. She never neglects to point out analogous stories that she encounters in her reading, the case of Lagerlöf, for example, twice over (*Sous bénéfice,* 190, 201) and that of Brantome (93). The hero is nearly always sacrificed for a lost cause. A fascinated Yourcenar devotes an entire essay to this theme dear to the Japanese, to their "sympathy for the subaltern," that is, for the nobility of failure. This nobility is apparently unknown to women. It comes only to men and is played out only among men: by fidelity to a friend or to Man, to his freedom and dignity. Perhaps Yourcenar's deep inspiration may be summarized in what she calls "the feeling for the tragic transience of life that leads simultaneously to poetry and to sacrifice" (*Temps,* 80).

Poetry and sacrifice: we must remember that Yourcenar's life began with the sacrifice of her mother's life, a circumstance that certainly affected, even unconsciously, her life as a child, then as poet and author. That seems all the more probable because the subject was nearly taboo in family conversations and because the women who took her mother's place acted similarly. They too left the child's life one after the other. She has said that "my father's wives" even seem to be one of the reasons for which writing *Quoi? L'Eternité* raised so many questions.

However that may be, everything happens in her fantasies and in her books as if Yourcenar were ceaselessly repeating the sacrifice and death of her mother—her basic situation—and the departure of the beautiful replacements. Certainly she intends to compensate, to relieve guilt and perhaps to compete, and she does so by transferring the sacrifice to the man's ideal universe. For what her mother did involuntarily man can freely choose to do. Man alone can embark without hope, can live freely while moving toward death.

In *Souvenirs pieux* there is an intriguing story about sacrifice that Yourcenar tells at length. It is the story of Sainte Rolende. Her uncle Octave used to tell it to Fernande, Marguerite's mother, and the family retold it to her daughter. Rolende was a princess who long ago became a hermit in order to keep her lover at a distance, and she succeeded in doing so all her life long. He too became a hermit. Rolende said that she would receive him only after her death when, having become a skeleton in her tomb, she would hold out her arms to his body once he too was dead. This legend, according to Yourcenar, had to have greatly impressed her mother much as it impressed her. The story summarizes the death themes that we have been looking at: the woman who abandons her lover in death, and the man's sacrifice for what seems a lost cause.

And if we seek less a tale than an image that illustrates and summarizes Yourcenar's mortuary universe we see immediately the image that recurs almost as an obsession in every essay as in almost every chapter of her novels. The image of fire—especially the image of the stake, of sacrifice by fire—spreads light, warmth, sparks.

Fires are lighted everywhere in her work, from the essay on Agrippa d'Aubigné who "opened his eyes onto the world at a time when stakes were burning bright and hot in the streets of Paris" (*Sous bénéfice,* 37) to the essay on the auto-da-fé in the Hespeddian Land. Even in her speech to the French Academy, Yourcenar could not refrain from suggesting a pyre—that of David de Dinant—as if a text without flames were a text without her signature. Once in her essays she cites another kind of fire—hell fire—but that torture, of course, is suffered by a woman, a wicked mother. In Yourcenar's works the stake is almost destined to receive only men; nowhere else does sacrifice achieve such splendor. The stake is imposed on the reader as the very center of the fantasies that underlie Yourcenar's writing.

To conclude: the experience of death, of abandonment, of sacrifice lies at the heart of Yourcenar's work. Confronted with that pitiless enemy that haunted her from childhood, she adopts a double attitude in her writing: idealization and defense.

On the one hand, and without denying the reality of the suffering that death causes, she tries to understand, to conciliate, to integrate. In order to do this she resorts to a feeling—or is it to an idea?—that allows her to go beyond the original opposition between life and death. She discovers eternity. "Morality becomes eternity."

She leaves history and makes an alliance principally with myth and metaphysics.

A defensive attitude may also be found in her work. Relegating death to a religious and atemporal sphere where questions are left unanswered, she abandons any dialogue with herself or with others, withdraws from answering genuine, historical, scientific, or especially personal questions, i.e., those dealing with her own biography and that alone could elucidate why death has such ascendancy in her life and work.

Even while walking the edge of the precipice in her autobiographical writings, she succeeds in bypassing or repressing the story of the being that she calls "I." Yet that unique, implacable story could help us understand the need for eternity, the burnings as punishment, the masculine friendships, the wicked mothers who frequent like so many blind spots a work written by a human being with her eyes wide open.

Others have spoken of a wall that Yourcenar erected around her books—a Hadrian's Wall as protection from invasion by barbarians. But the barbarians here are less indiscrete readers than her own anguish and the far too painful memories possibly threatening her. Certainly, each author, each one of us, needs such a wall. But in Yourcenar's case it has come to resemble a monument before which the reader feels alternately disoriented, frustrated, and filled with admiration. Surely the best thing to do is to choose admiration. After all, has Hadrian's Wall not proven also to be a claim to fame?

* * *

[The French version of this essay, "Les essais de Marguerite Yourcenar: analogie et éternité," appeared in C. Biondi and C. Rosso, eds., *Voyage et connaissance dans l'oeuvre de Marguerite Yourcenar* (Pisa: Editrice Golliardica, 1988), 123–36.]

Part III
Transpositions: Reading the Self, Reading the Other

Good Intentions: Marguerite Yourcenar's American Translations

Francesca Counihan

INTRODUCTION

THE FOLLOWING IS AN ATTEMPT TO ENGAGE WITH SOME OF THE ISSUES raised by Marguerite Yourcenar's translations into French of Negro spirituals and other texts. The starting point for this study was my initial reaction as reader on discovering the unorthodox appearance on the page of her versions of the spirituals, which led me to investigate further as to the approach that had led to the production of these texts.

Having looked in some detail both at the translations and the prefatory texts that accompany them, my focus here will be on what I perceive as a gap or a discrepancy between Yourcenar's intentions as translator and presenter of these texts, and the results of her enterprise. This is, as we shall see, a complex question. While her purpose in undertaking these translations was undoubtedly a liberal one, and was widely perceived as such, a closer reading of the translations and their prefaces suggests that the enterprise is conditioned by attitudes and prejudices of which the translator herself seems unaware.[1]

After settling in the United States in 1939, Yourcenar translated a number of texts relating to African-American culture. In 1964, Gallimard brought out *Fleuve profond, sombre rivière*, a collection of French translations of Negro spirituals.[2] This was followed in 1983 by *Le Coin des «Amen»*, a translation of James Baldwin's *The Amen Corner*,[3] and in 1983 by *Blues et Gospels*.[4] The following comments center on *Fleuve profond* and *Le Coin des «Amen»*, taken as Yourcenar's main translations of this kind. I will start by examining the translator's prefatory texts: her "Commentary" [commentaires] on the Negro spirituals, and the "Translator's Note" to *Le Coin des «Amen»*. The second part of this study is an analysis of the translated texts, examined in the context of the translator's comments. My aim here is not to establish whether these are "good" or "bad" translations, but to highlight the types of linguistic choice made by the translator, and what these may indicate about her attitudes toward the texts.

Yourcenar's North American translations first came to the attention of the French public with the publication in 1964[5] of *Fleuve profond*. In addition to the translated texts themselves, the volume contains a long introductory essay that sets out to inform the French reader about the historical and cultural background of the spirituals and their aesthetic and religious qualities. It is clear from reading this introduction that Yourcenar's aim is to affirm the value of the spirituals, and to persuade her French reader to take them seriously both as artistic expression and as a statement of human experience.

Yourcenar later described this undertaking as a conscious political gesture, remarking in 1984:

> Quelque chose de l'élan de ces années qui furent celles de la lutte pour l'intégration m'habitait. Je me proposais de montrer, autant qu'on le peut en l'absence du chant, combien ces hymnes [. . .] contenaient de chaleur et de ferveur, foi, espérance, amour et désespoir mêlés, issus de toutes les infortunes et de toutes les énergies vitales d'un peuple. (*Blues*, 7–8)[6]

> [I was moved by the enthusiasm of those years of the struggle for integration. My aim was to show, insofar as this was possible without the music, how full these hymns . . . are of warmth and fervour, mingled faith, hope, love and despair, born of all the misfortune and the vital energy of a people.]

Yourcenar here presents her translation as an act of solidarity with an oppressed group. This is also how the volume was perceived in France generally. *Fleuve profond* was very successful with both critics and the public, and the translations were seen as a vast improvement on previously available French versions of the spirituals.[7] Yourcenar was praised for her anti-racist stance, and for the serious scholarship that she brought to her study of this music. These positive French reactions are epitomized by the comments of Paul Renard in an article published in *Nord* in 1985:

> Elle a contribué à faire connaître une véritable culture et pris sa part dans la lutte antiraciste : c'est une forme humble et efficace de la littérature engagée.[8]

[She helped make known a real culture and played her part in the struggle against racism, which is a modest and effective form of politically committed literature.]

By the 1980s she had come to be regarded in France as an authority on Negro spirituals and was invited to participate in radio and television discussions on the subject (Renard, 64). Perhaps more significantly, her contribution was also recognized by the American expert John Lovell, who in 1972 described *Fleuve profond* as "one of the best foreign collections of spirituals" (*Black Song*, 560). This praise is important, given that Lovell is one of the chief North American authorities on the subject, and given his own stance on the origins and cultural role of the spirituals. Thus, in the case of the Negro spirituals, Yourcenar's role as cultural mediator was generally considered to be a positive one, and politically, she was perceived as being on the liberal and progressive side of the argument. This is also the appraisal found in more recent critical comments on this aspect of her work.[9]

Yourcenar's Commentaries on Her Translations

As noted above, Yourcenar's overall aim in these texts is to promote the work of a group or individual whose cause she wishes to further. In the case of the Negro spirituals, she does this by means of two complementary and potentially contradictory rhetorical strategies. On the one hand, she stresses the uniqueness of the spirituals, their specific musical qualities, which she sees as due to their African origins, and their human value as witness to a particular historical experience, that of the African-American community. On the other hand, she also emphasizes their universal qualities, the aesthetic and philosophical characteristics by which they are linked to a broader artistic tradition and to what she sees as universal human experience.

The particularizing strategy is evident in the first half of Yourcenar's essay, which deals with the history of the African-American community from slavery through emancipation to the present day. Yourcenar takes a clear antiracist stance and ends with a pessimistic assessment of the situation at the time of writing (in the early 1960s). This part of her essay has been deservedly praised by critics such as G. Shurr and C. Biondi. Yourcenar situates the spirituals in a very specific social and historical context, showing how they grew out of the experience of captivity and slavery. In so doing, she is, to quote her own remarks, striving to counteract a common French perception of the spirituals that trivializes them as quaint or "exotic" folk songs (*Blues*, 7–8). Yourcenar's aim here is to persuade her French reader of the importance of the spirituals as an expression of authentic human experience.

In the second part of her introduction, where she deals with the form and content of the spirituals, Yourcenar continues this particularist theme by drawing attention to the African origins of this type of singing. She presents this in a very positive way, asserting that its unique musical qualities can be directly traced to this African influence. This is a very important point. By adopting this standpoint, Yourcenar is positioning herself within an ongoing scholarly debate as to the origins of this form of music. While one side of this debate sees the spirituals as deriving from a preexisting tradition of American church music, in other words from a white Protestant tradition, the other view is that the spirituals derive directly from African rhythms and musical forms, to which they owe their distinctive quality. Yourcenar supports this latter view, affirming that "le Spiritual est beau en proportion de sa négritude" (*Fleuve*, 38). By taking this view, she is adopting a position similar to that of scholars such as John Lovell, who stress the cultural specificity and independence of the African-American singing tradition (*The Forge*, 89–110). This is also the view taken by earlier scholars such as James Weldon Johnson and Henry Krehbiel, whom Yourcenar quotes among her sources of information on the spirituals.[10]

The use of the term "négritude" in this context is also significant, suggesting as it does a possible reference to the literary movement of the same name, which similarly aimed to draw attention to the positive value of African culture and its contribution to human cultural expression. This included a celebration of the emotional, of the rhythmic,[11] of the intuitive, which the proponents of negritude presented as the specific contributions of the African tradition to universal culture.[12] Whether or not Yourcenar is referring here to the literary movement instigated by Senghor and Aimé Césaire is uncertain; there is no precise reference in the preface, which otherwise is very meticulous in its listing of sources and documents consulted. However, some of the American writers quoted by Yourcenar express similar views to those of the "négritude" poets; for example J. W. Johnson lays particular stress on the role of African rhythms in the spirituals.[13]

To return to the overall rhetorical strategies at work in the preface: in addition to her particularizing approach, which emphasizes the historical and cultural specificity of the spirituals, Yourcenar also uses what may be called a "universalizing strategy." This consists of asserting the value of the spirituals in terms of their worth as a statement of universal concerns, common to all humanity. This strategy is most clearly expressed in Yourcenar's closing comments to the preface:

> Mais l'erreur la plus sérieuse serait sans doute d'insister trop exclusivement sur leur arrière-plan historique et social, si tentant que cela soit, de les expliquer par le seul effet des douleurs et des aspirations frustrées de l'esclave ou du Noir pauvre. Comme dans toute grande poésie, le sujet traité dans les Spirituals est finalement celui des servitudes et des espoirs de l'homme. Nous sommes tous esclaves, et nous mourrons tous. Nous aspirons tous aussi, chacun à sa manière, à un royaume où règne la paix. C'est parce qu'il touche à ces thèmes universels que le Negro Spiritual a sa place parmi les grands témoignages humains. (*Fleuve*, 62–63)

> [However, the most serious mistake would no doubt be to overemphasize their historical and social background, tempting though that may be, to explain them exclusively in terms of the suffering and the frustrated aspirations of the slave or of the poor Black. As in all great poetry, the subject of the *Spirituals* is ultimately that of the servitudes and the hopes of mankind. We are all slaves, and we will all die. We all also aspire, each in his own way, to a kingdom where peace reigns. It is because it touches on these universal themes that the *Negro Spiritual* has its place among the great human statements.]

This passage raises complex issues. It is evident that by stressing the "universal" qualities of the spirituals, Yourcenar is endeavoring to establish them as "great poetry," as being on a par with the great cultural monuments of the Western tradition,[14] and thus eminently worthy of the attention and interest of her French reader. At the same time, however, by identifying their main theme as "celui des servitudes et des espoirs de l'homme," she is denying their political and social specificity, their grounding in a particular historical experience. Although throughout her preface she has drawn attention to the African cultural origins of the spirituals, she still considers it necessary to articulate their value in terms of the great universal themes.

Here, Yourcenar suggests that "universality" is a superior state, a higher good than any culturally specific characteristic. Furthermore, while a statement such as "Nous sommes tous esclaves" may be valid on an abstract metaphysical level, it also constitutes a denial of the political and social dimension of the subject.[15]

It becomes important at this point to examine Yourcenar's concept of the universal, and how it operates in this text. Blanca Arancibia has analyzed this concept as it appears in Yourcenar's work. Among the characteristics she identifies, two are relevant here; these are its constant Eurocentric bias, and its elitism, expressed as a tendency to establish hierarchies, particularly hierarchies that value the familiar over the different.[16] In Yourcenar's comments on North American texts, these attitudes express themselves in a tendency to value closeness to the familiar European model, and to depreciate or reject phenomena that do not conform to this paradigm.

In the introductory essay to *Fleuve profond*, for example, references to European art and history are frequent. Throughout the preface, Yourcenar expresses pleasure and approval at finding traces of the European tradition in the spirituals. Thus she finds it "miraculous" that despite its different origins and its connection to an American Protestant tradition, the Spiritual is nevertheless very close to the poetic forms of the European Middle Ages:

> Mais le miracle est justement que la poésie ornée et oratoire des hymnes wesleyens et méthodistes du XVIIIe siècle . . . ai[t] abouti dans la bouche du Noir à ces poèmes dont la piété enjouée et pathétique retrouve, à des siècles de distance, quelque chose de l'émotion nue de Villon ou de la tendresse de la poésie franciscaine. (*Fleuve*, 39)

> [But the miracle is precisely that the ornate oratory of eighteenth-century Wesleyan and Methodist hymns . . . gave rise in the mouths of black singers to these poems whose joyous, touching piety recalls, at a distance of centuries, something of the raw emotion of Villon or the tenderness of Franciscan poetry.]

In another passage, Yourcenar points out that despite apparent differences, the Negro spirituals express the same ideas in almost the same terms as the art forms of the Middle Ages:

> Si l'image du saint intercesseur . . . manque à cet empyrée protestant, le groupe des ancêtres du Christ s'y aligne comme au portail d'une cathédrale ou comme sur les volets d'une mystique Adoration de l'Agneau. (*Fleuve*, 39)

> [Though the image of the patron saint . . . is absent from this Protestant firmament, Christ's ancestors are arrayed there as if on the porch of a cathedral or on a triptych depicting a mystic Adoration of the Lamb.]

And where the expression of an idea differs from the medieval model, Yourcenar seems to regard it as a shortcoming; for example she finds it "regrettable" that the images of angels in the Negro spirituals do not reproduce what she calls "the great winged trio of medieval legend."[17]

In all these cases, closeness to the familiar model (the European Middle Ages) is noted with approval, while differences are minimized or deplored. Throughout the preface, Yourcenar expresses the worth of the spirituals in terms of their closeness to the European tradition. In so doing, she tends to establish a hierarchy of values, where the familiar is perceived as superior to what is different.

It is here that tension arises between Yourcenar's universalizing and particularizing strategies. As can be seen from the text, the superior value she accords to the universal leads to a devaluing of the culturally specific. This is evident for example in her comments on the "primitive" aspects of the spirituals. This term is used in a positive sense by other writers on African and African-American culture, for example, in the context of the "négritude" movement, where it is seen as synonymous with closeness to nature and freedom from the artificiality of modern, technocratic society.[18] Yourcenar's use of the term is more complex.

Some of Yourcenar's statements in the preface suggest a view close to that of the "négritude" movement; for example, she describes the spirituals' characteristic "jump" as creating effects that were "typically primitive, and moreover typically poetic" (*Fleuve*, 39). Elsewhere she remarks that "as in all primitive poetry, there is in the Negro Spirituals an almost topographic sense of wanderings beyond the grave."[19] In these cases, the equation of "primitive" with "poetic" is clear.

However, elsewhere in the preface, Yourcenar's use of this term tends to suggest that she regards the primitive as inferior to what is rational and enlightened. This is particularly the case in her comments on Africa. In a key passage, she sets out to show how the religious sensibility of the songs is influenced by African culture and ritual. She refers specifically here to the "négritude" of the spirituals, and her apparent intention is to express the value of difference, and to praise the spirituals by drawing attention to their African origins. However, the overall tone of her description of Africa is reminiscent of Victorian fantasies about the "Dark Continent." The following passage illustrates this point:

> Et c'est ici que nous retrouvons la profonde *négritude* du *Negro Spiritual*, l'obscur souvenir de cultes ancestraux étayant ou colorant les mythes et les rites chrétiens. L'obsession de la retraite mystique dans la solitude . . . semble faire écho à de vieilles réminiscences des initiations

indigènes; la vision délirante et presque frénétique de l'Agneau égorgé pour le salut des hommes ... évoque irrésistiblement les sacrifices sanglants de la vieille Afrique; la sombre image du baptême par immersion dans les eaux du fleuve ... rappell[e] les épreuves rituelles et les précautions apotropaïques des primitifs de tout temps.... Le paysage d'ossements de la vison d'Ézechiel revue par le poète noir fait l'effet d'une nécromancie vaudou. (*Fleuve*, 55)

[And here again we encounter the profound *Negritude* of the *Negro spiritual*, with the obscure memory of ancestral cults underpinning or coloring Christian myths and rites. The obsession with the idea of solitary, mystical retreat ... seems to evoke ancient echoes of native initiation customs; the delirious and almost frenzied vision of the Lamb slaughtered for the salvation of men ... calls irresistibly to mind the bloody sacrifices of old Africa; the somber image of baptism by immersion in the waters of the river ... recalls the ritual ordeals and apotropaic precautions of all primitive peoples.... The valley of bones of Ezechiel's vision, revisited by the black poet, is reminiscent of voodoo necromancy.]

Here Yourcenar's comments suggest an image of Africa as a place of superstition and primitive "frenzy," given to "delirium," "bloody sacrifice," and "black magic" [nécromancie vaudou]. The imagery used repeatedly evokes the idea of darkness—"the obscure memory of ancestral cults," the "somber image" of baptism by immersion—and of violent death: "the slaughtered Lamb," "bloody sacrifices," "voodoo necromancy."

And yet, most of the elements Yourcenar chooses to highlight in this passage (the sacrificial Lamb, the retreat into the desert, baptism by immersion) are also part of standard Christian imagery. It seems that the reference to "dark" Africa, to which she accords such prominence, is due primarily to her subjective vision, to a fascination with what she calls elsewhere "l'immémoriale Afrique noire" [immemorial black Africa] (*Fleuve*, 36).

Yourcenar's subjectivity as commentator intrudes in this passage more obviously than anywhere else in the preface. For whom are such evocations "irresistible"? Who sees the image of the sacrificial lamb in the spirituals as "delirious" and "almost frenzied"? Who is reminded of "voodoo necromancy" by the image of dry bones? The passage speaks of "obsession," of "somber" images; these are all terms of Yourcenar's choice, which say more about her subjective vision than about the texts on which she is commenting. Most revealing of all is the final statement in this passage:

Sous la voie lactée de la douceur chrétienne, nous croyons pénétrer des profondeurs de nuit noire. (*Fleuve*, 55–56)[20]

[Beneath the Milky Way of Christian gentleness, we seem to be advancing into depths of black night.]

This image in itself speaks volumes, contrasting as it does light and darkness, enlightenment and obscurity, Christianity and Africa. Indeed, as Patrick Brantlinger has pointed out, images of a very similar nature were common in Victorian discourse on Africa, with Christianity presented as the civilizing force that would bring light to the savages. However, though these are the terms of the opposition, this is not how Yourcenar places herself within it; rather than seeing herself as the bringer of light, she perceives herself as "advancing into" depths of darkness.[21] What she expresses is not repulsion, but fascination with the irrational, instinctual world that is Africa as she imagines it. It is tempting to suggest that for Yourcenar, the enlightened European rationalist, "Africa" is fascinating because it allows her to look into chaos and irrationality; yet this chaos is her own, it is what she brings to her construct of Africa. Africa is for her the dark Other, but also the inverted mirror onto which is projected the repressed side of herself.

Finally, this statement is important as the culmination of the passage dealing with Africa, expressing as it does a clear hierarchy between Christian (and therefore European) enlightenment, and African primitivism. Within this framework, African culture (including the African-American culture that produced the spirituals) is associated with irrationality and chaos, while Christianity represents light and progress. This idea is made explicit elsewhere in the preface; Yourcenar notes what a positive influence Christianity was for the first African slaves who encountered it in North America. As she puts it:

La bonne nouvelle du dieu fait homme a été assurément l'un des dons les plus révolutionnaires de la race des maîtres à la race des esclaves, et peut-être le seul passage vers un authentique Nouveau Monde. Des êtres habitués à la panique, à l'orgie sacrée, à tous les tressaillements primitifs en présence de l'inconnaissable, accédaient subitement aux délices de l'amour de Dieu. (*Fleuve*, 48)

[The good news of the god made man was surely one of the most revolutionary gifts from the race of masters to the race of slaves, and perhaps the only passage to an authentic New World. Beings accustomed to panic, to sacred orgies, to all the shuddering of primitives in the presence of the unknowable, suddenly gained access to the delights of God's love.]

In this case the primitive state is seen as oppressive and unenlightened, and greatly improved by the encounter with Christianity, even through the medium of slavery. Later remarks in the preface suggest that despite the civilizing influence of Christianity, primitive emotions remain strong; according to Yourcenar, even in their Christianized state, the slave singers of the Negro spirituals, when faced with death, "contemplate the shadows, sometimes with the trembling of an animal before the unknown, sometimes with an attitude of trusting, almost childlike acceptance" (*Fleuve*, 59).[22]

Such comments as these appear to belie Yourcenar's efforts to present the primitive in a positive light. The terms of description used here, where the singer of the spirituals is assimilated to an animal trembling with fear, suggest that she does indeed consider this to be a less advanced state of humanity. Despite her efforts to praise the other, unfamiliar culture, her own rationalist value system is too strong to allow her to do so without reserve.

This implicit hierarchy between "civilized" and "primitive" also expresses itself through the rhetoric of the preface. Many of the positive statements about the spirituals and their singers are couched in terms that express surprise or reserve on the writer's part. This is evident in the forms of language used, particularly in the modifiers, which convey the attitude of the discursive subject. We learn for example that:

> Ce qui étonne, en matière de Spirituals, c'est que l'inspiration religieuse ait, dans l'ensemble, été si haute, et que tant de témoignages soient là pour attester que le peuple à demi barbare des plantations a eu ses justes, ses pénitents, ses visionnaires naïfs et ses humbles prophètes. (*Fleuve*, 58)

> [What is surprising, as regards the spirituals, is that their religious inspiration was, on the whole, so lofty, and that there are so many accounts attesting that the half-wild people of the plantations had its righteous men, its penitents, its naive visionaries, and its humble prophets.]

Such expressions of surprise temper praise with condescension. In other passages, the modifiers used convey an attitude of reserve on the part of the speaker, as if the fact reported were something strange, contrary to the norm. Thus Yourcenar remarks that:

> Tout homme, et même l'ouvrier noir des marécages de la Géorgie, est le légataire universel de toute l'histoire. (*Fleuve*, 57)

> [Every man, even the black fieldworker in the swamps of Georgia, is the universal heir to all of history.]

or that:

> Malgré le jour en feu, et la nuit seule, une âme éternelle, mais enveloppée d'un corps noir, y vaque à observer son voeu. (*Fleuve*, 55)

> [Despite the fiery heat of the day, and the loneliness of the night, an eternal soul, albeit enclosed in a black body, attends to the observance of its religious commitment.]

Here, modifiers such as "even" [même] and "albeit" [mais] imply that what is being stated is unusual, contrary to what would be expected. This phrasing indicates surprise and reserve on the part of the speaker; the facts reported are, to her at least, anomalous.

Similar value judgments also color Yourcenar's remarks on the language of the spirituals. Throughout the preface, this is repeatedly described as "patois" or "jargon." In French, both of these terms are derogatory; "jargon" refers to a form of language that is "corrupted," "disparate," and "incomprehensible," while "patois" implies a nonstandard form of language, used by a group whose "level of culture and civilization is judged to be inferior."[23] Yourcenar also occasionally uses the adjective "barbare" in this context, which in French refers to what is "uncivilized" and outside accepted norms.[24]

Thus the "Africanism" of the spirituals is expressed through their use of the "characteristic Negro patois" [le caractéristique patois nègre] (*Fleuve*, 38); the common language of slaves from different parts of Africa is "an English jargon" [un jargon anglais] (*Fleuve*, 31), and early connoisseurs of the Spirituals appreciated the "dramatic power of their barbaric patois" [la puissance dramatique de leur patois barbare] (*Fleuve*, 33). Given the connotations of all of these terms in French, Yourcenar's comments amount to a statement about the inferiority of this language and the culture that produced it.

Judgments of a similarly negative nature are expressed in a more direct form in Yourcenar's "Translator's Note" to her version of James Baldwin's play, *The Amen Corner*.[25] Though short, this note contains a wealth of information about the translator's attitudes about the language and culture she is dealing with. It also helps to understand the linguistic choices she has made in translating both Baldwin's play and the spirituals.

Reading Yourcenar's "Note" (which precedes Baldwin's preface, so that the French reader's first impressions are influenced by the translator, not the author)[26] the first thing we learn about Baldwin's characters is that:

> Leur langage est bien entendu très négligé, non seulement parce qu'ils sont noirs, mais surtout peut-être parce qu'ils appartiennent au niveau le plus bas du prolétariat new-yorkais. (*Coin* 7)

> [Their language is, of course, very careless, not only because they are black, but perhaps especially because they belong to the lowest level of the New York proletariat.]

This comment expresses clear value judgments ("very careless" language, "the lowest level" of society); and it also expresses them in such a way as to convince the reader of their naturalness, their obviousness, through the use of modifiers such as "of course," "not only," indicating that the fact reported is something which is so self-evident as to need no explanation.

Yourcenar also extends this condescension to the writer being translated, informing us that:

> La préface de James Baldwin est certes écrite en un excellent anglais ou plutôt un excellent américain; néanmoins par la chaleur et la simplicité du langage, parlé plutôt qu'écrit, elle reste étroitement associée à l'humble milieu noir que le dramaturge décrit et dans lequel il a grandi. (*Coin*, 7)

> [James Baldwin's preface is no doubt written in excellent English, or rather excellent American; nevertheless, through the warmth and simplicity of the language, spoken rather than written, it remains closely associated with the humble black milieu that the dramatist describes and in which he grew up.]

The fact that Baldwin can write correct English is noteworthy, at least for Yourcenar. Nor does she let this fact prevent her from bringing him back into the paradigm in which she feels he belongs, that of the "warm," "simple" spoken word of his "humble" origins. In fact, she says, it would be doing him a disservice to render his work in "artificially refined French" (*Coin*, 8).[27]

Yourcenar's Translations of African-American Speech

This is the fundamental problem, not only with this preface, but with all Yourcenar's efforts to translate the speech of Baldwin's characters. She approaches the text with her own preconceptions and value judgments as to the quality of the language, and proceeds to "translate" accordingly. Specifically, this means that she passes judgment on their speech; she decides that their English is "incorrect," "neglected," "careless" [relâché], "faulty, but so direct, and so appropriate to the reality of their lives."[28] This "faulty" English is then rendered by a suitably "faulty" French of her own concoction. Such is her enthusiasm for this exercise that, as she admits, she has not only retained the "incorrect expressions" of the original, but has in fact:

> encore en ai-je rajouté, pour que le lecteur s'aperçoive bien que ces libertés prises sont voulues, et que le traducteur a essayé de laisser, comme je l'ai fait aussi dans mes traductions de *Spirituals*, de *Gospels* et de *Blues*, le son afro-américain des voix. (*Coin*, 8)

> [added more of them, so that the reader will be quite aware that the liberties taken are purposely so, and that the translator has tried, as I also did in my translations of *Spirituals*, *Gospels* and *Blues*, to leave intact the Afro-American sound of the voices.]

This last comment may be seen as part of Yourcenar's overall preoccupation with what might be termed "tonal authenticity," with capturing the "tone" or "voice" most appropriate to the character she wants to present to her readers.[29] This preoccupation has, however, led her to make some curious choices in the case of Baldwin's play. Her perception of the characters' speech is as "incorrect," substandard English, and certainly, the French they speak in her version of the play, if not substandard, is at least rather unusual.

Most of these "incorrections voulues" (*Coin*, 7) concern pronunciation. Thus we find "quéqu'" used instead of "quelque" (*Coin*, 38, 42, 44), "Je vas" instead of "Je vais," (*Coin*, 113), "P'être" for "Peut-être" (*Coin*, 29). The most frequent device of this type is the elision of silent "e"; as in "c't" for "cette," "pauv'" and "vot'" for "pauvre" and "votre," and of personal pronouns, particularly "il," rendered as "i,'" "i' en a" for "il y en a" (*Coin*, 56). However, these forms are not used systematically, but juxtaposed with the normal, nonelided forms, as in the following example: "L' petit David est un peu troublé en ce moment. Mais i' n' pense pas à retourner dans le monde profane; il a vu l'état où l' péché a réduit son père"[30] (*Coin*, 54). In addition to these nonstandard pronunciation forms, Yourcenar has the characters use various regionalisms, but again inconsistently; thus we find "C'est-y pas vrai?" (*Coin*, 52), which seems based on the Norman regional form, "comment ça-va-t-i'?" alternating with apparently Parisian forms like the elision of the pronoun "ils": "i' tenait par le bras une des filles . . . et on aurait dit qu'i' z-étaient très copains tous les deux" (55);[31] "Les gens, i' z-aiment de tout leur coeur Soeur Margaret" (56).[32]

The characters also use expressions which are grammatically incorrect in French such as "J'aimerais pas d'essayer" (53),[33] and "celui, qu'il dit, qui vont à l'école ensemble" (55),[34] and anglicisms such as "je n' crois pas que vous puissiez blâmer ça sur Papa" (100).[35] Both the nonstandard pronunciation forms and the grammatical variants are scattered through the text in a random manner, alternating with standard forms—which tends to suggest that they are indeed errors, deviations from a norm rather than part of a different idiom with its own internal coherence, as is the case in the original English text of the play.[36] Particularly in the French context, the cumulative effect of these nonstandard forms of pronunciation and expression is to suggest that the characters are poorly educated.

Yourcenar's version of the play also introduces curious shifts in tone and register. Among other things, the characters appear to speak a mixture of formal and informal French. One example of this is in the use of the formal "vous," which occurs even when characters are emotionally close, like the heroine Margaret and her sister, Odessa, or when the person addressed is an adolescent, like Margaret's son, David. (The use of "tu" is almost exclusively reserved by Yourcenar for Margaret's dissolute husband Luke, presumably as a means of marking his difference from the other, more conventional, characters. However, this distinction is entirely of Yourcenar's making; in Baldwin's English text, Luke's speech does not differ from that of the other characters.)

The use of "vous" also creates strange contrasts of tone when associated with familiar or colloquial expressions, as in the following example, where the heroine is addressing her young son:

> *Margaret.* Vous ne vous rappelez pas la mère Phillips ? Et comme vous trottiez derrière elle ? Comment ? Mais elle vous a gâté pourri.[37]
> (*Coin*, 34)

The "vous" form here contrasts with the image of the trotting toddler, and with a colloquial phrase like "gâter pourri." It also seems odd that the heroine addresses her eighteen-year-old son as "vous" whereas she uses "tu" with an unknown young woman who has just come into her church:

> *Margaret.* T'as bien fait, ma fille. La Bible dit: «Si tu t'avances d'un pas, Dieu de son côté fera deux pas vers toi.» Avance: aie foi en la promesse.[38] (*Coin*, 38)

The formal "vous" also contrasts oddly with familiar forms of address such as "mon petit sucre,"[39] as in the following example:

> *Margaret.* Mon p'tit sucre, i' n'y a rien que vous voulez que j' fasse pour vous, en votre temps d' tribulations?[40]

A striking example of these shifts in tone occurs toward the end of the text, at one of the most poignant moments in the play. After a final moment of reconciliation, the heroine's husband dies and she says:

> *Margaret.* My baby. You done joined hands with the darkness. (*Amen*, 132)

In Yourcenar's translation this becomes:

> *Margaret.* Mon petit homme! vous vous êtes associé avec les puissances des ténèbres. (*Coin*, 112)

A childish form of address like "mon petit homme" seems at odds with the rest of the sentence and its powerful biblical imagery. It is also worth noting that Yourcenar's sentence means something quite different from Baldwin's, or at the very least, that it excludes some of the possible meanings of the original. At this point in the play, the heroine has finally stopped condemning her husband and rediscovered her own love for him; thus her statement can be read as expressing her sorrow at his death, her regret that it is too late for them to begin again.[41] Yourcenar's sentence, on the other hand, is much more pessimistic, implying as it does Luke's final damnation.

Thus a number of the linguistic features of the French version are due to the translator's choices: the random and inconsistent use of nonstandard forms of grammar and pronunciation, and the clash of formal and informal registers of language. These are peculiar to Yourcenar's translation, and are not a feature of Baldwin's English text. Their combined effect is to introduce an air of incoherence and strangeness that is absent in the original version of the play. Yourcenar's "Translator's Note" suggests that the introduction of these linguistic variations is a direct result of her perception that the language of Baldwin's characters is "incorrect," and the natural concomitant of their inferior socioeconomic status.

As we have seen, the preface to *Fleuve profond* describes the language of the spirituals in similar terms: as "uncouth" [grossier] and "uncivilized" [barbare]. It is hardly surprising, then, that the translation of the songs displays linguistic features similar to those found in Yourcenar's version of *The Amen Corner*. Nonstandard pronunciation forms abound, particularly the elision of the silent "e," but also such (regionally influenced) forms as "alle" for "elle," "ben" for "bien," "su" for "sur," and "je m'en vas" for "je m'en vais."

Some of these features may be accounted for by Yourcenar's concern with maintaining the rhythm of the original.[42] This appears to be the case, for example, in her version of "Swing Low, Sweet Chariot," where the rather inconsistent elision of the silent "e" allows the words of the French version to fit the tune of the spiritual. Thus we have:

> Descends, doux char de feu,
> Qui dois m' ram'ner chez moi, chez Dieu !
> J' regarde vers le Jourdain
> Du côté du matin (*Fleuve*, 210)

For:

> Swing low, sweet chariot,
> Coming for to carry me home
> I looked over Jordan
> And what did I see[43]

In this case, the somewhat odd written appearance of the French version with its alternation of "de" and "le" with "J'" and "m'" may be justified by the fact that this irregular pattern is needed for the words to fit the tune.[44] Attention to rhythm is, after all, what critics have singled out as the salient feature of Yourcenar's versions of the spirituals. However, not all of Yourcenar's linguistic and stylistic choices may be explained in these terms. In many cases she appears to introduce irregular forms for their own sake, even when the result is a distortion of the original rhythm. Frequently an extra syllable containing a silent "e" is added while at the same time one or more silent "e's" in the line are elided. For example:

> Nobody knows the trouble I've seen,
> Nobody knows but Jesus[45]

becomes:

> Personne ne sait l' chagrin qu' j'ai eu,
> Personne ne l' sait, sauf que Jésus (*Fleuve*, 158)

In the second line "que" is added, although it is unnecessary and even awkward within the normal patterns of French speech. At the same time, "le" is shortened to "l'," as if to make room for "que" in the line. In terms of the rhythm of the line, these two nonstandard forms cancel each other out. The same effect could be achieved more simply by using standard French: "Personne ne le sait, sauf Jésus." This suggests that Yourcenar's translation choices are based on something other than respect for the rhythm of the original.

This pattern (addition of a superfluous "que" coupled with elision of one or more syllables in the same line) recurs in other translations. For example:

> Didn't my Lord deliver Daniel
> [. . .]
> An' why not a-every man[46]

becomes

> Dieu n'a-t-il pas sauvé Daniel
> [. . .]
> Pourquoi donc qu'il n' te sauverait pas (*Fleuve*, 103)

where both "que" and "ne" are elided. Other examples include: "O Moïse, où qu' t'étais quand le feu a brûlé not' église,"[47] (*Fleuve*, 97), in which "que" and "notre" are both shortened, and: "Marie, Marie, d'puis quand qu'il est mort?"[48] (*Fleuve*, 109), in which both "que" and "depuis" are elided. As these changes tend to overload the line, they cannot readily be explained by a concern with rhythm. What they do show is a deliberate choice to introduce nonstandard, irregular forms, even at the expense of other considerations.

This is also true of other translation choices made by Yourcenar: for example, changes in vowel quality, as in "Chanson de la vache crevée," where "alle" is used for "elle," "ben" for "bien," and "pu" for "plus." None of these changes affect syllabic quantity or rhythm; they do, however, create an impression of garbled and barely comprehensible French.

> Oh, tourne autour
> D' la vache crevée!
> [. . .]

> Faut êt' ben sûr
> Qu'alle a crevé!
> [...]
> J' suis ben content
> Qu'all' a crevé!
> [...]
> D' la vache, i' n'en reste presque pu!⁴⁹ (*Fleuve*, 73)

This may be deliberate in the case of this particular text, as Yourcenar mentions in the preface that she finds its content "horrible" and that she associates it with primitive African rites.[50] However, similar features occur in other spirituals, as when "Eun'" is used instead of "Une" (*Fleuve*, 189), and "J' vas," "j' m'en vas" for "je vais," "je m'en vais" (169). In all of these cases, the change in vocalic quality has no effect on the rhythm, but does create a pattern of faulty, careless French.

Furthermore, for the French reader, the text of the spirituals as it appears on the page is so replete with apostrophes and abbreviations as to be close to unreadable. While this may be an inevitable hazard in any effort to render orality in written form, it creates an impression of incoherence and suggests a generally condescending attitude to the songs and their singers (this has been the common reaction of the French readers to whom I have shown these texts).[51]

We may summarize by saying that although some of the irregular forms introduced by Yourcenar can be accounted for by the need to preserve the rhythm of the original, many others are gratuitous and seem specifically designed to highlight the oral and (in Yourcenar's eyes) "incorrect" character of the original texts. As in her translation of Baldwin's play, Yourcenar's concern here seems to be with expressing in French what she perceives as the faulty English of the originals. We have seen from her preface that she considers the language of the spirituals to be "jargon" or "patois"; in other words, a distorted or adulterated form of language, characteristic of a group whose culture or civilization is considered inferior. Analysis of the linguistic forms used in her translations of the spirituals suggests that her choices are such as to convey this impression to the reader of the French texts.

Yourcenar's choices as translator also affect other aspects of style. As in her work on Baldwin's play, she tends to alter the tone of the text, or to introduce sudden shifts in tone or register. In the case of the spirituals, one effect of this is to trivialize the text, introducing a casual, flippant tone where the original is grave or reflective. This occurs for example in her translation of "Nobody knows the trouble I've seen." Quoted below are the last two lines of the refrain, and the first lines of the verse, as they appear in English versions and in Yourcenar's translation:

> Nobody knows the trouble I've seen
> Glory Hallelujah
>
> Sometimes I'm up, sometimes I'm down
> Oh yes, Lord[52]

These lines appear in Yourcenar's version as:

> Personne ne sait l' chagrin qu' j'ai eu
> Ah, ah, Alléluia !
>
> Tantôt j' suis haut, tantôt j' suis bas,
> Ben oui, Seigneur (*Fleuve*, 158)

Here, the tone of the lines has changed in such a way as to diminish or negate their emotional impact: the prayerful "Glory Hallelujah" has become the jocular "Ah, Ah, Alléluia," while the solemn acquiescence expressed by "Oh yes, Lord" is replaced by the more flippant "Ben oui, Seigneur." The effect of these changes, combined with the curious typographic effect of the abbreviations, is to take away from the gravity and dignity of the song, lending it an air of childishness and frivolity. As in Yourcenar's version of Baldwin's play, the effect of the translation is to trivialize the text and diminish its poetic qualities.

Conclusion

Having examined both these translations—*Fleuve profond* and *Le Coin des «Amen»*—certain general points can be made. Despite the differences between the original English texts (Negro Spirituals from a variety of periods and regions, and Baldwin's play set at a particular time in a particular community), the French texts display remarkably similar linguistic and stylistic features. Both translations are characterized by a particular use of French, whose main features are an abundance of nonstandard forms of grammar and pronunciation. These are used profusely but unsystematically in such a way as to suggest errors, deviations from a norm, rather than a self-consistent linguistic system. The overall effect of this type of usage, particularly in the French context, is to convey the impression that the speakers (or singers) are incapable of correct or coherent expression and thus socially or culturally inferior. This impression is compounded by the presence in Yourcenar's versions of a curiously mixed tone and register. The effect of these is to trivialize the text and weaken its emotional and dramatic impact, introducing a frivolous or childish element in contexts where it is not appropriate.

Taken together, these linguistic and stylistic choices tend to depreciate the texts thus presented and the culture of which they are a part. Given Yourcenar's stated aims in undertaking these translations, this is obviously not her conscious intention. However, the reasons for this discrepancy between intention and execution become clearer on examination of the two commentaries which accompany her translations (the "Commentaires" in *Fleuve profond* and the "Note du traducteur" in *Le Coin des «Amen»*).

The essay on the Negro spirituals is an impressive historical and cultural study; however, despite the wealth of knowledge it displays, the underlying attitudes that inform it are not dissimilar to those expressed in the brief "Translator's Note" of *Le Coin des «Amen»*. Both reveal on the part of the translator an attitude that is at the very least condescending, and at times derogatory, toward the texts she is translating. Her assertions about the language of Baldwin's characters, and about the "primitive" cultural origins of the spirituals, are not neutral. Rather they reveal prejudices and reservations that are perhaps inevitable, given the mental framework within which Yourcenar is operating.

Despite her undoubted goodwill and openness, Yourcenar remains so rooted in her own "universalist" worldview that she cannot help but perceive as inferior any form of expression that does not conform to its norms. Given that this worldview has a strong eurocentric and elitist bias, her efforts to value other cultural manifestations are bound to fail, at least in part. Hence the difficulty she encounters in her attempt to celebrate African-American culture. Try as she may, the terms in which she describes it, indeed the mental framework with which she approaches it, make this an impossible and self-contradictory undertaking.

As we saw at the outset of this study, Yourcenar's motivations for undertaking these translations are undoubtedly positive, and she appears to have been largely successful in her aim of making these texts known to, and appreciated by, a French public. However, the value of her efforts is compromised by the attitudes that influence her approach to the texts. While Yourcenar's intentions are praiseworthy, the texts she produces as translator and commentator reveal prejudices of which she herself may not even have been aware. It remains for the individual reader to decide whether her contribution in this regard is globally positive, given the resonance of her work among the French public, or whether her good intentions are not to some extent undermined by the way in which she executes them.

Notes

1. For a differing view on this subject, see Carminella Biondi, "Marguerite Yourcenar et le problème noir," in C. Biondi, F. Bonali-Fiquet, M. Cavazzuti, and E. Pessini, eds., *Marguerite Yourcenar essayiste. Parcours, méthodes et finalités d'un discours critique* (Tours: Société Internationale d'Études Yourcenariennes, 2000), 237–44. This article appears to take issue with points raised in previous contributions to the debate. See for example F. Counihan, "Accueillir l'Autre dans son altérité: les traductions américaines de Marguerite Yourcenar," in J-Ph Beaulieu, J. Demers et A. Maindron, eds., *Marguerite Yourcenar. Écritures de l'Autre* (Montreal: XYZ Éditeur, 1997), 117–26; and "Écriture et autorité dans les traductions de Marguerite Yourcenar," in R. Poignault and J-P Castellani, eds., *Marguerite Yourcenar. Écriture, réécriture, traduction* (Tours: Société Internationale d'Études Yourcenariennes, 2000), 297–312.

2. Marguerite Yourcenar, *Fleuve profond, sombre rivière: Les "Negro Spirituals," commentaires et traductions* (Paris: Gallimard, 1964). (Reissued in the Poésie Gallimard Collection in 1974. Quotes refer to this edition.)

3. James Baldwin, *Le Coin des «Amen,»* traduit de l'anglais par Marguerite Yourcenar (Paris: Gallimard, 1983). (Translation of *The Amen Corner*, first published in 1968—edition quoted here: New York: Laurel, 1990).

4. *Blues et Gospels* (textes traduits et présentés par Marguerite Yourcenar, images réunies par Jerry Wilson) (Paris: Gallimard, 1984). Most of this book consists of photographs by Jerry Wilson, with an introduction and translations by Marguerite Yourcenar.

5. Though as Georgia Shurr points out, and as is evident from Josyane Savigneau's biography of Yourcenar, the author had started work on the translations out of personal interest as much as twenty years before this, soon after her arrival in the United States. G. Hooks Shurr, "Marguerite Yourcenar et 'drame noir' américain," *Bulletin du CIDMY* (Centre International de Documentation Marguerite Yourcenar, Brussels), no. 10 (1998); *Marguerite Yourcenar et l'Amérique*, 27–57; Josyane Savigneau, *Marguerite Yourcenar: L'Invention d'une vie* (Paris: Gallimard, 1990), 295–97.

6. My translation. In what follows, translations from the French are my own, except where otherwise indicated.

7. See for example J. Savigneau, *Marguerite Yourcenar: L'Invention d'une vie*, 295–97.

8. Paul Renard, "Yourcenar, Spirituals, Gospels, Blues" in *Nord* 5 (1985): 63–69.

9. See for example G. H. Shurr, "Marguerite Yourcenar et le 'drame noir,'" and C. Biondi, "Marguerite Yourcenar et le problème noir." Shurr's article gives a very

complete account of Yourcenar's North American translations, while Biondi comments (very favorably) on the author's contribution both as commentator and as translator of the spirituals.

10. James Weldon Johnson, *The Book of American Negro Spirituals* (New York: Viking, 1925), see preface, especially 13–28; Henry Edward Krehbiel, *Afro-American Folksongs: A Study in Racial and National Music* (New York: G. Schirmer, 1914), 56–69.

11. Léopold Sédar Senghor, "Ce que l'Homme noir apporte," in *L'Homme de couleur*, 1939. Quoted by Roger Toumson, *La Transgression des couleurs: Littérature et langage des Antilles*, II (Paris: Éditions Caribbéennes, 1989), 393–94.

12. See Toumson, *La Transgression des couleurs*, vol. II, 392–96; Robert Cornevin, *Littératures d'Afrique noire de langue française* (Paris: Presses Universitaires de France, 1978), 159–64.

13. Johnson, *The Book of American Negro Spirituals*, 18–19.

14. Elsewhere in the preface, she similarly declares them to be "one of the purest expressions of Christian fervor," or like "a poignant oratorio," 45.

15. This also occurs in Yourcenar's comments on other writers whose work she translates, for example the Indian poet Amrita Pritam. See F. Counihan, "Translation and Authority: The Case of Marguerite Yourcenar," in C. Shorley and M. McCusker, eds., *Reading Across the Lines* (Dublin: Royal Irish Academy, 2000), 47–58; 51.

16. See Blanca Arancibia, "Quelle universalité?" in R. Poignault and M-J Vásquez de Parga, eds., *L'Universalité dans l'oeuvre de Marguerite Yourcenar* (Tours: Société Internationale d'Études Yourcenariennes, 1994), vol. I, 15–21.

17. "De la grande triade ailée de la légende médiévale, Michel et Raphaël, dans leurs rôles d'ange juge et guerrier et d'ange guide, sont regrettablement absents" (*Fleuve*, 51–52). Rather than recognizing the specificity of a tradition that honors a particular angel, Gabriel, Yourcenar tries to reconstruct the triadic model that is familiar to her, despite the absence of two of its members.

18. See Toumson, *La Transgression*, 363–87. See also René Ménil, *Tracées: Identité, négritude, esthétique aux Antilles* (Paris: Robert Laffont), 78–89, for a rather more critical analysis of this concept.

19. "Comme dans toute poésie primitive, il y a dans le *Negro Spiritual* un sens presque topographique des pérégrinations d'outre-tombe" (*Fleuve*, 61).

20. Phonetically, the words "voie lactée" also suggest "voile," thus Christianity as a "veil" over the darkness of Africa.

21. Patrick Brantlinger, "Victorians and Africans: The Genealogy of the Myth of the Dark Continent," in Henry L. Gates, Jr., ed., *Race, Writing and Difference* (Chicago: University of Chicago Press, 1986), 185–222, 197–98.

22. "Démuni, esclave, le nègre des Spirituals contemple ces ténèbres tantôt avec un frémissement qui est celui de l'animal devant l'inconnu, tantôt avec une acceptation confiante et quasi enfantine."

23. "Jargon" is defined by the *Petit Robert* as "Corrupted, adulterated language composed of disparate elements; by extension, any incomprehensible language" [Langage corrompu, déformé, fait d'éléments disparates; par extension, tout langage incompréhensible]. "Patois" is defined as "local dialect or form of speech used by a generally small, rural population whose level of culture and civilization is judged to be inferior to that of the surrounding group (which uses the standard language)" [parler, dialecte local employé par une population généralement peu nombreuse, souvent rurale et dont la culture, le niveau de civilisation sont jugés comme inférieurs à ceux du milieu environnant (qui emploie la langue commune)],

Le Petit Robert, I, Alain Rey and Josette Rey-Debove, eds. (Paris: Dictionnaires Le Robert, 1990).

24. "Barbare" is defined as "That which is not civilized; which shocks, which is contrary to rules, to good taste, to custom" [Qui n'est pas civilisé; Qui choque, qui est contraire aux règles, au goût, a l'usage] (*Le Petit Robert*, 1990).

25. James Baldwin, *Le Coin des «Amen,»* traduit de l'anglais par Marguerite Yourcenar (Paris: Gallimard, 1983).

26. Conversely, when Yourcenar's own works are translated into English, the "Translator's Notes" (if any) are modestly placed at the end of the text, thus occupying what Genette considers as the belated and ineffectual position of the "postface" (cf. Gérard Genette, *Seuils* [Paris: Seuil, 1987], 221). See also F. Counihan, "Translation and Authority: The Case of Marguerite Yourcenar," a paper read at the conference on "Transitions, Transpositions and Translations," Queen's University, Belfast, November 1998.

27. "[L]a traduire en un français artificiellement châtié serait lui faire perdre ... sa vérité *tonale*" [to translate it (Baldwin's preface) into an artificially refined French would make it lose its *tonal* authenticity]. *Le Coin des «Amen,»* 8.

28. "[L]eur parler si fautif, mais également si direct, et si bien adapté aux réalités de leur vie." Ibid., 7.

29. See for example her essay, "Tone and Language in the Historical Novel," in *That Mighty Sculptor, Time*, trans. Walter Kaiser (New York: Noonday Press, 1993), 27–56, in the original: "Ton et langage dans le roman historique," in *Le Temps, ce grand sculpteur* (Paris: Gallimard, 1983), 29–58.

30. Baldwin's text reads: "Little David's just been a little upset. He ain't thinking about going back into the world, he see what sin did for his daddy." James Baldwin, *The Amen Corner*, 1968 (New York: Laurel, 1990), 53.

31. Baldwin's text: "that boy ... had his hand on one of them girls ... well, like he knowed her pretty well" (*Amen* 54).

32. "Folks just love Sister Margaret" (Ibid., 56).

33. "I wouldn't like to try it" (Ibid., 52).

34. "[T]he one he say he go to school with" (Ibid., 54).

35. "I don't think you can blame it on Daddy, Mama" (Ibid., 116).

36. For a fuller discussion of this question (of African-American English as a distinct and self-consistent idiom), see John Edwards, "Linguistic Hierarchies," in *Multilingualism* (Harmondsworth: Penguin, 1995), 89–97; R. L. Trask, "Attitudes To Language," in *Language: The Basics* (London: Routledge, 1995), 157–81, especially 170–71; P. Trudgill, "Language and Ethnic Groups," in *Sociolinguistics: An Introduction to Language and Society* (Harmondsworth: Penguin, 1995), 39–61.

37. "MARGARET: You don't remember Mother Phillips? The way you used to follow her around? Why, she used to spoil you something awful" (*Amen*, 23).

38. "MARGARET: That's right, daughter. The Word say, If you make one step, He'll make two. Just step out on the promise" (Ibid., 14).

39. This diminutive (nonexistent in French usage) is presumably Yourcenar's attempt to render "Honey" or "Sugar," which occur frequently in Baldwin's text.

40. Compare Baldwin's text, where no such shift of tone is apparent: "MARGARET: Honey, is there anything you want me to do for you now, in your time of trouble?" (Ibid., 100).

41. See *The Amen Corner*, 131, where Margaret says: "Oh Luke! If only we could start again," and 132 (just after his death): "My Lord! If I could only start again! If I could only start again!"

42. This concern is expressed in the brief "Note sur les traductions qui suivent" at the end of the preface (*Fleuve*, 63–64).

43. Version noted by Hugo Frey. H. Frey, *A Collection of 25 Famous Negro Spirituals* (New York: Robbins Music Corporation, 1924), 14, and quoted by Yourcenar in preparatory notes for *Fleuve profond* (Harvard University, shelf mark bMS Fr 372 [1318]). Reproduced by kind permission of the Houghton Library. The same wording is used for this song in the recording, *"Les plus beaux Negro Spirituals,"* Auvidis, A 53025, 1991. One of the singers on this recording is Marion Williams, with whom Yourcenar had earlier collaborated on another recording project.

44. As was demonstrated by M. Maurice Delcroix at a Yourcenar conference in Tours in 1997. ("Marguerite Yourcenar. Écriture, réécriture et traduction," Université de Tours, November 22–26, 1997.)

45. Version noted by Florence Botsford, F. Hudson Botsford, *Folk Songs*, vol. I: *Songs from the Americas, Asia and Africa* (New York: G. Schirmer, 1929), 41–42, quoted by Yourcenar in preparatory notes for *Fleuve profond*. (Harvard University, shelf mark bMS Fr 372 [1318]. Reproduced by kind permission of the Houghton Library.) The same wording features on the 1991 Auvidis recording quoted above.

46. Johnson, *The Book of American Negro Spirituals*, 158.

47. ["Oh Moses, where were you when our church burned down?"] In the absence of a precise source, this English wording is my own.

48. ["Mary, Mary, how long is he dead?"] My English wording.

49. ["Oh turn around / The dead cow! / You have to be sure / That she's dead! / I'm very glad / That she's dead! / There's almost nothing left of that cow!"] My English wording.

50. "L'horrible *Chanson de la vache crevée* est une 'ronde de vautours,' peut-être importée de l'immémoriale Afrique noire" [The horrible *Song of the Dead Cow* is a "vulture dance," perhaps imported from immemorial black Africa] (*Fleuve*, 36).

51. I am indebted for these comments to my friends and colleagues Brigitte Le-Juez, Olivier Colette, Mireille Brioude, and Patricia Subirade.

52. Version noted by Florence Botsford, quoted by Yourcenar in preparatory notes for *Fleuve profond*. (Harvard University, shelf mark bMS Fr 372 [1318]. Reproduced by kind permission of the Houghton Library.)

Performing the Masculine Voice

Elène Cliche

Translated by Gervais E. Reed

TO TAKE AN INTEREST IN YOURCENAR'S PERFORMANCE IN MASCULINE VOICE is to consider that the binary category of masculinity and femininity exists. Although the sexual dichotomy is often successfully subverted, I would, like many others, prefer to see it eliminated or ended. Yourcenar was right when she said in an interview: "I mistrust all labels, all categories, and everything titled 'new.'"[1] Even if on a practical level these two poles serve as gender markers, I feel compelled to deconstruct this category or at least to reconceptualize it.[2]

Thus in all sincerity I shall propose a theory that I will call the oscillation of the subject in Yourcenar's work, for it allows her to assume various narrative voices, whether they be masculine narrators as different as those of *Alexis, Le Coup de grâce,* or *Mémoires d'Hadrien* or ambiguous feminine characters such as Sophie in *Le Coup de grâce*. I would like to grant full value to the concept of the *floating* subject that fortunately corresponds to an expression that Yourcenar used to refer to herself in *Discours de réception à l'Académie française,* January 22, 1981: "This uncertain floating I."[3] This uncertainty of subject that obviously contrasts to a conception of a full and stable I allows her to shape desire and its many fantastical identities in the imaginative activity of writing thanks to the performance of voices, whether they be masculine or feminine or both simultaneously as happens in the poem "Hermaphrodite" of 1930, a figuration of the body's "enigma."[4] The idea of the floating I comes close to Judith Butler's theory of gender as social construct, gender being seen as a free-floating artifice in comparison to sex that may be changed by the production of gender: "When the constructed status of gender is theorized as radically independent of sex, gender itself becomes a free-floating artifice, with the consequence that *man* and *masculine* might just as easily signify a female body as a male one, and *woman* and *feminine* a male body as easily as a female one."⁵ I would like to emphasize that the problematics that I am approaching here are very well expressed in literature by Virginia Woolf in *Orlando*. This novel exemplifies the oscillation of the subject as a process of "vacillation": "Different though the sexes are, they intermix. In every human being a *vacillation* from one sex to the other takes place, and often it is only the clothes that keep the male or female likeness, while underneath the sex is the very opposite of what it is above." One may note elsewhere in *Orlando* this sentence about sexual ambiguity: "And here it would seem from some ambiguity in her terms that she was censuring both sexes equally, as if she belonged to neither, and, indeed, for the time being, she seemed to *vacillate*, she was man; she was woman."⁶ This preoccupation with not belonging to any sex whatsoever or with vacillation between the sexes is also present in Yourcenar's work. It marks a "tendency toward total impersonality" in the case of Hadrian, who says: "A man who reads, reflects, or plans belongs to his species rather than his sex; in his best moments he rises even above the human."⁷ In *Un Homme obscur,* Nathanaël's floating identity is indicated thus: "Nor did he particularly consider himself male in contrast with the gentle society of women." Here the sociocultural reality of gender is laid out: "Custom more than nature seemed to him to dictate the differences we set up between classes of men, the habits and knowledge acquired from infancy, or the various ways of praying to what is called God. Ages, sexes and or even species seemed to him closer to one another than each generally assumed about the other...."⁸ Now, a reader notices in Yourcenar's work an instability of the binary logic masculine/feminine, and the author reflects in *Carnets de notes de l'Oeuvre au noir* that there is "in each being a difference in the amount of sexual components" (*La Nouvelle Revue française*, September 1990, 41). In fact, one finds an example of this idea in the figure of Sappho included in the collection *Feux*. I would say that Sappho is par excellence the floating being. She is a woman who "looks like an athlete" and "a female impersonator,"⁹ wavering between her desire for Attys and her transvestite substitute, Phaon, with "square shoulders" and "feminine gentleness" (124). The vacillation that Woolf speaks of takes on a tragic dimension in Sappho. "This creature, tired of being only half woman" (128), Yourcenar writes of her when she comes face to face with this character who attempts suicide as a trapeze artist but who fails as she falls into the net. Sappho appears one last time in the metaphor of a woman drowned in the sea, a definitive feminine element at the edge of each confine.

Similarly, I refer to Yourcenar's description of the poet Sappho in *La Couronne et la lyre*, a text in which the author (wanting to reflect on matters of gender) tries to classify Sappho's specifically feminine characteristics that we in turn may think of as cultural traits, whereas other aspects of her poetry may be found, she says, in the work of "all of the poets of her century."[10]

In her story "Sappho ou le suicide," Yourcenar specifies details of clothing as signs of passage from one sexual identity to another, a crossing that may be found in the quotation from *Orlando*: "and often it is only the clothes that keep the male or female likeness." Phaon wrapped himself in Attys' dressing gown in order to seduce Sappho: "relieved of its confining men's clothing, this flexible body is almost a woman's body. This Phaon, comfortable in his impersonation, is nothing more than a stand-in for the beautiful absent nymph" (*Feux*, 211; *Fires*, 126). But as we know, Sappho flees from this double image in order to cling "to her death as to an overhanging ledge" (*Feux*, 215; *Fires*, 129). Yourcenar shifts between this ambiguous sexual entity and the aspiration to death that serves as a metaphor for the failure of passion, in this case the it-is-not-she of desire, for Attys has become absence itself. Following the example of *Mémoires d'Hadrien*, this story forms part of the matrix of the homosexualization of desire and of the narcissistic choice of the beloved: "All women love one woman: they love themselves madly, consenting to find beauty only in the form of their own body" (*Feux*, 197–98; *Fires*, 118). The intensity of this love gets its power, however, from mourning the beloved who has died, such as Attys in "Sappho ou le suicide" or Antinoüs in *Mémoires d'Hadrien*.

In *Le Coup de grâce*, Sophie is also a vacillating character who traverses the lines of sexual difference. Here Yourcenar mixes gender traits. Whereas Conrad is presented as having "retained a childhood innocence, a girl's gentleness" (*Le Coup de grâce*, 148), Sophie is described as a failed boy (180) or as a soldier having put on presentable men's clothing (222). Readers become aware of the instability constituting Sophie's character, of "her fierce, wild grace" (154), and as a result come to distrust Eric, the narrator: "Everything led me to misunderstand Sophie, and I did so all the more so because of her soft yet brusque voice, her close-cropped hair, her short smocks and heavy, muddy shoes that made her seem like her brother's brother" (157–58). On the one hand, Eric's desire for Conrad reverses the image of Sophie as a man by superimposing her on him. On the other hand, Eric has to face her as a woman, that is to say specifically as a woman raped by a Lithuanian sergeant. He says that the account of this misfortune has brought him closer to her (156). He admits that he is especially struck by her appearance as an injured adolescent girl (154). Moreover, she plays the role of prostitute in order to get a jealous reaction from Eric; she performs the role of seductress outrageously, and is thus perceived by Eric: "I hated those low, suggestive tones that she had adopted ever since she had begun playing whore" (189). But in another narrative twist, Sophie behaves in the last analysis like "a very young soldier," "dressed and shod like the others," with "a boy's carefree manner" (238–39). She remains, however, marked by feminine gender as a woman having suffered masculine violence to the extreme degree of being attacked by Eric von Lhomond. When Eric assumes that she has been attacked and left as dead in a ditch, there emerges the metaphor of Sophie's body "like the corpse of a partridge or pheasant wounded by a poacher" (224–25).

The dead Sophie haunts Eric during sleepless nights as the ghostly image of "a girl wading in cold mud" (218). Sophie is inscribed as feminine in the last sentence of *Le Coup de grâce*. After Sophie has been murdered, Eric says that she has left him remorseful, and he thinks of himself, executioner that he is, as a victim of women: "One is always trapped with these women" (248). It is unfortunate that the English translation of *Le Coup de grâce* renders "ces femmes" [these women] that special category within a general category, as "women": "One is always trapped, somehow, in dealings with women."[11] It deprives the character of Sophie of her uncommon nature. After the failed boy's cross-dressing as a soldier, the text oscillates toward the final signifier, "ces femmes," these women, finalizing gender like a landmark as in *Sappho ou le suicide*, "a woman drowned in the sea" (*Feux*, 216, *Fires*, 129). The expression "ces femmes" conveys a particular meaning because "these women" stand up to male domination, rape being at the heart of the problematics. We know that Eric, first-person narrator, bears responsibility for masculine power and violence; compared to him, Sophie is a figure of defiance who refuses his mercy and forces him to kill her.[12]

I would simply like to state that despite Eric's dominant expression in *Le Coup de grâce* that sets off his "taut heroism" to the detriment of Sophie's resistance, the narrative offers nonetheless a dialectical tension that intermittently undermines the unilateral performance of masculine voice. This subversion results from the character of Sophie, metaphor of the element earth, whereas Sappho combines the elements air and water. I refer here to the scene of the mirror that casts back to Sophie the reflection of a face "like earth itself in spring, a landscape of gently sloping fields crossed by streams of tears" (173). This is the narrator's vision of Sophie: "I told myself that at least this woman would be firm like the earth on which one could build or lie down" (201). Yourcenar says in her preface that Sophie "needed to surrender body and soul" (132). Without necessarily believing in an essential femininity or masculinity, I think that Yourcenar tends to associate through metonymy a gift or an excess of generosity with earth and the feminine, the wellspring of riches, as she did also with Marcella in *Denier du rêve*. I cite as relevant to this question Yourcenar's radio interview with Patrick de Rosbo: "In *Le Coup de grâce* Eric has the advantage of being the narrator, of being intellectually more clearly drawn, but to me Sophie seems as important as he. She represents somehow earth itself; she embodies that feminine element that means so much to me but that unfortunately I have to confess that I rarely find in women we see around us: that nearly inexhaustible abundance of emotion and feeling, that intrinsic goodness, that patient capacity for acceptance" (*Entretiens,* 89). I hasten to add that if excessive giving and feeling is considered here as "a feminine element" (which could also under certain circumstances be taken as submission), it is certainly not something natural or intrinsic but rather the result of sociocultural conditioning. I would say, however, that in Sophie's case, the capacity for acceptance or resignation (founded on a powerful unrequited love) is linked to will. Eric derives from it a lucid strategy that consists of taking revenge and finding remorse. He is impressed by Sophie's serenity as death approaches: "However that may be, she no longer loved me then: she was no longer thinking about producing an effect on me" (241). But again the paradox of Sophie's sexual ambiguity troubles Eric, especially at the time of her execution resulting from her resemblance to her brother, when he gets the impression of seeing Conrad die twice. Gender is thus constructed through power relations: "I clung to the idea that I had wanted to finish off Conrad and that it was the same thing" (247). Here in the assimilation of brother and sister, feminine and masculine are interchangeable. The optical illusion characterizing a confusion of gender reminds me of the puzzlement Mishima feels when he sees sexual ambiguity illustrated in a picture book. The boy thinks that he sees a knight, and his nanny explains that he is looking at a woman named Joan of Arc. Yourcenar writes in her essay *Mishima ou la vision du vide* (1980) that he reacts to this fact by feeling cheated and offended in his boyish masculinity. "What interests us is that what caused the reaction is Joan and not one of many Kabuki heroines disguised as a man" (14). The illustration of Joan of Arc thus makes the youthful Mishima aware of a destabilization of the binary logic of the sexes.

Literature has always allowed Yourcenar to set up passage—crossing of limits—toward "the something other than oneself" that could be represented by the masculine voice. I think of Alexis, whom she defines in her preface as the "portrait of a voice." This oscillation of the subject of writing has always made critics uneasy as they were trying to classify her texts that could not be categorized as "feminine writing" or "feminist." Some labeled her writing "masculine" (based, we might ask, on what essentialist criteria?). Others concluded that her writing was androgynous, for example Georgia Hooks Shurr: "Her style is androgynous more than it is masculine or feminine" (89). For me Yourcenar's writing is neither masculine nor feminine but a writing that opens out or calls to the other, whoever that may be. It gives free rein to various transfers of sexual identity. I quote here a letter that Yourcenar wrote to Patrick de Rosbo, who reproduced a passage from it in his book: "What is important in what I have written is the almost impersonal search that I began early on, this passage from myself to what is more important than I. . . ." (171). I shall insist here on precisely this idea of passage, a threshold allowing discourse to enter wherever it seems right.

Now I shall take *Mémoires d'Hadrien* as an example of the fulfillment of the performing masculine voice. I will consider first the materiality of a body constructed from words. In this instance, the written subject takes on a being that has already existed (a Roman emperor) and whose gender is already decided. There is a social reason for this choice. According to Yourcenar in her *Carnets de notes de Mémoires d'Hadrien*, women's lives were too limited. Therefore a constitutive constraint materializes and sexes the body. The formulation of Hadrian's body as well as his masculinity is assumed by the expression that produces a subjectivity, an I that speaks in a particular tone and with particular inflections. This individuation functions within a masculine intersubjectivity, for he speaks to Marcus Aurelius, "my dear Marcus." In fact, from the beginning of the narrative, the materiality of the body is seen by the doctor as "a mass of humors, a sorry mixture of blood and lymph" (11). This reference to the body precedes statements about culture or power. From the beginning the emperor says, "I like my body." Out of this same defeated body with its swollen legs that hardly hold him up he utters the sentence that, according to the author, triggered the book in 1934: "I begin to discern the profile of my death" (*Mémoires,* 13; *Memoirs,* 5; *Carnets,* 322). The writer got the feeling that she had found "the book's point of view" that would lead the subject-narrator to construct himself retrospectively. Although Hadrian's sentence is anchored in his body's materiality, the reader could take it out of context in order to reflect on its metaphysical dimension with the thought that it might be said by either a man or a woman at any moment of history. The sentence belongs, however, to the narrator who refers to his own body, and therein lies the focus that Yourcenar chose in 1934 to engender language.

Performance is therefore the act by which discourse will produce its effects of masculinity: "Grown to manhood, I found in hunting release from many a secret struggle with adversaries.... My hunts in Tuscany have helped me as emperor to judge the courage or the resources of high officials" (*Memoirs*, 13–14). Thus Hadrian's monologue introduces us immediately to the story of his body, several elements of which are given in the very first chapter. In a personal synesthesia he speaks of the sensation of eating fruit: "To eat a fruit is to welcome into oneself a fair living object, which is alien to us but is nourished and protected like us by the earth" (16). Such a sensual nonsexual sentence might just as well be found in a text by Colette. Elsewhere Hadrian speaks of the sensations of drinking the wine of Samos or simply water or of caressing the beloved. To perform the masculine voice is to insist first on the materiality of the body, the "emotions of the senses." Yourcenar used this as a technique of relating to and possibly identifying with the subject: "Those men who, like us, nibbled olives and drank wine, or gummed their fingers with honey" (*Carnets*, 332). In seeking an existential reality, a space of infiltration permits the identifying projection "as we all are." Such infiltration is to be found in statements such as "a man would prefer British rain to the mosquitoes of Rome" or "an individual unique as we all are, made as we all are of fortuitous elements assembled a bit randomly and which need to be rediscovered in their complexity" (*Entretiens*, 65–66). But more thoroughly and by means of the utterance of the I, the subject of the writing appropriates the other in the alternance of the I and not I. For as the author mentions in an interview, she certainly did not make peace in the world as Hadrian did, but here and there she used her "own experience in order better to understand Hadrian's" (*Entretiens*, 64). Thus imagination comes into play as one passes from the self to the other. It is linked here to masculinity, "Greek love," homosexual eroticism, ancient culture, etc., that writing must undertake. A performative act is fulfilled in writing, an act that produces discourse in materializing the body, its sex (even if nibbling olives is not a sexual act), its desire outside the hegemony of heterosexuality, family and reproductive ideology: "I have no children, nor is that a regret. To be sure, in time of weakness and fatigue, when one lacks the courage of one's convictions, I have sometimes reproached myself for not having taken the precaution to engender a son, to follow me. But such a vain regret rests upon two hypotheses, equally doubtful: first, that a son necessarily continues us, and, second, that the strange mixture of good and evil, that mass of minute and odd particularities which make up a person, deserves continuation" (*Memoirs,* 253).

Yourcenar's discourse assumes a (gendered) social position that is masculine in a given culture, in this instance that of a Roman emperor, although beyond the limits of gender the human body prevails in the text: "It is difficult to remain an emperor in presence of a physician, and difficult even to keep one's essential quality as man" (*Memoirs,* 3–4). If there is an underlying "I am woman" of Yourcenar the writer, this sex is easily replaced by masculine gender (I would say that is a typically Orlandian vacillation), and this gender displaces the feminine sex. Here I follow Judith Butler for whom gender is the social construction of sex, sex being absorbed in gender. Here we can speak of imaginative identification as phantasmatic trajectory and fulfillment of desire.[13] Yourcenar thus performs masculine gender and its reference to a body, and desire connects this body to another body of floating gender, Antinoüs: "the full chest of the young runner took on the smooth, gleaming curves of a Bacchante's breast" (*Mémoires,* 171; *Memoirs,* 156).

Ever since a visit to Hadrian's villa when she was about twenty, a memorable experience if there ever was one, and the plan "to write something some day about Hadrian,"[14] he became a phantasmatic investment. To invent his voice, however, required long gestation: consulting texts about him, seeing regions where his life had taken place, reflecting on subjects in order to make him talk about them (Yourcenar and Galey, 225). In order to accomplish all of that, she had to find certain subjective factors such as "toga style," half narrative, half meditation, that would retain the emperor's dignity.[15] This performance takes place, then, in the materiality of the writing and with a certain transfer of identity: "[learning] how to calculate exactly the distances between the emperor and myself" (*Carnets,* 323; *Reflections,* 322). Moreover, this process occasioned self-analysis: "trying to bridge not only the distance which separated me from Hadrian but, above all, the distance which separated me from my true self" (*Carnets,* 326; *Reflections,* 325). The process is therefore one of subjectification, transformation, sexual differentiation that passes through the other, through the appropriation of a masculine position linked to the fantasy of "the importance of the prince" (*Carnets,* 328; *Reflections,* 327). Yet she needed to retain the proper distance that had to be calculated differently when dealing, for example, with the episode of mourning the lover and grieving over loss. Therefore the emperor Hadrian appears as a performed ideal free of both constraint and moral censure and offering to the writer a "reterritorialization of gender and sexuality," to borrow an expression from Deleuze-Guattari, i.e., the territory of a libidinal scenography based on the choice of an object of the same sex where homosexuality is both conspicuous and legitimate. We may safely assume that Yourcenar took pleasure in the experience of writing, what she calls her "method akin to controlled delirium" or "sympathetic magic" (*Carnets,* 330; *Reflections,* 328–29), that takes her inside her character, a phenomenon, I would say, of doubling or psychic appropriation. This experience consists of silencing her own thought and listening to a voice, an occurrence that she called "visitation" (Yourcenar and Galey, 224). What to another might seem passive seems to me an active projection into the masculine world with, in this instance, the engendering of a confessional I. Here also I see a subversive act of possession in keeping the male utterance and simulating his desire, a challenge to restrictive conventions, an overstepping of gender boundaries. It is a way of critiquing the rigid notion of gender rooted in nature or the body. For Yourcenar, to explore masculinity as a form of representation or sociohistorical construction is to deconstruct gender as a static concept; above all, it is to inscribe desire in the transfer of sexual identity. I suggest that a woman is challenged when she constructs masculinity in history and language just as a man is challenged when he enters the feminine world. Thus woman affirms herself as subject other than the I-woman, the empirical referent of what has been theorized as femininity. There is a semiotic difference of reference and signification. For example, the text *Mémoires d'Hadrien* is a cultural production; the identity of Hadrian is discursively constituted by the writer's act when she takes many particulars to represent what is masculine. The term "performative" implies that there is no being behind the act and no gender identity behind expressions of gender. This may well have been how Yourcenar saw the act of writing when she defined herself in 1981 in her *Discours de réception à l'Académie française* as "this uncertain floating I, this entity whose existence I have myself questioned, and that I feel is determined only by the few works I happen to have written" (10). This statement confirms an act where multiple identities vacillate in her work.

I shall end simply by stating that the title of my paper, "Performing the Masculine Voice," might have suggested a single voice in Yourcenar's work, that of Michel, the voice of the father "so little a father in the idiomatic or tyrannical sense of the word" (*Quoi? L'Eternité*, 275). In *Quoi? L'Eternité* she often lets him speak in the form of an interior monologue, using first or third person. What will be remembered from this book is that the girl Marguerite quickly assimilated another cultural gender conditioning, as she says, for she was absorbed in reading books rather than in sewing or in playing with dolls (*Quoi? L'Eternité,* 273). The father's voice echoed literature: "in the evening, when he did not go out, we would read. Through his voice I heard Racine, Saint-Simon, Chateaubriand, Flaubert" (*Quoi? L'Eternité,* 233). In Paris that voice directed Marguerite's governess to take her twice weekly to the Louvre. The father's encouraging voice opened the world of culture and art, and something fundamentally positive took shape in the girl and led her far: "Between the ages of nine and eleven, something abstract and at the same time divinely physical rubbed off on me: the taste for color and form, Greek nudity, the pleasure and glory of living" (*Quoi? L'Eternité*, 234).

Notes

This essay was first translated by Adele Parker, Brown University. In the present translation I have retained the French titles of Yourcenar's works in order to avoid confusion. Unless English editions are cited, all translations from Yourcenar's texts are mine. (Translator's note.)

1. Patrick de Rosbo. *Entretiens radiophoniques* (Paris: Mercure de France, 1972), 28.
2. This paper was presented in an earlier version in French at a special session of the MLA convention on "Marguerite Yourcenar: The Paradox of Sexual Ambiguity," December 27–30, 1995, San Diego, California.
3. "Ce moi incertain et flottant, cette entité dont j'ai contesté moi-même l'existence, et que je ne sens vraiment délimité que par les quelques ouvrages qu'il m'est arrivé d'écrire. . . ." [This uncertain floating I, this entity whose existence I have myself questioned, and that I feel is determined only by the few works that I happen to have written. . . .] in *Discours de réception de Mme Marguerite Yourcenar à l'Académie française et réponse de M. Jean d'Ormesson* (Paris: Gallimard, 1981), 10.
4. "Il propose au désir l'énigme de son corps" [He proposes his body's enigma to desire], the last line of "Hermaphrodite" in Marguerite Yourcenar, *Les Charités d'Alcippe* (Paris: Gallimard, 1984), 64.
5. Judith Butler, *Gender Trouble: Feminism and the Subversion of Identity* (New York: Routledge, 1990), 6.
6. Virginia Woolf, *Orlando: A Biography* (New York: Penguin, 1946), 120, 99. Underscoring mine.

7. Marguerite Yourcenar, *Les Yeux ouverts*, "Le Livre de poche" (Paris: Ed. du Ceinturion, 1980), 272. Translated as *With Open Eyes: Conversations with Matthieu Galey, 1980* (Boston: Beacon Press, 1984), 227.

8. Marguerite Yourcenar, *Un Homme obscur* (Paris: Gallimard, 1985), 170. Translated as "An Obscure Man" in *Two Lives and a Dream* (New York: Farrar, Straus and Giroux, 1987), 117.

9. Marguerite Yourcenar, "Sappho ou le suicide" in *Feux* (Paris: Gallimard, 1957), 195. Translated as "Sappho or Suicide" in *Fires*, 1936 (Chicago: University of Chicago Press, 1994), 115.

10. Marguerite Yourcenar, *La Couronne et la lyre* (Paris: Gallimard, 1979), 77. Yourcenar lists feminine traits in Sappho such as delicacy in the expression of love, nervousness in the confession of jealousy, a nearly conventional sense of propriety, a taste for perfumes, oils, beautiful clothes, etc.

11. Quoted by Judith L. Johnson, "Marguerite Yourcenar's Sexual Politics in Fiction, 1939" in *Faith of a (Woman) Writer*, eds. Alice Kessler-Harris and William McBrien. *Contributions in Women's Studies* 86 (1988): 225.

12. I refer here to the article by Georgia Hooks Shurr, "The Male Voice in *Le Coup de grâce*" in *A Reader's Guide* (Lanham: University Press of America, 1987), 47–55. I refer also to the article by Elaine Marks, "Getting Away with Murd(h)er, Author's Preface and Narrator's Text. Reading Marguerite Yourcenar's *Coup de grâce* 'After Auschwitz,'" *Journal of Narrative Technique* (spring 1990): 210–20. The author studies, among other things, the danger that the feminine poses for Eric. She does a reading of sadism, sexism, and anti-Semitism in the text, but unfortunately she ends by equating facilely and without textual authority M. Yourcenar and the novel's protofascist narrator-character Eric, which is most regrettable. Moreover, this essay fails in its study of Sophie's resistance to Eric's monolithic discourse. Mieke Bal, in her study of the narratology in *La Chatte* by Colette, rightly said that the one who focuses the text, the one who sees, influences the judgment of the reader who thinks by means of the one who provides focus, which is the case of Eric in *Le Coup de grâce*. In my opinion, Judith L. Johnston's article, "Marguerite Yourcenar's Sexual Politics in Fiction," 221–28, is a more judicious study of the complexity of Yourcenar's text as well as of the energy emanating from the triangle of characters. She demonstrates that the first-person narrative, confession by a dominant voice, stimulates the reader to respond actively by generating an alternative to passive acceptance of authoritarian violence.

13. Judith Butler, *Bodies that Matter: On the Discursive Limits of "Sex"* (New York: Routledge, 1993), 99.

14. *Quoi? L'Eternité*, 186.

15. See "Ton et langage dans le roman historique" in *Le Temps, ce grand sculpteur*, 37.

Death-defying Acts: Performing Gender in Marguerite Yourcenar's "Sappho ou le suicide"

Judith Holland Sarnecki

> Pain penetrates
> Me drop
> by drop
> —Sappho

IN 1936 WHEN HER SMALL BOOK OF PROSE POEMS *FEUX* (TRANSLATED AS *Fires*) was first published, Marguerite Yourcenar was thirty-three years old. She had purportedly composed the poems to assuage her suffering from an unrequited love. In her 1967 preface she attempted to explain this early text as one that can be read either as a collection of love poems or, if the reader prefers, as a series of lyric prose pieces linked by a particular notion of love: "Produit d'une crise passionnelle, *Feux* se présente comme un recueil de poèmes d'amour, ou, si l'on préfère, comme une série de proses lyriques reliées entre elles par une certaine notion de l'amour" (9). It is Yourcenar's description of her text, which speaks of "preference" and a "certain notion of love," that catches the eye. What is this notion of love that Yourcenar only hints at? Why should the reader be given an interpretive choice, and what has preference got to do with it? These are interesting prefatory remarks from an author who so closely controlled her literary production.

Josyane Savigneau, in her fascinating 1990 biography of Yourcenar, reveals the identity of the man who precipitated the emotional crisis that moved Yourcenar to adopt nine different male and female personae in *Feux* as the author's editor at the time, André Fraigneau, a homosexual male several years her junior.[1] Yourcenar's choice of prominent figures from Greek myth to represent lost love cleverly hides—in Poesque fashion—a series of bisexual plots that involve her various personae.[2] While each of the masks Yourcenar dons in *Feux* challenges the reader to search for glimpses of the very private woman behind the mask, in this essay I concentrate on the last adopted persona, the one who takes center stage in the concluding poem, "Sappho ou le suicide." In choosing Sappho, Yourcenar picked, I contend, her most revealing mask.

Why Sappho?

Then why Sappho? What is her relation to suicide and why does she provide Yourcenar with an ideal mask for her final performance in *Feux*? Both Mary Barnard, one of Sappho's translators, and Joan DeJean, author of *Fictions of Sappho, 1546-1937*, give us several good clues. In the commentary that follows her translation of Sappho's poetry, Barnard readily concedes that the real-life poet's biographical information is full of contradictions (96). In addition, most of Sappho's texts are simply fragments, probably recorded sometime after their original composition, which other scholars and translators have tried to fill in or flesh out. Resembling the structure of *Feux*—prose poems interspersed with random thoughts or sentences—Sappho's poetry (as well as her identity) remains fragmentary. Somewhat like the reclusive Yourcenar, Sappho is a woman about whom much has been written but little is actually known.[3] She may have been exiled to Syracuse, may have been married, may have had a child, may have been a prostitute, may have been both mentor and lover to a group of younger women, may have been rejected by Phaon, may have committed suicide after he abandoned her, or may have died at home in bed (96–97). When it comes to the real-life Sappho, the reader or researcher is put in the position of reading her life and work as either/or. Either she was a mother or she was a prostitute. Either she committed suicide over Phaon or she lived to a ripe old age. Either she was heterosexual or she was lesbian.

DeJean interprets Sappho somewhat differently: such deliberate ambiguity in her poetry, coupled with the little we know of her life, has allowed for the many fictions of Sappho that abound in both French literature and scholarship (8). DeJean uncovers what she considers the most complex and neglected aspects of Sappho's major odes, "the evasively undefinable internal signature and the calculated avoidance of stable erotic orientation" (17). DeJean also calls attention to Teresa de Lauretis's definition of Sappho as a writer who at one and the same time attempts to escape gender, deny it, transcend it, or perform it in excess (21).[4] DeJean notes "the polyphony of voices of sexual desire" that can be heard in Sappho's poetry, where the gender of the object of desire cannot always be determined (20).[5] But it is the virgin-whore dichotomy, DeJean contends, that enables another figure to emerge: the decadent, lesbian Sappho, "whose formation originates in the Racinian tragedies and Baudelairean poems of the mid-nineteenth century and who is still alive in Marguerite Yourcenar's 1936 collection *Feux*" (203).

Yourcenar's Sappho can certainly be read as "the decadent, lesbian Sappho," but I would suggest that she represents more, for she is also the bisexual Sappho who destabilizes the either/or, who keeps both identity and sexual orientation up in the air—a quality DeJean attributes to the real-life Sappho. Not surprisingly, Sappho does not appear in Yourcenar's version as either poet or writer, but as a down-at-the-heels circus performer whose artistry consists in acrobatic feats to delight and appease the hungry crowd of spectators who watch her from the safety of their earthbound seats. "Up in the air" turns out to be that liminal space where Yourcernar's circus Sappho performs her death-defying act—her marginalized, nomadic existence its perfect complement. A nomadic existence, in fact, was elected by the author of *Feux* and extolled in a posthumous work titled *En pèlerin et en étranger [As Pilgrim and Outsider]* published by Gallimard in 1989.[6] Furthermore, Sappho's position in *Feux* bears a striking resemblance to Baudelaire's albatros; both serve as metaphors for poets who are at home in the air (who can "fly" above the vulgar crowd with ease), but miserable on the ground (who cannot walk comfortably among their fellow creatures).[7]

> Créature aimantée, trop ailée pour le sol, trop charnelle pour le ciel, ses pieds frottés de cire ont rompu le pacte qui nous joint à la terre. (*Feux*, 195)
>
> [Magnetic creature, too winged for the ground, too fleshy for the sky, her feet rubbed with wax have broken the pact that joins us to the earth.][8]

It is not without purpose that Yourcenar chooses Sappho as an alter ego or concludes *Feux* with her own version of Sappho's story. The poem's title (like all eight others) contains an either/or option: Sappho *or* suicide. Does this intriguing title indicate that Sappho is to be identified with suicide, or is she the alternative choice? Might she represent both? Might Yourcenar's poetic performance include transforming the either/or configuration into a both/and: poetry *and* prose, Sappho *and* suicide, heterosexual *and* homosexual? I believe that Yourcenar's performance does, in part, accomplish that; in addition, I agree with Marjorie Garber's contention in *Vice Versa* that an illusory heterosexual/homosexual opposition occludes the very real possibility of bisexuality (the possibility of both/and). Sappho appears to function in *Feux* as Yourcenar's double, a metaphor for the author who performs (in writing) the acrobatics demanded by pre-scripted gender roles—roles that force us to hide forbidden proclivities and taboo desires, demanding that we be either/or. Considering the date of *Feux*'s composition and publication, both her Sappho's high-wire act and Yourcenar's poem are high-risk performances that presuppose our voyeuristic presence and demand our close attention.[9]

Poetry in Motion (or Literary Cross-dressing)

The unsettling first sentence of the poem "Sappho ou le suicide" links Sappho to the narrator and pairs love with death: "Je viens de voir au fond des miroirs d'une loge une femme qui s'appelle Sappho" [In the depths of the dressing room mirrors I have just seen a woman named Sappho] (193). The reader can imagine the narrator sitting or standing in front of a dressing room mirror (or mirrors) staring at the fragmented reflection of a woman who is both self and stranger. This uncanny doubling of the speaking subject recalls the famous Rimbaud line, "Je est un autre."[10] It also serves to distance the reader from the author, keeping the latter's identity in limbo in much the same way that Sappho distances herself from the crowd beneath her when she performs her trapeze act. Furthermore, the fixing of identities and identifications in "Sappho ou le suicide" is forestalled by the way the narrative has been framed. Although Sappho will continually be referred to in the third person, we know from the preface and the semiconfessional nature of *Feux* that she stands in for the invisible other woman poet, the one writing the text.

While Yourcenar wears the mask of Sappho in this prose poem, Sappho, the high-wire acrobat, is immediately linked to the twin ideas of masquerade and performance. Curiously, what the "Sappho mask" most resembles in the poem is a death mask. Without her stage makeup, Yourcenar's Sappho is as pale as death; with it, she resembles a murdered woman: "Et comme elle se farde pour cacher cette pâleur, elle a l'air du cadavre d'une femme assassinée, avec sur ses joues un peu de son propre sang" [And as she puts on her make-up to hide this pallor, she looks like the corpse of a murdered woman with a bit of her own blood smeared on her cheeks] (193). Thus the image of Sappho in the mirror is one of a woman already dead—a foreshadowing of the suicidal leap that occurs just prior to the poem's close. Such a suicide also suggests a "murder" committed by the spectators (with their exaggerated expectations) since the artist's livelihood, and hence her life, depend on their approval.

Yourcenar links Sappho's "lesbianism," referred to indirectly early in the text, to the dual notions of aging and degeneration, both of which correspond nicely to the decadent and dilapidated circus milieu (and recall DeJean's reading of Yourcenar's poem). Pulling from her head the white hairs that will soon be numerous enough to weave her own shroud, Sappho mourns her youth as she would a fickle female lover.[11] Yourcenar's Sappho is clearly not what she appears to be during her act (a young and athletic female); rather, her performance masks a less "desirable" woman. Aging rapidly and tired of the act she must continue to perform, Sappho turns to her circus trunks filled with fake pearls and disintegrating birds' feathers [perles fausses et de débris d'oiseaux] (194). Although she is exhausted by dragging herself from town to town, her finances and lifestyle force her to keep on the move. In circus parlance, "the show must go on." But what exactly is "the show"? A show of "normalcy"—of gender that perfectly matches sex—requiring a constant balancing act? A kind of mental and physical gymnastics in order to stay alive? Isn't Yourcenar's Sappho primarily tired of performing her female drag, a performance that requires high-risk maneuvers under society's ever-watchful eye?

In *Gender Trouble* and *Bodies that Matter*, Judith Butler suggests that all gender is performative, that gender does not necessarily follow from the body we inhabit. Yet there are certain prescribed behaviors for those of us defined as "women" in societies that pose male/female and masculine/feminine as opposites. But what if one is neither one nor the other? (What if either/or does not work for you or me?) Then where does one fall? Or does one simply remain up in the air, a misfit, miscreant, or circus "freak"? Butler's theories help us understand Sappho the acrobat's despair from the futility of trying to match her subjective experience to her public's expectations. According to Butler, "The Lacanian version of sex and sexual difference implicates his descriptions of anatomy and development in an unexamined framework of normative heterosexuality" (*Bodies*, 97). Such heterosexual positioning excludes and abjects lesbian and gay possibilities (96). Butler goes so far as to question "under what conditions and under the sway of what regulatory schemes does homosexuality itself appear as the living prospect of death?" (98)

Homosexuality represents a "living death" (the Sappho in the mirror) because in a society that accepts only either/or, it signals a subject position of abjection and imposed invisibility. In a Freudian or Lacanian schema, we identify with one sex and desire someone of the opposite sex. Butler would undo this either/or dilemma by reminding us that to identify with someone does not preclude—indeed, *it includes*—our desire for that person.

> Identification is a phantasmatic trajectory and resolution of desire; an assumption of place; a territorializing of an object which enables identity through the temporary resolution of desire, but which remains desire, if only in its repudiated form. (*Bodies*, 99)

For Butler, to assume a sex is a kind of identification, but it is also "a site at which prohibition and deflection are insistently negotiated" (100). The subject's position and sexual identity or identification are never stable entities—they are always being contested and renegotiated. Such fluidity is in and of itself destabilizing and menacing to the supposed "natural" order of things; hence it brings about the threat of punishment and the specter of abjection for those who fail to conform to societal norms (Lacan's Law of the Father) (101). This is the threat faced by Yourcenar's Sappho, forced night after night to repeat her performance.

Yet Butler rejects two overdetermined figures of abjection—"the feminized 'fag' and the phallicized 'dyke'"—because they "foreclose precisely the kind of complex crossings of identification and desire which might exceed and contest the binary frame itself" (103). In other words, such figures force us back into thinking in terms of either/or. Butler sees these figures as what the Lacanian symbolic produces "as its threatening outside to safeguard its continuing hegemony" (104).[12] Oppositional categories and stereotypical figures function as the glue that maintains the status quo, naturalizing what is, in fact, social phenomena.

This constant cultural reinscription requires us to be ever vigilant, to resist the urge to categorize strong, sexualized females as one of the stereotypical figures—the castrating female or Medusa of Greek mythology and Freudian psychoanalysis, for example. Butler includes the "phallic mother" and the "femme fatale" among such threatening figures—figures that can only be represented as destructive in a linguistic system that takes the male as its point of departure.[13] She speculates that "the failure to submit to castration appears capable of producing only its opposite, the spectral figure of the castrator with Holophernes' head in hand" (102). Thus, to attempt to fix the identity of Yourcenar's Sappho (perhaps as a mannish lesbian or butch dyke) is to miss the point, to deny the fluidity of both the subject's position and her desire.

"Sappho ou le suicide" challenges the figures of the "phallicized dyke" and the "femme fatale" by reproducing them in cross-sex configurations that defy boundaries of gender and desire. Yourcenar's Sappho can be categorized as neither mannish lesbian nor femme fatale; for if and when she embodies these traditional figures, she does so in a different and impermanent way. Not convincing as a woman, neither is she a man: "on lui trouve l'air d'être déguisée en femme" [She has the look of being disguised as a woman] (*Feux*, 195). A seducer of women, Yourcenar's Sappho secretly longs for a more passive role. While she is not attracted to what many females perceive as "masculine" attributes, she is attracted to certain men. Tired of playing the male role with her female lovers, she despairs of finding a better one: "elle ouvre sur le vide la porte du desespoir, avec le geste d'un homme obligé par l'amour à vivre chez les poupées" [She opens the door of despair onto the void with the gesture of a man obligated by love to live with dolls] (197). She bitterly adores in her female companions that which she is not; they offer her a glimpse of happiness she does not possess (198). Thus the poem's contorted sentences trace the path of Sappho's convoluted emotions, complicated desires, gender mergings, and crossings.

In Yourcenar's poem, Sappho's female lovers abandon her with such monotonous regularity that she comes to expect this as the inevitable outcome of her personal relationships. Yet Attys, one of a long series of companions, feels irreplacable, perhaps because this melancholy waif mirrors a loss of innocence and a troubled childhood to which Sappho (or is it Yourcenar?) briefly alludes. In many ways, Attys functions as Sappho's double; her lips, like those of Sappho in her stage makeup, are reminiscent of a bloody wound—"ses lévres serrées, pâles comme la cicatrice d'une blessure" [her compressed lips, pale as the scar of a wound] (200).

Yet how can Attys be a double when Sappho already functions in this poem as the author's double? Where should we place this unsettling third entity? Subject positions constantly shift as the reader catches glimpses of multiple reflections—reflections of an author who has created a *mise en abyme*, a house of mirrors in which identity and desire remain mobile. But then Yourcenar's characters never fall into neat categories. Not only might one read Attys as Sappho's double or her lover, one can also discern how she functions as the child Sappho never had:

> A force de soigner cette enfant maladive, d'écarter de son chemin les hommes qui pourraient la tenter, le morne amour de Sappho prend à son insu une forme maternelle, comme si quinze années de voluptés stériles avaient abouti à lui faire cette enfant. (202)

> [As a result of constantly caring for this sickly child and keeping the men who might tempt her from her path, Sappho's dismal love takes on a maternal form, as if fifteen years of sterile sensual pleasure had ended up producing this child.]

But Attys only tolerates Sappho's love because she has been abandoned by the dashing Philippe. His all too conspicuous absence transforms their incestuous twosome into a spectral triangle of desire.

Love's Möbius Strip

One day Sappho returns to their modest apartment to find Attys gone. The telltale button from Philippe's blue jacket signals the predictable dénouement to Sappho's and Attys' affair, changing Attys from mournful waif to something of a *femme fatale*. For instance, when Sappho glances at the staircase leading to their apartment, she sees the stairway's spiral suddenly transformed into the rings of a snake: "la spirale de l'escalier ressemble soudain aux anneaux d'un serpent" (203). Attys is surprisingly transfigured as the Medusa, while her sudden disappearance changes Sappho from phallic woman to female victim. She stubbornly refuses to believe Attys' departure is final for fear of being unable to bear the loss (204).[14] With this new turn of events, Sappho begins desperately to crave someone to love her rather than someone to love. The triangle of Sappho, Attys, and Philippe shatters like a broken mirror, leaving a solitary Sappho to her nomadic existence, fragmented identity, and precarious performances.

Then the scene shifts abruptly: several years have passed and we find ourselves in the "Orient," where exoticism reigns and anything can happen (15). Sappho learns that Philippe has also been moved to the East and has married a rich and imposing woman; the now abandoned Attys has been spotted nearby in a tawdry dance troupe. In haste, Sappho launches an all-out search for her lost love, but is unable to find her. Ultimately Sappho's search takes her to Istanbul, where chance places her each evening beside an unhappy-looking young man named Phaon. Coincidentally, he has the same delicious foreign accent (half Greek, half British) as Attys. Sappho intuits that she and Phaon are alike—the narrator tells us that only a provisionary and precarious permission granted by their fellow beings allows people of their ilk to exist [une race menacée, à qui une indulgence précaire et toujours provisoire permet de rester en vie] (206).[15] Both Phaon's hybrid accent and his threatened "type" would suggest that he, like Sappho, is someone whose sexual desires and identities do not fit the norm. We are told, in fact, that he is a fake [il est fraudeur], and does not need to confide in Sappho in order to establish between them a "brotherhood" of misfortune (206–7). They are alike, but are they doubles? Not for the moment, as Sappho clearly perceives Phaon to be a "man," an object normally outside the range of her desire. Although his presence allows her to feel more like a "woman," these subject positions (man and woman) turn out to be as precarious as Sappho's high-wire act.

When Sappho relates her painful story to Phaon, he immediately volunteers to help her find the lost Attys. But during the journey itself, in the movement that takes them from one run-down port café to another, desire begins to vacillate like the lantern in the bow of their small boat on the Bosphorus. "Assise à la poupe, Sappho regarde vaciller à la lueur d'une lanterne ce beau visage de jeune mâle qui est maintenant son seul soleil humain" [Sitting in the stern, Sappho watches in the lantern's glow the swaying of this beautiful young male's face, which has become her only human sun] (207). Little by little and to her own amazement, Sappho comes to desire Phaon's more rigid male body, where just enough feminine softness remains to allow her to fall in love with him (208). Clearly we are into the creation of a new love triangle (Sappho, Attys, and Phaon) and a second bisexual plot. Whereas it was once Attys who preferred a more masculine body, it is now Sappho. Imagery of male sexuality appears for the first time in a poem that seemed to concern itself primarily with lesbian desire. "Couchée au fond de la barque, elle s'abandonne aux pulsations nouvelles du flot que fend ce passeur" [Stretched out in the back of the boat, she abandons herself to the pulsations, new to her, of the waves parted by this ferryman] (208).

Later, when a letter arrives from the long-lost Attys, Sappho tears it up in Phaon's presence. For his part, he consents to spend Sappho's last evening in Istanbul in her small seaside apartment.

For a brief moment, sex and gender coalesce for Sappho as she feels herself for once entirely a woman:[16]

> Cette femme qui jusqu'ici prenait sur elle le choix, l'offre, la séduction, la protection de ses amies plus frêles, se détend et sombre enfin, mollement abandonnée au poids de son propre sexe et de son propre coeur, heureuse de n'avoir plus à faire désormais auprès d'un amant que le geste d'accepter. (210)

> [This woman who until now took upon herself the choice, the offer, the seduction, and the protection of her frailer friends, finally relaxes and lets herself go, languorously giving in to the weight of her female sex and her heart—happy from this point forward to have only to accept a lover's advances.]

Yet her happiness is short-lived, for Phaon, after roaming aimlessly about her bedroom, finally emerges dressed in one of Attys' discarded peignoirs. His sudden, unexpected appearance as Attys' double signals the end of the illusion of his manliness as well as Sappho's own self-identification as "entirely a woman." "Ce corps flexible et lisse est presque un corps de femme" [This supple, smooth body (Phaon's) is almost the body of a woman] (211).

At this point the new love triangle collapses; the cross-dressed Phaon appears to Sappho as nothing more than a poor substitute for the missing girl. But the real "travesty" here lies not in Phaon's cross-dressing, but rather in the deception of sexual difference and sexual identity. As the already elusive boundaries between "man" and "woman" begin to evaporate before her very eyes, Sappho returns to the circus, determined to end her (gender) performance once and for all. She will dive from the highest platform to a place where no net awaits her. Tired of being "half a woman," Sappho sees suicide as the only answer to the conundrum of longing, lack, and loss:

> Elle se hisse d'un coup de rein sur le seul point d'appui auquel consente son amour du suicide: la barre du trapèze balancée en plein vide change en oiseau cet être fatigué de n'être qu'à demi femme. (213)

> [She hoists her hips onto the only support her love of suicide allows: the trapeze bar balanced in midair makes a bird of this creature tired of being only half woman.]

Yourcenar the poet, however, has prepared another surprise for her readers. Although Sappho does take the plunge, her arms open as if to embrace half of infinity, she misses the mark and falls against a blue floodlight, which bears a striking resemblance to a jellyfish [une grosse méduse bleue] (215).[17] Linked metonymically to the legendary Medusa, Sappho returns as a femme fatale (or perhaps a demifemme fatale), taking the word "fatal" literally. Yet "fatality" in this poem has as much to do with destiny as with death. The narrator tells us that those who somehow miss the mark in life run the risk of failing at suicide; however, she does not instruct us how to read this enigmatic statement.[18]

What conclusion can be drawn from Sappho's suicidal leap and unpredictable landing? Is she reborn, this statue fished back from the depths of the sky [cette statue repêchée des profondeurs du ciel] or does she remain an abject "freak of nature" (216)? Does her rebound into the safety net mean a return to a repetitious and fake gender performance, or does it signal an acceptance of a more hybrid existence and fluid (bi)sexual identity? Furthermore, does the unsuccessful suicide attempt symbolize Sappho's failed gender performance or her rejection of the heterosexual plot? As Sappho's pale marble body emerges dripping sweat like a drowning victim drips seawater, the reader is left to wrestle with Yourcenar's intentional lack of closure and her refusal to answer the many questions the text poses. At this point "Sappho or suicide" seems to become "Sappho" by default rather than by choice. But Yourcenar has not finished toying with her readers.

Putting an End to Performance?

Gender performance as aerial acrobatics is not the only act going on in "Sappho ou le suicide." Yourcenar also uses performance in this poem as a metaphor for the act of writing itself. Writing becomes the performative vehicle by which the author attempts to transcend both the fate of her characters and her socially defined gender. Beginning her long writing career early in the twentieth century, Yourcenar was not unaware of the nineteenth-century invention of the category of "homosexual" and its concomitant medicalization—what Foucault refers to as "the opening up of the great medico-psychological domain of the 'perversions,' which was destined to take over from the old moral categories of debauchery and excess" (*History of Sexuality*, 118). Still cognizant of older stereotypes, Yourcenar also wrestled with the more recent categories that came into being with Freudian psychoanalysis. But does she buy into those stereotypes or work against them? At times she appears to accept the definition of "homosexuality" as "perversion" and "illness," at others she pushes on the boundaries that such terms impose on the bodies that are subjected to them. As she struggles with language that categorizes human beings and limits the ways we configure bodies, Yourcenar appears paradoxically to be both behind and ahead of her time.

Yet phrasing our questions in an either/or mode only serves to muddy the waters and preserve binary thinking. What if we return to the idea that Yourcenar's poetics may embody a different (a both/and) mentality? Then Sappho's aborted suicide might signal both the failure to perform an enforced gender code and the personal rejection of that code. In such a scenario Yourcenar's "fires" would burn up the heterosexist rulebook, lighting up subversive desires and transgressive passions couched in eloquent, classical prose—a virtuoso performance in which sexuality is a narrative rather than an identity (Marjory Garber's definition).

The mask of Sappho that Youcenar dons in *Feux*'s final "fire" both conceals and reveals personal suffering and the belief in its possible transcendance through art. Sappho's failed suicide ultimately confirms the author's rejection of a premature death as well as her belief in writing as a way to recreate oneself. In the closing sentences of *Feux* (that immediately follow "Sappho ou le suicide"), Yourcenar, returning to her first person narrative, writes that she will not kill herself; the dead are too quickly forgotten: "Je ne me tuerai pas. On oublie si vite les morts" (217). She affirms that her own personal happiness will have to be constructed on a foundation of despair.[19] By *Feux*'s open-ended conclusion, Yourcenar appears to have arrived at a new sense of self-acceptance, one that goes beyond societal censorship and a limited binary view of sexuality as she claims full responsibility for her life: "Qu'on n'accuse personne de ma vie" (217).

Are we, however, to swallow whole the authorial voice that speaks in *Feux*'s introduction and interstices? Is this subject who writes "I" simply another mask that the author dons to tantalize and torment her readers? I would contend that behind the brave voice that so stoically rejects suicide, the reader of "Sappho ou le suicide" has momentarily glimpsed a woman who, having withstood the pain of rejection, failure, and abandonment, feels older than her years. Although in *Feux* the narrator finally rejects suicide as a possible escape from a melancholy existence, Yourcenar the author continued to be haunted and tempted by it until her death from natural causes in 1987. "Sappho or suicide" is perhaps Sappho *and* suicide after all.

Notes

Based on a paper given at the Midwest Modern Language Association in 1997.

1. See Josyane Savigneau's *Marguerite Yourcenar: L'invention d'une vie* (Paris: Gallimard, 1990).
2. I am indebted to Marjorie Garber's *Vice Versa: Bisexuality and the Eroticism of Everyday Life* for the notion of "bisexual plots."
3. When Yourcenar left her private papers to the Houghton Manuscript Library she stipulated that her private journal not be made available to the public until fifty years after her death.
4. DeJean quotes from De Lauretis's article "Sexual Indifference and Lesbian Representation" published in *Theatre Journal* 40 (May 1988): 159.
5. John J. Winkler writes of a "double consciousness in Sappho's lyrics" that is of necessity both public and private, noting, for example, one poem's "many-mindedness."
6. This work has not yet been translated into English, but the word "étranger" immediately recalls Camus' *L'Etranger* (literally "the foreigner," but translated as *The Stranger*); Meursault was estranged, an alien in French society.
7. See Baudelaire's *Les fleurs du mal*, "L'Albatros."
8. All translations from *Feux* are my own. For the translation produced in collaboration with the author, see *Fires*, trans. Dori Katz (New York: Farrar, Straus and Giroux, 1981).
9. I am grateful to students in my class on "L'amour fatal" for their insights into this poem and their willingness to discuss and debate various interpretations.
10. See the Pléiade edition of Rimbaud's *Oeuvres complètes*.
11. Sappho "pleure sa jeunesse comme une femme qui l'aurait trahie" (*Feux*, 194).
12. The marginalized world of the circus performer could readily symbolize this threatening "outside."
13. Salome also instantly comes to mind. See Mary Ann Doane's discussion of the emergence of the femme fatale as a central figure in the nineteenth century in *Femmes Fatales: Feminism, Film Theory, Psychoanalysis*.
14. One could argue that Sappho is a "femme fatale" in either position, but this would require an expansion of the meaning of the expression so that it could encompass both a phallic woman and woman as victim.
15. Written at the height of French colonial power, *Feux*'s nebulous "Orient" provides the perfect backdrop for the bizarre events to follow. See Edward W. Said's *Culture and Imperialism* (New York: Vintage Books, 1994) for an expansion of the thesis he originally developed in *Orientalism* (1978).
16. This allusion is reminiscent of the treatment of homosexuals in society at large, and in what was yet to come: the Nazi death camps. In her texts Yourcenar frequently alludes in a roundabout way to persons who were forced to remain invisible due to their sexual orientation.
17. The French word "méduse" refers to both "jellyfish" and the legendary Greek Gorgon, that femme fatale whose visage and serpentine hair turned men to stone with a single look. In Yourcenar's description the "méduse" is large and blue like its counterpart, the circus floodlight.
18. "Mais ceux qui manquent leur vie courent aussi le risque de rater leur suicide" (*Feux*, 215).
19. "On ne bâtit un bonheur que sur un fondement de désespoir. Je crois que je

vais pouvoir me mettre à construire" [One only builds happiness from a foundation of despair. I believe that I am going to be able to begin construction] (*Feux*, 217). Whether the author means despair at society's militant heterosexism or despair over unrequited love is not clear. Once again, perhaps *both/and* is more appropriate.

Bibliography

Alesch, Jeanine. "Le cours des devises in Marguerite Yourcenar's *Mémoires d'Hadrien*." *French Review* 72, 5 (April 1999): 877–85.

Allamand, Carole. "Yourcenar et Gide: paternité ou parricide?" *Bulletin de la Société Internationale d'Etudes Yourcenariennes* 18: 19–38. Université de Tours: déc 1997.

Altbach, Edith H. "The New German Women's Movement." In *German Feminism: Readings in Politics and Literature*, edited by Edith H. Altbach, 3–26. Albany: State University of New York, 1984.

Andersson, Kajsa. *Le "Don sombre": Le thème de la mort dans quatre romans de Marguerite Yourcenar*. Uppsala, Sweden: Acta Universitatis Upsaliensis, 1989.

Balzac, Honoré de. *La comédie humaine I et II*. Paris: Seuil, 1965.

Barnard, Mary. *Sappho: A New Translation*. Berkeley and Los Angeles: University of California Press, 1958.

Barney, Natalie Clifford. *Pensées d'une Amazone. Les Sexes adverses, la guerre et le féminisme. Choses de l'Amour. Pages prises au roman que je n'écrirai pas. Autres éparpillements*. Paris: Émile-Paul Frères, éditeurs, 1921.

Barthes, Roland. "La mort de l'auteur." *Le bruissement de la langue*, 61–67. Paris: Seuil, 1984.

———. *Le plaisir du texte*. Paris: Seuil "Points," 1973.

Baudelaire. "L'Albatros." *Les fleurs du mal*. Paris: Garnier frères, 1961.

Benjamin, Walter. *Illuminations*. Translated by Harry Zohn. New York: Schocken, 1969.

Benoit, Claude. "De l'image du moi à l'image du monde." In *Ensayos de literatura europea e hispanoamericana*, edited by Félix Menchacatorre, 39–46. San Sebástian: Universidad del País Vasco, 1990.

———. "Le Personnage yourcenarien: De l'individuel à l'universel." In *L'Universalité dans l'oeuvre de Marguerite Yourcenar*, edited by María José Vázquez de Parga and Rémy Poignault, 61–70. Tours: Société internationale d'études yourcenariennes, 1994.

Benstock, Shari. *Women of the Left Bank: Paris, 1900-1940*. Austin: University of Texas Press, 1987.

Berger, Michèle. "Histoire et roman: Comment s'en défaire?" In *Roman, histoire et mythe dans l'oeuvre de Marguerite Yourcenar*. Edited by Simone Delcroix and Maurice Delcroix, 29–37. Tours: Société internationale d'études yourcenariennes, 1995.

Bernier, Yvon. "Genèse et fortune littéraire des *Mémoires d'Hadrien*." *Revue de l'Université de Bruxelles* (1988): 3–4.

Biondi, Carminella. *Marguerite Yourcenar ou la quête de perfectionnement.* Pisa: Editrice Libreria Goliardica, 1997.

Blot, Jean. *Marguerite Yourcenar.* Paris: Seghers, 1971.

Bonali-Fiquet, Françoise. "Du 'je' à 'l'autre' dans *Le labyrinthe du monde.*" *L'Universalité dans l'oeuvre de Marguerite Yourcenar* 2: 93–106. Tours: Société internationale d'études yourcenariennes, 1995.

———. "Choix bibliographique 1997." *Bulletin de la Société Internationale d'Etudes Yourcenariennes* 18: 167–76 . Université de Tours: déc 1997.

———. "Choix bibliographique 1998." *Bulletin de la Société Internationale d'Etudes Yourcenariennes* 19: 173–81. Université de Tours: déc 1998.

———. "Choix bibliographique 2000." *Bulletin de la Société Internationale d'Etudes Yourcenariennes* 21: 209–17. Université de Tours: déc 2000.

———. "Choix bibliographique 2001." *Bulletin de la Société Internationale d'Etudes Yourcenariennes* 22: 227–34. Université de Tours: déc 2001.

———. Réception de l'oeuvre de Marguerite Yourcenar (1922–94). Tours: Société internationale d'études yourcenariennes, 1995.

Bonali-Fiquet, and E. Restori. "Choix bibliographique 1995–96." *Bulletin de la Société Internationale d'Etudes Yourcenariennes* 17: 155–71. Université de Tours: déc 1996.

Boone, Joseph, and Michael Cadden. *Engendering Men: The Question of Male Feminist Criticism.* New York: Routledge, 1990.

Bots, W. J. A. "L'Histoire: Prétexte au roman yourcenarien de l'universel." In *Roman, histoire et mythe dans l'oeuvre de Marguerite Yourcenar*, edited by Simone Delcroix and Maurice Delcroix, 71–79. Tours: Société internationale d'études yourcenariennes, 1995.

Bourdet, Denise. "Marguerite Yourcenar." *Revue de Paris* 59 (April 1952): 125–28.

Boussuges, Madeleine. *Marguerite Yourcenar: sagesse et mystique.* Grenoble: Cahiers de l'Alpe, 1987.

Braidotti, Rosi. *Patterns of Dissonance: A Study of Women in Contemporary Philosophy.* Cambridge: Polity Press, 1991.

Bridenthal, Renate, et al., eds. *When Biology Became Destiny: Women in Weimar and Nazi Germany.* New York: Monthly Review Press, 1984.

Brignoli, Laura. "Les *Mémoires d'Hadrien* entre mythologie et 'mythopoiesis'." In *Roman, histoire et mythe dans l'oeuvre de Marguerite Yourcenar*, edited by Simone Delcroix and Maurice Delcroix, 81–91. Tours: Société internationale d'études yourcenariennes, 1995.

Bulletins du CIDMY. http://users.skynet.be/yourcenar/cidmy.publications.html (April 8, 2003).

Butler, Judith. *Bodies that Matter: On the Discursive Limits of "Sex."* New York: Routledge, 1993.

———. *Gender Trouble: Feminism and the Subversion of Identity.* New York: Routledge, 1990.

Carlier, Christophe. "Une oeuvre à la première personne." In *Analyses et réflexions sur Marguerite Yourcenar* Mémoires d'Hadrien: *L'écriture de soi*, edited by Maryse Adam-Maillet, et al., 98–102. Paris: Ellipses, 1996.

Carlston, Erin G. *Thinking Fascism: Sapphic Modernism and Fascist Modernity.* Stanford: Stanford University Press, 1998.

Céline, Louis-Ferdinand. *D'un château l'autre*. Paris: Gallimard, 1957.
Centre International de Documentation Marguerite Yourcenar. http://www.users.skynet.be/yourcenar (April 8, 2003).
Chaillot, Nicole. "Marguerite Yourcenar." *Femmes et littérature: George Sand, Colette, Marguerite Yourcenar*. Romorantin, France: Editions Martinsart, 1980.
Cixous, Hélène. "Entretien" avec F. van Rossum-Guyon. *RSH* 168 (1977): 479–93.
———. "Le rire de la méduse." *L'Arc* 61 (1975): 39–54.
———. "Le sexe ou la tête?" *Les Cahiers du GRIF* 13 (1976): 5–15.
———. *Ou l'art de l'innocence*. Paris: des femmes, 1981.
———. *Three Steps on the Ladder of Writing*. New York: Columbia University Press, 1993.
Clément, Catherine. "L'androgynie imaginaire de Marguerite Yourcenar." *Magazine Littéraire* 153 (1979): 19–21.
Clément, Catherine, and Hélène Cixous. *La Jeune née*. Paris: Union Générale d'Editions, 1975.
Corbin, Laurie Lynette. "The Daughter's Authorization: Colette, Simone de Beauvoir, Marguerite Duras." Ph.D. diss., University of Wisconsin-Madison, 1993.
Counihan, Francesca. *L'autorité dans l'oeuvre romanesque de Marguerite Yourcenar*. Villeneuve d'Ascq: Presse universitaires du Septentrion, 2000.
Debreuille, Jean-Yves. "Le Voyageur et l'empereur: Parcours spatiaux et parcours temporels dans les *Mémoires d'Hadrien*." In *Voyage et connaissance dans l'oeuvre de Marguerite Yourcenar*, edited by Carminella Biondi and Corrado Rossi, 61–75. Pisa: Goliardica, 1988.
De Feyter, Patricia. "Nathanaël ou la désinvolture." *Bulletin de la Société Internationale d'Etudes Yourcenariennes* 13 (1993): 22, 71–80.
DeJean, Joan. *Fictions of Sappho, 1546-1937*. Chicago: University of Chicago Press, 1989.
Delany, Samuel R. *The Motion of Light in Water: Sex and Science Fiction Writing in the East Village, 1957-1965*. New York: William Morrow, 1988.
Delcourt, Marie. *Hermaphrodite: Mythes et Rites de la bisexualité dans l'antiquité classique,* 9–10. Paris: Presses Universitaires de France, l958: 9–10.
Delcroix, Maurice. "Illuminations." *Bulletin de la Société Internationale d'Etudes Yourcenariennes* 17: 143–54. Université de Tours: déc 1996.
———. "Notes et connotations. Les Carnets de l'Oeuvre au noir." In *Marguerite Yourcenar. Aux frontières du texte*, edited by A.-Y. Julien, 43–52. Paris: Roman 20–50, 1995.
———. "Un entretien inédit de Marguerite Yourcenar." *Bulletin de la Société Internationale d'Etudes Yourcenariennes* 19: 17–48. Université de Tours: déc 1998.
Deleuze, Gilles, and Félix Guattari. *Anti-Oedipus: Capitalism and Schizophrenia*. Translated by Robert Hurley, Mark Seem, and Helen Lane. Minneapolis: University of Minnesota Press, 1983.
———. *A Thousand Plateaus*. Translated by Brian Massumi. Minneapolis: University of Minnesota Press, 1987.
Deleuze, Gilles, and Claire Parnet. *Dialogues*. Paris: Flammarion, 1977.
De Man, Paul. "Autobiography as De-facement." *Modern Language Notes* 94 (1979): 919–30.

———. *Wartime Journalism, 1939-1943*. Edited by Werner Hamacher, et al. Lincoln: University of Nebraska Press, 1988.

Demedeiros, Ana Maria. *Les Visages de l'Autre: Alibis, Masques et Identités dans* Alexis ou le Traité du vain combat, Denier du rêve *et* Mémoires d'Hadrien. New York: Peter Lang, 1996.

Dementi, Margit. "Luminous Obscurity: Marguerite Yourcenar and the Academy." *Critical Matrix* 10, nos. 1–2 (fall 1996): 3–30.

Deprez, Bérengère. "L'Elargissement de la perspective dans *Mémoires d'Hadrien*." In *L'Universalité dans l'oeuvre de Marguerite Yourcenar*, edited by María José Vázquez de Parga and Rémy Poignault, 187–98. Tours: Société internationale d'études yourcenariennes, 1995.

———. "Surhomme hadrianique et Surhomme nietzschéen: Un Pari sur l'inhumain." *Lettres Romanes* 47, no. 3 (August 1993): 177–84.

Derrida, Jacques. "Hors livre." *La Dissémination*, 9–67. Paris: Seuil, 1972.

———. "Outwork." *Dissemination*. Translated by Barbara Johnson, 7. Chicago: University of Chicago Press, 1981.

Desmers, Jeanne. "La Mort, contrainte suprême de *Mémoires d'Hadrien*." In *Les Visages de la mort dans l'oeuvre de Marguerite Yourcenar*. Edited by C. Frederick Farrell, Jr., et al., 56–65. Morris: University of Minnesota Press, 1993.

Dezon-Jones, Elyane, and Rémy Poignault. *Mémoires d'Hadrien, Marguerite Yourcenar: des repères pour situer l'auteur, ses écrits, l'oeuvre étudiée: une analyse de l'oeuvre sous forme de résumés et de commentaires: une synthèse littéraire thématique: des jugements critiques, des sujets de travaux, une bibliographie*. Paris: Nathan, 1996.

Dinnerstein, Dorothy. *The Mermaid and the Minotaur: Sexual Arrangements and Human Malaise*. New York: Harper, 1976.

Doane, Mary Ann. *Femmes Fatales: Feminism, Film Theory, Psychoanalysis*. New York: Routledge, 1991.

Doré, Pascale. "Affinités helléniques: L'Eros au masculin dans *Le Coup de grâce* et *Mémoires d'Hadrien*." *Bulletin de la Société Internationale d'Etudes Yourcenariennes* 20 (1999): 85–98.

———. *Yourcenar ou le féminin insoutenable*. Geneva: Droz, 1999.

Ecksteins, Modris. *Rites of Spring*. New York: Anchor Books, 1990.

Fackenheim, Emil. *To Mend the World: Foundations of Post-Holocaust Jewish Thought*. New York: Schocken, 1982.

Farias, Victor. *Heidegger and Nazism*. Edited by Joseph Margolis and Tom Rockmore. Philadelphia: Temple University Press, 1989.

Farrell, C. F., and E. R. Farrell. "Marguerite Yourcenar's *Feux*: Structure and Meaning." *Kentucky Romance Quarterly* 29 (1982): 25–35.

———. *Marguerite Yourcenar in Counterpoint*. Lanham, Md.: University Press of America, 1983.

Faverzani, Camillo, ed. *Marguerite Yourcenar et la Méditerranée*. Clermont-Ferrand: Centre de Recherches sur les Littératures Modernes et Contemporaines, 1995.

Felman, Shoshana. *La folie et la chose littéraire*. Paris: Seuil, 1978.

———. *Jacques Lacan and the Adventure of Insight: Psychoanalysis in Contemporary Culture*. Cambridge: Harvard University Press, 1987.

Felman, Shoshana, and Dori Laub, M.D. *Testimony: Crises of Witnessing in Literature, Psychoanalysis and History*. New York: Routledge, 1992.

Foucault, Michel. *The History of Sexuality Volume One: An Introduction*. Translated by Robert Hurley. New York: Vintage Books, 1990.

———. "Qu'est-ce qu'un auteur?" *Bulletin de la Société française de philosophie* LXIII. 3 (1969).

Freud, Sigmund. *Beyond the Pleasure Principle*. Translated by J. Strachey. New York: Liverwright Publishing, 1961.

———. *Civilization and Its Discontents*. Translated by J. Strachey. New York: W. W. Norton, 1962.

———. "Medusa's Head." *Standard Edition of the Complete Psychological Works of Sigmund Freud*. Vol. 28. Translated by James Strachey, 273–74. London: Hogarth, 1955.

———. "Question of Lay Analysis." *Standard Edition*. Vol. 20, 179–258 (1926).

———. "Three Essays on Sexuality." *Standard Edition*. Vol. 7. Translated by James Strachey. London: Hogarth Press, 1960.

Friedlander, Saul. *Reflections of Nazism: An Essay on Kitsch and Death*. Bloomington: Indiana University Press, 1993.

Gaillard, Françoise. "La modernité de Marguerite Yourcenar." *Equinoxe* 2 (1989): 11–18.

Galey, Matthieu. *Les Yeux ouverts: entretiens avec Marguerite Yourcenar*. Paris: Le Livre de Poche, 1980.

Garber, Marjorie. *Vice Versa: Bisexuality and the Eroticism of Everyday Life*. New York: Simon and Schuster, 1995.

Gardiner, Judith Kegan. "A Wake for Mother: The Maternal Deathbed in Women's Fiction." *Feminist Studies* 4, 2 (1978): 146–65.

Garner, S., C. Kahane, and M. Sprengnether. *The (M)other Tongue: Essays in Feminist Psychoanalytic Interpretation*. Ithaca: Cornell University Press, 1985.

Garréta, Anne F., and Josyane Savigneau. "'A Conversation.' Same Sex/Different Text? Gay and Lesbian Writing in French." *Yale French Studies* 90 (1996): 214–34.

Gaudin, Colette. "Hadrien 'rêveur des dieux'." *Bulletin de la Société Internationale d'Etudes Yourcenariennes* 17 (1996): 111–23.

———. *Marguerite Yourcenar à la surface du temps*. Amsterdam: Editions Rodopi BV, 1994.

———. "Préfaces: genèse de la fiction ou l'effacement du moi." *Marguerite Yourcenar: une écriture de la mémoire*. *Sud* (1990): 17–30.

———. "Yourcenar, écho d'outre-Atlantique." *Le Monde des Livres* 19, 12 (1997).

Gelas, Bruno. "Le traitement de la fiction dans les oeuvres romanesques." *Sud* (1990): 7–15.

Genette, Gérard. *Seuils*. Paris: Seuil "Poétique," 1987.

———. "Discours du récit." *Figures III*. Paris: Seuil, 1972.

Gill, Brian. "Marguerite Yourcenar, *Mémoires d'Hadrien* et la rhétorique." *L'Universalité dans l'oeuvre de Marguerite Yourcenar*. Edited by María José Vázquez de Parga and Rémy Poignault, 185–96. Tours: Société internationale d'études yourcenariennes, 1994.

———. "Narrateur et narrataire chez Yourcenar." *Marguerite Yourcenar: Ecriture, réécriture, traduction.* Edited by Rémy Poignault and Jean-Pierre Castellani, 121–32. Tours: Société internationale d'études yourcenariennes, 2000.

Goslar, Michèle. *Yourcenar. Biographie.* "*Qu'il eût été fade d'être heureux*". Brussels: Racine et Académie royale de langue et littérature françaises, 1998.

Guslevic, Caroline. *Étude sur Marguerite Yourcenar:* Mémoires d'Hadrien. Paris: Éllipses, 1999.

Hamacher, Werner, et al., eds. *Responses: On Paul de Man's Wartime Journalism.* Lincoln: University of Nebraska Press, 1989.

Hamzaoui, A. Fettah. "Du prétexte au pre-texte." *Bulletin de la Société Internationale d'Etudes Yourcenariennes* 13 (1994): 39–46.

Henriot, Emile. "Mémoires supposés d'un empereur romain." *Le Monde*, January 9, 1952, 7.

Hertz, Neil. "Medusa's Head: Male Hysteria under Political Pressure." *Representations* 4 (fall 1983): 27–54.

Hillenaar, Henk. "L'Oeuvre d'une femme forte." *Recherches sur l'oeuvre de Marguerite Yourcenar.* Edited by H. Hillenaar. CRIN 8 (1983): 1–31.

Hogsett, Charlotte. "Reading between the Books: Discontinuity in the Oeuvre of Marguerite Yourcenar." In *Discontinuity and Fragmentation*, edited by Freeman G. Henry, 137–47. Amsterdam: Rodopi, 1994.

———. "Scholarship and Vision in Marguerite Yourcenar's *Mémoires d'Hadrien*." *Classical and Modern Literature* 13.3 (spring 1993): 203–15.

Horkheimer, Max, and Theodor Adorno. *Dialectic of Enlightenment.* Translated by John Cumming. New York: Continuum, 1972.

Hörmann, Pauline. *La biographie comme genre littéraire:* Mémoires d'Hadrien de Marguerite Yourcenar. Amsterdam: Rodopi, 1996.

Horn, Pierre L. *Marguerite Yourcenar.* Boston: Twayne, 1985.

Howard, Joan E. *From Violence to Vision: Sacrifice in the Works of Marguerite Yourcenar.* Carbondale: Southern Illinois University Press, 1992.

Howard, Richard. "Yourcenar composed." *Salmagundi* 103 (summer 1994): 51–69.

Humphreys, S. C. *The Family, Women, and Death.* Ann Arbor: University of Michigan Press, 1993.

Hure, Jacques. "L'Histoire de l'Orient antique, à la charnière de la représentation romanesque d'Hadrien et du discours autobiographique." In *Roman, histoire et mythe dans l'oeuvre de Marguerite Yourcenar*, edited by Simone Delcroix and Maurice Delcroix, 251–58. Tours: Société internationale d'études yourcenariennes, 1995.

Irigaray, Luce. *Et l'une ne bouge pas sans l'autre.* Paris: Editions de minuit, 1979.

———. *Ce sexe qui n'en est pas un.* Paris: Editions de minuit, 1977.

———. *Le Corps-à-corps avec la mère.* Ottawa: Editions de la pleine lune, 1981.

———. *Je, tu, nous: Pour une culture de la différence.* Paris: Grasset, 1990.

———. *Je, tu, nous: Toward a Culture of Difference.* Translated by Alison Martin. New York: Routledge, 1993.

Jaccomard, Hélène. *Lecteur et lecture dans l'Autobiographie française contemporaine.* Geneva: Droz, 1993.

Jameson, Fredric. *Late Marxism: Adorno, or, the Persistence of the Dialectic*. London and New York: Verso, 1990.

Jardine, Alice A. *Gynesis: Configurations of Woman and Modernity*. Ithaca: Cornell University Press, 1985.

Jardine, Alice, and Paul Smith, eds. *Men in Feminism*. New York and London: Methuen, 1987.

Jeanmaire, H. *Couroi et Courètes: Essai sur l'éducation spartiate et les rites d'adolescence dans l'Antiquité hellénique*. Lille-Paris: Bibliothèque Universitaire, 1939.

Johnson, Barbara. *A World of Difference*. Baltimore: Johns Hopkins University Press, 1987.

Johnston, Judith L. "Marguerite Yourcenar's Sexual Politics in Fiction, 1939." In *Faith of a (Woman) Writer*, edited by Alice Kessler-Harris and William McBrien, 221–28. New York: Greenwood Press, 1988.

Julien, Anne-Yvonne. "Présentation." In *Marguerite Yourcenar. Aux frontières du texte*, edited by A.-Y. Julien, 9–13. Paris: Roman 20–50, 1995.

Jung, Carl J. *Psychology of the Unconscious*. Translated by B. M. Hinkle. New York: Dodd, Mead, 1961.

Kakridis, Johannes. *Homeric Researches*. Lund: CWK Gleerup, 1949.

Kaplan, Alice Y. "Theweleit and Spiegelman: Of Men and Mice." In *Remaking History*, edited by Barbara Kruger and Phil Mariani, 151–72. Seattle: Bay Press, 1989.

King, Katherine. *Achilles: Paradigms of the War Hero from Homer to the Middle Ages*. 131–33, 181–84. Los Angeles: University of California Press, 1987.

———. "Antigone's Lyric Heart: Marguerite Yourcenar's Revision of Sophokles' *Antigone*." In *Lyric Symbols and Narrative Transformations*, edited by K. L. Komar and R. P. Shideler, 64–80. Columbia, S.C.: Camden House, 1998.

———. "Marguerite Yourcenar's Greek Earth." *Journal of Modern Greek Studies* (fall 1997): 239–46.

Koonz, Claudia. *Mothers in the Fatherland*. New York: St. Martin's Press, 1987.

Kristeva, Julia. *Black Sun: Depression and Melancholia*. Translated by Leon S. Roudiez. New York: Columbia University Press, 1989.

———. *Pouvoirs de l'horreur*. Paris: Seuil, 1980.

———. "Le temps des femmes," *Cahiers de recherche de S.T.D.* 33/44. 5 (Université de Paris VII): 5–19.

Lacan, Jacques. *Le séminaire I: Les écrits techniques de Freud*. Paris: Seuil, 1975.

Lanser, Susan Sniader. "Sexing the Narrative: Propriety, Desire and the Engendering of Narratology." *Narrative* 3, 1 (1995): 85–94.

Ledesma, Manuela. "Plénitude temporelle et éthique dans *Mémoires d'Hadrien*." *Bulletin de la Société Internationale d'Etudes Yourcenariennes* 6 (1990): 81–94.

Lelong, Armelle. *Le parcours mythique de Marguerite Yourcenar*: de Feux à Nouvelles orientales. Paris: L'Harmattan, 2001.

Leontis, Artemis. "Surrealist Poetics of Identity and Andreas Embeirikos' Defense of Man." *Modern Greek Studies Yearbook* 6 (1990): 315–29.

———. *Tragic Ways of Killing a Woman*. Translated by A. Forster. Cambridge: Harvard University Press, 1987.

———. *L'invention d'Athènes: Histoire de l'oraison funèbre dans la cité classique*. Paris and New York: Mouton, 1981.

Leuwers, Daniel, and Jean-Pierre Castellani, eds. *Marguerite Yourcenar: Une écriture de la mémoire*. Sud Hors series. Saint-Etienne, France: mai 1990.

Loraux, Nicole. *Façons tragiques de tuer une femme*. Paris: Hachette, 1985.

Lovell, James. *Song: The Forge and the Flame; The Story of How the Afro-American Spiritual was Hammered Out*. New York: MacMillan, 1972.

Lukacher, Maryline. *Maternal Fictions: Stendhal, Sand, Rachilde, Bataille*. Durham and London: Duke University Press, 1994.

Lukács, Georg. *The Historical Novel*. Translated by Hannah and Stanley Mitchell. Lincoln: University of Nebraska Press, 1962.

Lydon, Mary. "Calling Yourself a Woman: Marguerite Yourcenar and Colette." *differences* 3, 3 (1991): 26–44.

Macciocchi, Maria-Antonietta. "Female Sexuality in Fascist Ideology." *Feminist Review* 1 (1979): 67–82.

Maindron, André. "De Julien à Hadrien: Roman, histoire (et mythe?) chez Stendhal et Yourcenar." In *Roman, histoire et mythe dans l'oeuvre de Marguerite Yourcenar*, edited by Simone Delcroix and Maurice Delcroix, 311–20. Tours: Société internationale d'études yourcenariennes, 1995.

———. "Hadrien entre Orient et Occident." In *Les Visages de la mort dans l'oeuvre de Marguerite Yourcenar*, edited by C. Frederick Farrell, Jr., et al, 25–33. Morris: University of Minnesota Press, 1993.

Manzoni, Alessandro. *On the Historical Novel*. Translated by Sandra Bermann. Lincoln: University of Nebraska Press, 1984.

Marks, Elaine. "'Getting Away with Murd(h)er': Author's Preface and Narrator's Text. Reading Marguerite Yourcenar's *Coup de grâce* 'After Auschwitz.'" *Journal of Narrative Technique* 20, 2 (1990): 210–20.

Marx, Karl, and Fredrick Engels. *Collected Works* Vol. 28. New York: International Publishers, 1986.

Mayer, Arno. *Politics and Diplomacy of Peacemaking*. New York: Vintage, 1969.

Medeiros, Ana. "L'Universalité dans *Mémoires d'Hadrien* à travers le style, le temps et l'espace." *L'Universalité dans l'oeuvre de Marguerite Yourcenar*. Edited by María José Vázquez de Parga and Rémy Poignault, 199–207. Tours: Société internationale d'études yourcenariennes, 1995.

———. *Les Visages de l'autre: Alibis, masques et identité dans* Alexis, ou, Le Traité du vain combat, Denier du rêve *et* Mémoires d'Hadrien. New York: Peter Lang, 1996.

Meitinger, Serge. "Le Voyage intérieur: Hadrien, Zénon, Nathanaël." In *Voyage et connaissance dans l'oeuvre de Marguerite Yourcenar*, edited by Carminella Biondi and Corrado Rossi, 155–67. Pisa: Goliardica, 1988.

Melzi D'Eril Kaucisvili, Francesca. *Dans le laboratoire de Marguerite Yourcenar*. Fasano/Paris: Schena/Presses de l'université de Paris-Sorbonne, 2001.

Messling, Markus. "La Fonction de la sculpture dans *Mémoires d'Hadrien* de Marguerite Yourcenar par rapport au *Temps, ce grand sculpteur*." *Bulletin de la Société Internationale d'Etudes Yourcenariennes* 21 (2000): 105–26.

Milne, Lorna. "(Fe)male Impersonation and Transcendence in Marguerite Yourcenar's *Mémoires d'Hadrien*." *Women in French Studies* 7 (1999): 209–18.

———. "The Power and Pitfalls of Mythical Vision: Ritual Structures in Marguerite Yourcenar's *Mémoires d'Hadrien*." *Orbis Litteratum: International Review of Literary Studies* 54, 5 (1999): 372–92.

Moi, Toril. *Sexual/Textual Politics: Feminist Literary Theory*. New York: Routledge, 1988.

Monsacré, Hélène. *Les larmes d'Achille: le héros, la femme et la souffrance dans la poésie d'Homère*. 63–77. Paris: Albin Michel, 1984.

Mouline, Lucette. "L'Ecriture et le pouvoir dans *Mémoires d'Hadrien*." In *Lectures transversales de Marguerite Yourcenar*, edited by Rémy Poignault and Blanca Arancibia, 187–200. Tours: Société internationale d'études yourcenariennes, 1997.

Murciaux, Christian. "D'Alexis à Hadrien." *La table ronde* 56 (August 1952): 144–48.

Nelson, Cary. "Envoys of Otherness: Difference and Continuity in Feminist Discourse." *For Alma Mater: Theory and Practice in Feminist Scholarship*. Champaign-Urbana: University of Illinois Press, 1985.

Ness, Béatrice. *Mystification et créativité dans l'oeuvre romanesque de Marguerite Yourcenar. Cinq lectures génétiques*. Chapel Hill: University of North Carolina Press, 1994.

Nietzsche, Friedrich. *Ecce Homo. Oeuvres II*. Paris: Robert Laffont, 1993.

O'Sickey, Ingeborg Majer. "Mystery Stories: The Speaking Subject in Exile." In *Women's Writing in Exile*, edited by M. L. Broe and A. Ingram, 369–94. Chapel Hill: University of North Carolina Press, 1989.

Owens, Craig. "Outlaws: Gay Men in Feminism." In Alice Jardine and Paul Smith, *Men in Feminism*, 219–32. London: Methuen, 1987.

Pacaly, Josette. "Les songes et les sorts. Préfaces et dossiers." In *Marguerite Yourcenar. Aux frontières du texte*, edited by A.-Y. Julien, 31–42. Paris: Roman 20–50, 1995.

Papadopoulos, Christiane. *L'Expression du temps dans l'oeuvre romanesque et autobiographique de Marguerite Yourcenar*. New York: Peter Lang, 1988.

Paquette, Jean-Marcel. "L'Autre genre: La forme de l'essai dans *Mémoires d'Hadrien*." *Bulletin de la Société Internationale d'Etudes Yourcenariennes* 18 (1997): 99–107.

Peyroux, Marthe. "*Mémoires d'Hadrien*: Le Hasard et l'histoire." *Francofonia* 22 (spring 1992): 101–10.

Picard, Charles. "L'Empereur Hadrien vous parle." *Revue Archéologique* 43 (January–March 1954): 83–85.

Poignault, Rémy. "Du soleil de Lambèse aux boues du Nil." In *Voyage et connaissance dans l'oeuvre de Marguerite Yourcenar*, edited by Carminella Biondi and Corrado Rossi, 195–206. Pisa: Goliardica, 1988.

———. *L'Antiquité dans l'oeuvre de Marguerite Yourcenar: Littérature, mythe et histoire*. Brussels: Latomus, Revue d'études latines, 1995.

———. "L'empire romain figure de l'universel dans *Mémoires d'Hadrien*." In *L'Universalité dans l'oeuvre de Marguerite Yourcenar*, edited by María José Vázquez de Parga and Rémy Poignault, 209–23. Tours: Société internationale d'études yourcenariennes, 1995.

———. "*L'Oratio togata* dans *Mémoires d'Hadrien*." In *Marguerite Yourcenar: Ecriture, réécriture, traduction*, edited by Rémy Poignault and Jean Pierre Castellani, 49–63. Tours: Société internationale d'études yourcenariennes, 2000.

———. "Hadrien chez Hécate." *Bulletin de la Société Internationale d'Etudes Yourcenariennes* 17 (1996): 125–41.

———. "Le Prince entre mythe et histoire." In *Roman, histoire et mythe dans l'oeuvre de Marguerite Yourcenar*, edited by Simone Delcroix and Maurice Delcroix, 363–77. Tours: Société internationale d'études yourcenariennes, 1995.

Pont, Carmen Anna. *Yeux ouverts, yeux fermés: la poétique du rêve dans l'oeuvre de Marguerite Yourcenar*. Amsterdam: Editions Rodopi BV, 1994.

Portmann, Tatjana. "*Mémoires d'Hadrien*: Roman historique?" *Bulletin de la Société Internationale d'Etudes Yourcenariennes* 22 (2001): 89–104.

Pratt, Annis. "The New Feminist Criticisms: Exploring the History of the New Space." In *Beyond Intellectual Sexism: A New Woman A New Reality*. New York: David McKay Co., Inc., 1976.

Proust, Simone. *L'autobiographie dans* Le Labyrinthe du Monde *de Marguerite Yourcenar*. Paris: L'Harmattan, 1997.

Real, Elena. "Les Grands romans de Marguerite Yourcenar: De *Mémoires d'Hadrien* à *Un Homme obscur*. In *Ensayos de literatura europea e hispanoamericana*, edited by Félix Menchacatorre, 411–20. San Sebástian: Universidad del Pais Vasco, 1990.

———. ed. *M. Yourcenar: Biographie et Autobiographie*. Valencia: Universidad de Valencia, 1988.

Reiss, Timothy J. "Introduction: Literature and the Idea of Europe." *PMLA* 108, 1 (January 1993): 14–29.

Renard, Paul. "Yourcenar, Spirituals, Gospels, Blues." Nord 5 (1985): 63–69.

Restori, Enrica. "Un Anthropomorphisme à rebours: De la voix humaine à la voix des choses." In *L'Universalité dans l'oeuvre de Marguerite Yourcenar*, edited by María José Vázquez de Parga and Rémy Poignault, 137–51. Tours: Société internationale d'études yourcenariennes, 1994.

Ricciulli, Paola. *Hadrien, ou, La vision du vide: Lectures yourcenariennes*. Rome: Bulzoni, 1999.

———. "Hadrien, ou la vision du vide." In *L'Universalité dans l'oeuvre de Marguerite Yourcenar*, edited by María José Vázquez de Parga and Rémy Poignault, 225–35. Tours: Société internationale d'études yourcenariennes, 1995.

Rich, Adrienne. "The Thieves of Language: Women Poets and Revisionist Mythmaking." *Signs* 8 (1982): 68–90.

Riffaterre, Michael. *Sémiotique de la poésie*. Paris: Seuil, 1982.

Rinaldi, Angelo. "Montherlant, soror . . ." *L'Express*, October 23, 1981.

Rosbo, Patrick de. *Entretiens radiophoniques avec Marguerite Yourcenar*. Paris: Mercure de France, 1972.

Ross, Andrew. "Containing Culture in the Cold War." *No Respect: Intellectuals and Popular Culture*, 42–64. New York: Routledge, 1989.

Rothberg, Michael. "After Adorno: Culture in the Wake of Catastrophe." *New German Critique* 72 (fall 1997): 45–81.

———. *After the "Final Solution": Traumatic Realism and Holocaust Representation*. Author's manuscript.

———. "Marxism after Post-Marxism." *Socialist Review* 92, 1 (1992): 113–20.
Rousseau, Jean-Jacques. *The Confessions*. Translated by Christopher Kelly. Hanover, N.H.: University Press of New England, 1995.
Rutledge, Harry C. "Marguerite Yourcenar: The Classicism of *Feux* and *Mémoires d'Hadrien*." *Classical and Modern Literature* 4, 2 (winter 1984): 87–99.
Said, Edward W. *Culture and Imperialism*. New York: Vintage Books, 1994.
———. *Orientalism*. New York: Vintage Books, 1979.
Sanz, Téofilo. "Carnets de notes des *Mémoires d'Hadrien* et de *L'Oeuvre au Noir*: Du factuel au fictionnel." In *Lectures transversales de Marguerite Yourcenar*, edited by Rémy Poignault and Blanca Arancibia, 55–63. Tours: Société internationale d'études yourcenariennes, 1997.
Sarde, Michèle. *Vous Marguerite Yourcenar. La passion et ses masques*. Paris: Robert Laffont, 1995.
Sargent, Bernard. *Homosexuality in Greek Myth*. Translated by A. Goldhammer. Boston: Beacon Press, 1986.
Sarnecki, Judith Holland. "When Our Gender is a Lie: Marguerite Yourcenar's 'Achille ou le mensonge.'" *Women in French Studies* (fall 1996): 80–87.
Savigneau, Josyane. *Marguerite Yourcenar: L'Invention d'une vie*. Paris: Gallimard, 1990.
———. *Marguerite Yourcenar: Inventing a Life*. Translated by Joan E. Howard. Chicago: University of Chicago Press, 1993.
Shurr, Georgia Hooks. *Marguerite Yourcenar: A Reader's Guide*. Lanham, Md.: University Press of America, 1987.
———. "Marguerite Yourcenar et 'drame noir' américain," *Bulletin du Centre International de Documentation Marguerite Yourcenar* 10 (1998): 27–57.
Spadaro, Donata. "Marguerite Yourcenar et l'écriture autobiographique." *Bulletin de la Société Internationale d'Etudes Yourcenariennes* 17: 69–84. Université de Tours: déc. 1996.
Sperti, Valeria. *Écriture et mémoire*: Le Labyrinthe du monde *de Marguerite Yourcenar*. Naples: Liguori, 1999.
Starobinski, Jean. "Pseudonymous Stendhal," *The Living Eye*. 82. Cambridge: Harvard University Press, 1989.
———. "Stendhal pseudonyme," *L'oeil vivant*. 197. Paris: Gallimard, 1961.
Stillman, Linda K. "Marguerite Yourcenar and the Phallacy of Indifference." *Studies in Twentieth Century Literature* 9, 2 (1985): 261–77.
Taat, Mieke. "La Bette à la lettre," *Balzac et "Les Parents pauvres."* Edited by F. van Rossum-Guyon. Paris: CDU/CEDES, 1981.
———. "Lire et délire: Marguerite Yourcenar." Edited by J.-P. Castellani et D. Leuwers, 165–75.
———. "Lire *L'Orestie* avec Marguerite Yourcenar." *La révolution dans les lettres*. Edited by H. Ritter and A. Schulte Nordholt, 303–16. Amsterdam: Rodopi, 1993.
Taleb-Khyar, M. B. "Poétiques de l'histoire: *Mémoires d'Hadrien* de Marguerite Yourcenar." *Revue Romane* 28, 1 (1993): 110–21.
Taylor, John. "Waiting for Hadrian." *Georgia Review* 42, 1 (spring 1988): 147–51.
Theweleit, Klaus. *Male Fantasies, Volume I: Women, Floods, Bodies, History*.

Translated by Stephen Conway. Minneapolis: University of Minnesota Press, 1987.

———. *Male Fantasies, Volume II: Male Bodies: Psychoanalyzing the White Terror*. Translated by Erica Carter and Chris Turner. Minneapolis: University of Minnesota Press, 1989.

Tournier, Michel. "Gustave et Marguerite." *Sud* 55 (1984): 68–77.

Trouvé, Alain. *Leçon littéraire sur* Mémoires d'Hadrien *de Marguerite Yourcenar*. Paris: Presses Universitaires de France, 1996.

Vicinus, Martha. "They Wonder to Which Sex I Belong." In *The Lesbian and Gay Studies Reader*, edited by Henry Abelove, Michèle Aina Barale, and David M. Halperin. New York: Routledge, 1993.

Vidal-Naquet, Pierre. *The Black Hunter: Forms of Thought and Forms of Society in the Greek World*. Translated by A. Szegedy-Maszak, 163–64. Baltimore: Johns Hopkins University Press, 1986.

Watson-Williams, Helen. "Hadrian's Story Recalled" *Nottingham French Studies* 23, 2 (October 1984): 35–48.

Whatley, Janet. "*Mémoires d'Hadrien*: A Manual for Princes." *University of Toronto Quarterly* 50 (1980–81): 221–37.

Whitman, Cedric. *Homer and the Heroic Tradition*. New York: Norton, 1965.

Winkler, John J. "Double Consciousness in Sappho's Lyrics." In *The Lesbian and Gay Studies Reader*. New York: Routledge, 1993.

Wright, C. M. T. "'Reading Between the Lines': A Study of *Alexis, Dernier du rêve, Coup de grâce,* and *Feux* by Marguerite Yourcenar." Ph.D. diss., University of Reading Press, 1987.

Wyss, Antoine. "Auteur, narrateur, personnage: Quelle historiographie pour *Mémoires d'Hadrien?*" In *Roman, histoire et mythe dans l'oeuvre de Marguerite Yourcenar*, edited by Simone Delcroix and Maurice Delcroix, 483–91. Tours: Société internationale d'études yourcenariennes, 1995.

Yourcenar, Marguerite. *Alexis ou le traité du vain combat* suivi de *Le Coup de grâce*. Paris: Gallimard, 1971.

———. "Carnets de notes de *L'oeuvre au noir*." *La nouvelle revue française* 452 (1990): 38–53.

———. *Coup de Grâce*. Translated by Grace Frick. New York: Farrar, Straus and Giroux, 1981.

———. *Le Coup de grâce*. Paris: Gallimard, 1939.

———. *Dear Departed*. Translated by Maria Louise Ascher. New York: Farrar, Straus and Giroux, 1991.

———. "Deux amours d'Achille." *Mercure de France* 263 (1935): 118–27.

———. *Discours de Réception à l'Académie Française*. Paris: Gallimard, 1989.

———. *En pèlerin et en étranger*. Paris: Gallimard, 1989.

———. *Essais et Mémoires*. Paris: Gallimard *Pléiade*, 1991.

———. *Feux*. Paris: Gallimard, 1974.

———. *Feux*. Paris: Grasset, 1935.

———. "Feux," *Revue de France* 4 (1935): 491–98.

———. *Fires*. Translated by Dori Katz. New York: Farrar, Straus and Giroux, 1981.

———. *Les songes et les sorts*. Paris: Grasset, 1938.

———. *Les yeux ouverts. Entretiens avec Matthieu Galey.* Paris: Centurion, 1980.

———. *Lettres à ses amis et quelques autres.* Edited by Michèle Sarde. Paris: Gallimard, 1995.

———. *Mémoires d'Hadrien.* Paris: Gallimard, 1974.

———. *Oeuvres romanesques.* Paris: Gallimard *Pléïade*, 1982.

———. *That Mighty Sculptor, Time.* Translated by Walter Kaiser. New York: Farrar, Straus and Giroux, 1992.

———. *Théâtre I.* Paris: Gallimard, 1971.

———. *Théâtre II.* Paris: Gallimard, 1971.

———. *With Open Eyes: Conversations with Matthieu Galey.* Translated by Arthur Goldhammer. Boston: Beacon Press, 1984.

Zeitlin, Froma. "Thebes: Theatre of Self and Society in Athenian Drama." *Greek Tragedy and Political Theory.* Edited by Peter Euben, 101–41. Berkeley and Los Angeles: University of California Press, 1986.

Žižek, Slavoj. *The Sublime Object of Ideology.* New York: Verso, 1989.

Zola, Emile. *Preface to Thérèse Raquin.* 6. Oxford: Oxford University Press, 1992.

Contributors

CAROLE ALLAMAND, Assistant Professor at Rutgers University, holds a Master's from the University of Geneva (Switzerland) and a Ph.D. from Cornell University. Her work, inspired by psychoanalysis, narratology, and stylistics, focuses mainly on twentieth-century novels and autobiography. She has published articles on Yourcenar, Duras, Gide, and Jack Kerouac and is currently completing a manuscript (Mal de mère) that defines the poetics of Marguerite Yourcenar as an attempt to retrieve a mother lost at birth.

ELÈNE CLICHE, Professor of Literature at the University of Québec in Montreal, holds a doctorate in Literary Semiology from Paris's École des Hautes Études en Sciences Sociales where her thesis director was Roland Barthes. She has a particular interest in psychoanalysis and feminism as well as women's writing. She has published numerous articles in France, Belgium, the United States, and Canada on Simone de Beauvoir, Colette, Lispector, Marie-Claire Blais, and Yourcenar, and has participated in a great variety of international conferences. She has also worked on the epistolary form in Colette, Simone de Beauvoir, and Yourcenar and is currently working on the representation of feminine characters in a series of short stories.

FRANCESCA COUNIHAN, Lecturer in French at the National University of Ireland, Maynooth, teaches modern French literature, civilization, and language. She received her doctorate from L'Université de Paris 7. She has published articles on Yourcenar and Annie Saumont and is the author of *L'Autorité dans l'oeuvre romanesque de Marguerite Yourcenar* (1998). At present she is preparing a study on authority in literature, comparing approaches in the French and English-speaking worlds.

HENK HILLENAAR, Professor Emeritus of French Literature at Groningen University, the Netherlands, taught there from 1984 until 2000. As a historian of ideas, he is also a specialist in the area of psychoanalysis and literature. *Le secret de Télémaque* (1996), is his most recent book.

Ksenya Kiebuzinski, the Petro Jacyk Bibliographer at the Ukrainian Research Institute, Harvard University, holds a Ph.D. in literary studies from Brandeis University. Presently she is continuing her work on the relationship between history and literature and the nature of transnational understandings; she is also preparing a comparative study on the representations of Ukraine, Poland, and Russia in nineteenth-century French cultural discourse.

Katherine Callen King, Professor of Comparative Literature and Classics at the University of California at Los Angeles, also teaches in the Women's Studies Program. Her two published books, *Achilles: Paradigms of the War Hero from Homer to the Middle Ages* and *HOMER*, reflect her scholarly interest in why and how a writer manipulates important cultural texts for ideological purposes. She is currently working on *Imaginary Women,* a cross-cultural analysis of female cultural archetypes. She is an antiwar activist.

Leakthina Chau-Pech Ollier received her Ph.D. from the University of California at Los Angeles in 1995. She taught in the Department of Romance Languages at Bowdoin College from 1995 to 2001 and coedited *Of Vietnam: Identities in Dialogue* (2001). She is currently teaching in Phnom Penh, Cambodia, and is at work on a book on contemporary Cambodian culture.

Michael Rothberg, Associate Professor of English and Comparative Literature at the University of Illinois, Champaign-Urbana, is the author of *Traumatic Realism: The Demands of Holocaust Representation* (2000), and coeditor, with Neil Levi, of *The Holocaust: Theoretical Readings* (forthcoming). He has recently published essays on W. E. B. Du Bois and Toni Morrison and is currently working on the relationship between post-Holocaust and postcolonial discourses.

Judith Holland Sarnecki, Associate Professor of French, teaches all levels of French and Gender Studies at Lawrence University, Appleton, Wisconsin. She received her Ph.D. from the University of Wisconsin-Madison. She has published articles on Marguerite Yourcenar and Aimé Césaire. With a nascent interest in tattoo culture, she has recently published an article on trauma and tattoo. Currently she is researching texts and films produced during the German occupation of France, 1940–44.

MIEKE TAAT has worked for twenty-five years as a lecturer in Modern French Literature in the Department of French Language and Literature at the University of Amsterdam. She presently holds a position there with the Department of General Literary Studies. Her current research focuses on issues concerning the practice of reading, with special emphasis on psychoanalysis, ethics, deconstruction, and gender. Within this context she has published—in Dutch and in French—several theoretical essays and literary case studies extending from the works of Marguerite Yourcenar to ancient Greek tragedy.

INGEBORG MAJER O'SICKEY, Associate Professor of German and Women's Studies at the State University of New York at Binghamton, teaches literature, feminist film and literary theory, visual culture, and language. She edited (with I. V. Zadow) *Triangulated Visions: Women in Recent German Cinema* (1998), and has published numerous articles on German film, most recently on Tom Tykwer's *Run Lola Run*. Majer O'Sickey's archival research in Berlin (1999–2000, 2001) on images of women in Nazi cinema will culminate in a monograph.

TRANSLATORS

CHANTAL RODAIS received her Masters of English at Université d'Orléans in France. After working in business for ten years in France and in the United States, she returned to her studies to finish her Ph.D. in Comparative Literature at the State University of New York at Binghamton, where she also teaches literature.

GERVAIS REED, Professor of French Emeritus, Lawrence University, currently serves as a review editor for *French Review*. He earned his B.A. at Princeton University and his M.A. and Ph.D. at Brown University. He is the author of *Claude Barbin: librairie de Paris sous le règne de Louis XIV* and has published articles on Molière, Pierre Corneille, and contemporary writer Patrick Drevet.

Index

Abyss, The (Yourcenar), 79, 81, 84, 94, 99 n. 22
Académiciens, 15, 27 n. 8
Académie Française: dictionary of, 11; members of, 27 n. 3; rituals of, 12, 28 n. 10; Yourcenar induction into, 11
Achille ou le mensonge (Yourcenar). See *Achilles or the Lie*
Achilleid (Statius), 34
Achilles on the Field of Sexual Politics (King), 16
Achilles or the Lie (Yourcenar), 16; classical *vs.* modern elements in, 33; gender in, 35–39, 51–52; sexual climax/death in, 36, 57 n. 16
Action Council for Women's Liberation, 129
Adorno, Theodor, 130
adulthood. See individual identity
African Americans: language of, 24–25, 179–99
Alexis (Yourcenar), 79, 81, 91, 99 n. 22
Alexis ou le Traité du Vain Combat (Yourcenar), 75 n. 1
Allamand, Carole, 18
Amazons, 50–51
ambiguity, use of, 53
Amen Corner, The (Baldwin), 24–25, 179, 189–93, 197–99
analogy, 23, 167
androgynous figure, or third sex, 16, 25, 35, 53
anima, 40
Anna, soror . . . (Yourcenar), 79, 81, 84, 86, 99 n. 22, 121 n. 19
Anti-Oedipus (Deleuze, Guattari), 130
anti-Semitism, 21, 125, 130–31
antisex ideology, 137
Arancibia, Blanca, 184
Aristotle, 167
As Pilgrim and Outsider (Yourcenar), 126, 216

asceticism, 131
Aside on Proletarian Reality, Proletarian Woman and Man of the Left (Theweleit), 143
Associated University Presses, 10
Auschwitz, 126, 128, 226 n. 16
author: intention of, 81, 102–3, 109–10; relationship to book, 103–4; style of, 114
Author, death of, 102–3
Author-Genitor-Father, 105
authoritarianism. See fascism
Autobiography and Matricide: Marguerite Yourcenar's Dear Departed (Ollier), 17
autobiography, process of, 62
Autonomous Women's Movement, 129

Bajazet (Racine), 79
Baldwin, James, 24–25, 179
Balzac, Honoré de, 107
barbarism, 125–27, 145. See also fascism
Barney, Natalie Clifford, 53
Barthes, Roland, 19, 102–4, 107
Baudelaire, 216
Bemba, the, 107
Benjamin, Jessica, 129, 145
Benjamin, Walter, 125
bibliography, 79, 92
Biondi, Carminella, 181
Blot, Jean, 157
Blues et Gospels (Yourcenar), 179
Blüher, Hans, 136
Bodies that Matter (Butler), 218
Bosch, Hieronymus, 167
Bourdet, Denise, 157
Brahman, the, 107
Bredin, Jean-Denis, 27 n. 4
Breitbach, Joseph, 151
Browning, 168

244

Brueghel, Pieter, 167
Buchenwald, 167, 226 n. 16
Butler, Judith, 25, 147 n. 19, 157, 203, 218
Byron, lord, 79

Caillois, Roger, 11
Callimachus, 168
Caravaggio, Michelangelo Merisi da, 167
Carlier, Pierre, 156
Carnets de Notes de Mémoires d'Hadrien (Yourcenar), 148, 150, 156, 209
Carré, Rev. Father, 13
Carrère d'Encausse, Helene, 27 n. 1
Cartesian mind/body split, 20
Cavafy, Constantin, 168, 171
sexe qui n'en est pas un, Ce (Irigaray), 63
Céline, Louis Ferdinand, 130, 141
censorship, 83, 90, 94
Césaire, Aimé, 182
Chamson, André, 12
characters, reality of, 20, 65–67, 85–86, 91
Chateaubriand, François, 79
Chénier, 168
Chenonceaux, 166, 170–71
childbirth: complications during, 70–71; process of, 100 n. 36
civil rights, 24
Cixous, Hélène, 63, 101, 110–11
Cliche, Elène, 25
Coin in Nine Hands, A (Yourcenar), 79, 84
Coin des "Amen," Le (Baldwin). See *The Amen Corner*
Cold War, 21, 125, 141
Colette, 14
Comédie humaine, 107
Comme l'eau qui coule (Yourcenar). See *Two Lives and a Dream*
Confessions (Rousseau), 64
contact, theory of, 149
contextual complexity, 126
Corbin, Laurie Lynette, 68
Corneille, 167
Corps-à-corps avec la mère, Le (Irigaray), 66–67
cosmic harmony, 149. See also *Memoirs of Hadrian*

Counihan, Francesca, 24
Coup de grâce as Male Fantasy: On the Sexual Politics of Fascism (Rothberg), 21, 77, 79, 81, 85, 121 n. 19, 125–42, 213 n. 12
Coup de grâce, Un (Yourcenar), 25
Couronne et la lyre, La (Yourcenar), 205
Crayencour, Fernande de: death of, 19, 20, 23, 64, 65, 75 n. 3; dedication of *Dear Departed* to, 62; illness of, 72; literary character of, 67–68, 72; revitalization of, 65, 66–67, 69; Yourcenar's feelings towards, 18, 64, 66, 70, 74
Crayencour, Marguerite de. See Yourcenar, Marguerite
Crayencour, Michel de, 64, 66, 110
creation: literary: aspects of, 88, 97; process of, 107, 111; womb metaphor for, 19, 20, 102, 106, 108, 110, 113, 117
critics, Yourcenar's disdain for, 82, 98 n. 15
Crosscurrents (Yourcenar), 84, 95
cultural nationalism, 125
culture Industry, 130

Dante, 167, 168
d'Aubigné, Agrippa, 167, 168, 174
daughter/mother, separation of, 62–63
De Rosbo, Patrick, 82, 91, 101
Dear Departed (Yourcenar), 18, 62, 67, 74, 92
death, 17, 23, 36, 36 n. 16, 45, 46; of Author, 102–3; as corrective to life, 45; death/abandonment/sacrifice theme in, 170, 173–74; importance of, 17; obsession with, 17, 23; sadism as death instinct, 36; sexual climax and, 36, 36 n. 16, 57 n. 16; of Yourcenar, 28 n. 17; Yourcenar's obsession with, 17, 23
Death Drives the Cart (Yourcenar), 94. See also *The Abyss; Two Lives*
Death-defying Acts: Performing Gender in Marguerite Yourcenar's "Sappho ou le suicide" (Sarnecki), 25–26
deconstruction, 113–14
DeJean, 215
Deleuze, Gilles, 19, 102, 104–5, 107
delirium, 116–19, 121 n. 27

246 INDEX

Denier du rêve (Yourcenar), 109, 121 n. 19
Derrida, Jacques, 19, 80, 101, 102–3
Deux amours d'Achille (Yourcenar). See *Two Loves of Achilles*
Dialogues (Deleuze, Parnet), 103–5
Dinnerstein, Dorothy, 96, 100 n. 37
Dissémination, La (Derrida), 105–6
d'Ormesson, Jean, 12
Dreams and Spells (Yourcenar), 83, 88, 92, 94–95
Dufresne, Noémi, 67
D'un château l'autre (Céline), 141

ecology for Yourcenar, 90–91, 95, 171–72
ecriture feminine (women's language), 15
ego: disconnection from, 115–17; of fascist, 131–32, 143–44; structure of, 117, 121 n. 24; survival of, 131
Ehrenreich, Barbara, 129
Eksteins, Modris, 131–32
Electre ou la chute des masques (Yourcenar), 108
Eliot, T. S., 168
Elizabeth I, 167
Embeirikos, Andreas, 56 n. 12
En pèlerin et en étranger (Yourcenar). See *As Pilgrim and Outsider*
engenderment, concept of, 109
Entretiens (Yourcenar), 111–15, 209
epitext, 82
Erasers, The (Robbe-Grillet), 85
Essais (Yourcenar), 113, 117
essay, Yourcenar: content of, 166, 169; death/abandonment/sacrifice theme in, 170, 173–74; genre of, 166; good *vs.* evil in, 170; good vs. evil in, personal world in, 170; presentation of, 166, 169
Essays of Marguerite Yourcenar: Analogy and Eternity, The (Hillenaar), 22–23, 166–75
Et l'une ne bouge pas sans l'autre (Irigaray), 64–65, 68
ethnic/national identity, 129
Euripides, 114
Europe: politics/economics of, 21

facts, nature of, 20
Farias, Victor, 128–29

fascism: contemporary forms of, 126; contradictions of, 133; ego and, 131–32, 143–44; fantasy/violence of, 128; Germany's neonationalist rebirth of, 128–29; molar mass as, 132; persistence/renewal of, 128; philosophy of, 125–29; reality of, 127; sexual politics of, 21, 125–45
fear, immunization against, 49–50
Felman, Shoshana, 115–16
female voice, 90–91
femininity: antiwar nature of, 41; female image of, 39; male understanding of, 53; murder *vs.*, 40
feminism: Action Council for Women's Liberation for, 129; Autonomous Women's Movement for, 129; critique of, 15; facets of, 90; French voice of, 15; German activism of, 129; influence of, 9; men in, 129–30; for Yourcenar, 90, 156–63, 172–73
femme fatale, 220
Feux (Yourcenar). See *Fires*
final solution for Other, 21, 35, 56 n. 14
Fires (Yourcenar), 17, 25; classical *vs.* modern in, 33–34, 55 n. 8; classical *vs.* modern in, dedication of, 88; eternal human characteristics in, 33, 54 n. 4, 204; gender in, 220, 225; introduction to, 83; paratext of, 95; preface of, 26, 80, 81, 109, 214; publication of, 26, 54 n. 1, 95; style of, 95; subject of, 214–15
Fitzgerald, F. Scott, 168
Flaubert, Gustave, 152
Fleuve profond, sombre rivière (Yourcenar), 24, 179–81; African imagery in, 185–86; context of, 181–85; historical/cultural approach to, 182–85, 188; introductory essay to, 184–85, 202 n. 43; language of, 194–98; universalizing strategy for, 182–83
floating I, concept of, 203
foetal relationship, 117
folie et la chose littéraire, La (Felman), 116
Ford, John, 79
Forster, E. M. 168
Foucault, Michel, 103
Fraigneau, André, 214
France, Anatole, 168

Franco, Francisco, 134
Frankfurt School, 128
Freikorps, men of, 21, 126–33
French dictionary, 11
French literary theory, 27
French Review (journal), 9
French Revolution, 167
Freud, Sigmund, 23, 36, 56 n. 12, 113–14, 131
Freudian psychology, 36, 40, 102, 113–14, 131, 224
Frick, Grace, 12, 26, 140
Friedlander, Saul, 125
Fukui, Y., 11
Furetière, dictionary of, 11

Galey, Matthieu: *With Open Eyes: Conversations with Matthieu Galey,* 12–13, 66, 82; Yourcenar analogy by, 13, 28 n. 15; Yourcenar interviews with, 20, 22, 28 n. 13, 66, 67, 82, 101, 168; Yourcenar repudiation of interviews with, 82
Garber, Marjorie, 217
Gardiner, Judith Kegan, 62
Gaudin, Colette, 84, 99 n. 17, 102, 109
gender: dismissal of, 90–91; as metaphor, 91–92; poetic relation to, 16; social construction of, 53, 203–7; Yourcenar's floating I for, 203; Yourcenar's issues for, 55 n. 9
Gender Trouble (Butler), 218
genocide, 126
Germany: neonationalist rebirth of fascism in, 128–29; Weimar era for, 127–28, 132
gestation of characters, 20, 97, 110
Gide, André, 82, 99 n. 16, 168
Giscards, the, 13
Glidden, Peter, 97
godhood, fear of, 42–43
Goethe, Johann-Wolfgang von, 79
Good Intentions: Marguerite Yourcenar's American Translations (Counihan), 24
Goya, 167
Guattari, Félix, 130
gynocritique, 15

Heidegger and Nazism (Farias), 128–29

Heliogabalus, 167
Henriot, Emile, 154
Heraclitus, 168, 169–70
heroism: classical, 17; vulnerability and, 49–50
Hillenaar, Henk, 22–23
Hiroshima, 167
Historia Augusta (Yourcenar), 166, 170–71
historical novel, 22, 88, 153
Hitler, Adolf, 126, 154
Holocaust, the, 21, 141
Homer, 16, 33, 59 n. 38
Homme obscur, Un (Yourcenar), 204
homoeroticism, 136
homophobia/misogyny, 136
homosexuality, 96, 136, 218–19, 224–25
Hors livre: Préfaces (Derrida), 105–6
Hugo, Victor, 167

identification *vs.* individuation, 64
identity, metaphysics of, 15
Ignace de Loyola's Exercises. *See* meditation
Iliad, the, 16, 33, 59 n. 38
imagery: fire-water as, 47–48; killer as sculptor for, 45–46; masculine/feminine use of, 46–52, 203
imaginative re-creation, 118
immortels, the: body of, 11, 12; dress of, 11, 27 n. 2; Yourcenar thoughts on, 13, 28 n. 16
incest, 79, 96, 135–36
individual identity, 17
individuation, 62
intelligence/sympathy, interdependence of, 118
Irigaray, Luce, 18, 63, 116–17
Is There No Body on the Scene of Writing?: Contemporary Conceptions of Textual Practice in/and Yourcenar's Paratexts (Taat), 19

Jaccomard, Hélène, 82, 98 n. 14
Jameson, Fredric, 130–31
jargon, 200 n. 23
Jeroboam, 167
Jeune née, La (Cixous), 63
Johnson, Barbara, 62, 64
Johnson, James Weldon, 182
Johnson, Joanne, 10

Journal de Mémoires d'Hadrien (Yourcenar), 118
Judaean campaign, 155. See also *Memoires of Hadrian*
Jung, Carl J., 23, 43, 56n. 12, 114

Kaplan, Alice, 129, 147n. 17
Katz, Dori, 54n. 2
Khayyám, Omar, 168
Kiebuzinski, Ksenya, 21–22
King, Katherine Callen, 16
Koonz, Claudia, 127–28
Kristallnacht, 126
Kristeva, Julia, 15, 18, 19–20, 64, 107, 111, 130

labyrinthe du monde, Le (Yourcenar), 17, 20, 65, 170
Lacan, Jacques, 15, 18, 64, 116, 121n. 19, 130, 133
Lagerlöf, Selma, 168, 172
language, use of, 139
Late Marxism (Jameson), 130–31
Lauretis, Teresa de, 215
l'école classique, 11
l'école précieuse, 11
l'immortalité, A: seal of, 11
Lettres à ses amis et quelques autres (Yourcenar), 101, 117
Lévi-Strauss, Claude, 12
life: formula for, 75n. 1; transformation of, 140
Lindbergh, Anne, 125
lingua materna, 12
lingua paterna, 12
literary device; analogy as, 23, 167; conception *vs.* delivery by, 95; evolution of characters, 20, 65–67, 85–86, 91; formula for life as, 75n. 1; metaphor as, 19, 43, 57n. 15, 103–4; metonymy as, 167, 224; sympathetic magic as, 118; thematic/stylistic characteristics as, 80; tonal authenticity as, 191; Yourcenar's observations as, 101–2
literary history, 11, 113
literary themes, Yourcenar, 170–75
Literature and the Idea of Europe (Reiss), 125–26
literature, reality of, 77
L'Oeuvre au noir (Yourcenar), 17, 101, 204

Logos, the, 106
love, masculine control of, 34
Lovell, John, 181
Lucretius, 167
Lukács, George, 153

Macciocchi, Maria-Antonietta, 145
macro/micro politics, 132
Mahler, Margaret, 130
maîtres-penseurs, 107–9
male bonding, 38, 40
Male Fantasies (Theweleit): fascist ego-construction by, 21, 126–27; feminist contexts for, 129, 142–43
Mallarmé, Stéphane, 89, 167, 168
Man, Paul de, 129, 139
Mann, Thomas, 79, 95, 169, 172
Mantegna, 168
Manzoni, Alessandro, 151
Marcus Aurelius, 148, 168
Marcus, Jane, 147n. 20
Margerie, Diane de, 76
Marguerite Yourcenar: Inventing a Life (Savigneau), 76n. 6
Marks, Elaine, 28n. 24, 125, 141
Martin du Gard, Roger, 79
Marxism, 114, 143
masculine *vs.* feminine, 25, 35, 51, 56n. 12, 102, 203
masculinist-poststructuralist, 15
masculinity, 34–35, 42, 43, 48
Master-Subject, 119
maternal instinct, 92, 96–97, 110–11
maternal *vs.* paternal functions, 106–7
maternaliter, 15
matricide: guilt in, 65; literary use of, 17; Modernity as, 119; symbolism of, 62–65; woman's individual identity and, 62
Mayer, Arno, 127
Mazzolani, Lidia Storoni, 152
meditation, 117–18
Medusa, 70, 75n. 2, 224, 226n. 17
Mémoires d'Hadrien. See *Memoirs of Hadrian*
Memoirs of Hadrian (Yourcenar), 79, 85, 99n. 22; cosmic harmony in, 149; genre of, 148–64; historical interpretation of, 151, 152–53, 165n. 5; masculine voice in, 208–11; meaning of existence in, 148; narrative structure

of, 89, 151–52; poetry *vs.* facts in, 152; research for, 114–15, 150; rewriting of, 89; theory of contact for, 149–50, 163; use of metaphor in, 161
Mère Terrible, 108
metaphor: birth/battlefield as, 73–74; black hole as, 105, 107; bodily parts as, 135; gender, 91–92; germination as, 111; killer as sculptor for, 45; Medusa as, 71, 137–38; rider/horse as, 161; sculpture as, 150–51; sexual/martial use of, 57 n. 15; use of, 19, 43, 57 n. 15, 103–4, 204; womb as, 19, 20, 102, 106, 108, 110, 113, 117
metaphysics, Western, 14
metonymy, 167, 224
Michelangelo, 170–71
The Milk of Death (Yourcenar), 70, 71
Milne, Lorna, 156
Milton, John, 167
Mishima, 117, 166
Mishima (Yourcenar), 170
misogyny, 12, 15, 136
Mithra cult, 159
Modernity, 119. *See also* matricide
molar/molecular mass, 132. *See also* fascism
Montesquieu, 79
La mort de l'auteur (Barthes), 103
motherhood anxiety over, 92–93; differences in, 71; elevation of, 70; repression of, 20; separation from daughter, 62–63
Murciaux, Christian, 148
Musset, 168
Mussolini, Benito, 153–54
Mystère d'Alceste (Yourcenar), 114

narrative, discipline of, 89, 91
narrative of genesis. *See* preface
National Socialist State. *See* fascism
Nazi Germany, 21, 226 n. 16
Nazi homosexuality, 136
Negro spirituals, 24, 179–99
New Novel, 85
nobility of failure, 173
Non-au-Père, 15
Nouvelle Revue française, La (journal), 204
Novalis, 83

Obscure Man, An (Yourcenar), 81, 87–88
Oedipus, myth of, 62
Oeuvres romanesques (Yourcenar), 12, 67, 79; *Carnet de notes* for, 22; gestation of book in, 111; historical authenticity/universal truths of, 21–22; masculine voice in, 25; Racine reference in, 75 n. 1, 79; use of meditation in, 117–18; as Yourcenar autobiography, 22
oeuvre à la première personne, Une (Carlier). See *A Work in the First Person*
Ollier, Leakthina Chau-Pech, 17, 62–76
On the Historical Novel (Manzoni), 151
On the Origin of Inequality (Rousseau), 151
Oriental Tales (Yourcenar), 70
Orlando (Woolf), 25, 204–5
O'Sickey, Ingeborg Majer, 142, 147 n. 20
Ostriker, Alicia, 33
Other, the: destruction of, 21, 25; as female, 131, 135; final solution for, 21, 35, 56 n. 14; imagery of, 53; permeation by, 118; revelation of, 115; voice of, 20, 85–86, 116
Owens, Craig, 136

Pantheon of the Pleïde, 16
paratext: as censorship, 90; composition of Yourcenar's, 88–89, 116; control/authority in, 82, 86, 92; Yourcenar's use of, 78–79, 81, 83
parler femme, 15
Parmenides, 168, 169–70
Parnet, Claire, 103
patois, 200 n. 23
patriarchy, 145. *See also* facism
Patrocle ou le destin (Yourcenar), 16, 33, 44–46
people, marginalization of, 21
Performing the Masculine Voice (Cliche), 25
Petronius, 168
phallic symbolism, 110, 119
phallicized dyke, 220
physiology/knowledge, connection of, 20
Picard, Charles, 152

Pinget, Robert, *85*
Pirandello, 168
Piranesi, 168, 170–71
Pirmez, Octave, 66
Pirmez, Rémo, 66
placental economy, 63
Plato, 167
plenitude *vs.* lack, 64
Plutarch, 168
Poignault, Rémy, 10, 53
postface, 78, 81, 84, 95, 109
poststructuralism, 127
poststructuralist theories, 9
power relations, 54
préciosité, 11–12
preconceptions, 113
preface: authority of, 102; as censorship, 90; as interpretation, 81; nature of, 109; as reader, 87; superfluousness of, 77–78, 80–81; use/goal of, 80–81, 84–85, 88, 90, 101; voices of, 87
presence *vs.* absence, 64
Proust, 168
psychoanalysis: Freud and, 36, 40, 102, 113–14, 131, 224; Imaginary Order in, 63; mother-daughter relationship in, 63; Oedipal structure in, 130; placental economy in, 63; politicization in, 144; Pre-Symbolic stage in, 64; repression in, 94, 130; Symbolic stage in, 62, 64
psychology *vs.* politics, 142
psychomachia, 39–40
psychosis: duality of, 64; identification *vs.* individuation in, 64; plenitude *vs.* lack in, 64; presence *vs.* absence in, 64; separation *vs.* symbiosis in, 64
Puritanism, 92

Quai Conti, 11
"Questions of *genre*: History and the Self in Marguerite Yourcenar's *Mémoires d'Hadrien*" (Kiebuzinski), 21–22
Quoi? L'Eternité (Yourcenar), 67, 173

Rabinbach, Anson, 129
Racine, Jean, 79, 80, 98 n. 6
racism, 138
rape, desire for, 37, 57 n. 22
Reading Prohibited: The Politics of Yourcenar's Prefaces (Allamand), 18
Reed, Gervais, 9, 22–23
Reflections of Nazism (Friedlander), 125
Reflections on the Composition of Memoirs of Hadrian (Yourcenar), 80, 83–85, 88, 99 n. 21
Reichspogromnacht. See *Kristallnacht*
Reiss, Timothy J., 125
Rendre à César, 109
repression of mothers/motherhood, 20
Retz, Christine, 10
Revue Archéologique (journal), 152
rewriting: as censorship, 90, 94; goal of, 90, 92–93; Yourcenar's use of, 89–90, 93
Richelet, dictionary of, 11
Richelieu, Cardinal de, 11
Riffaterre, Michael, 93
Rilke, 168
Rire de la méduse, Le (Cixous), 63
Rochefort, Christiane, 12
Rodais, Chantal, 9, 19, 101
Röhm, Ernst, 136
Role of Eroticism in Male Society, The (Bluher), 136
Romilly, Jacqueline de, 27 n. 1
Ronsard, 167
Room of One's Own, A (Woolf), 25
Rose-Schmalz, Dana, 10
Rothberg, Michael, 21, 28 n. 24
Rouch, Hélène, 63, 116–17
Rousseau, Jean-Jacques, 64, 151
Russian Revolution, 127, 134

sacrifice, theme of, 173–74
sadism, 36
St. Bartholomew's Day Massacre, 167
salons, French, 11
Sand, George, 14
Sappho et le suicide (Yourcenar). See *Sappho or Suicide*
Sappho or Suicide (Yourcenar), 25, 27, 205, 214–25
Sappho, voice of, 25, 215–25
Sarnecki, Judith Holland, *25-26*
Savigneau, Josyane, 13–14, 76, 214
scholarship, 111
Scott, Walter, 153

self, unitary, 14
Senghor, Léopold Sédar, 182
separation *vs.* symbiosis, 64
Serrano, Lucienne, 98 n. 15
sexual identity, 16–17, 38, 144
sexual politics, 16, 21, 54, 125–45
sexual relationship, 37, 57 n. 22
Shakespeare, William, 89, 167–68
Shurr, Georgia Hooks, 157, 181, 199 n. 5, 208, 213 n. 12
Signorelli, 167
slaves, displacement of, 24
songes et les sorts, Les (Yourcenar), 28 n. 22, 113–14
Staël, Mme de, 14
Société Internationale d'Etudes Yourcenariennes, 10
Sous bénéfice d'inventaire (Yourcenar), 101, 170
Spanish Civil War, 134
spatial proximity, 109
Stanton, Donna, 11
Starobinski, Jean, 97, 100 n. 40
Statius, 34
Straton, 168
Stygian baths, 50
subjectivity, 64
sympathetic magic, 118
sympathy/intelligence, interdependence of, 118

Taat, Mieke, 9, 19–20, 101–20
temporal proximity, 109
Le Temps, ce grand sculpteur (Yourcenar), 101, 150–51, 170–71
Le Temps des femmes (Kristeva), 111
Théâtre I (Yourcenar), 110
Théâtre II (Yourcenar), 108
Theses on the Philosophy of History (Benjamin), 126
Theweleit, Klaus, 21, 126–33, 142–43
Three Steps on the Ladder of Writing (Cixous), 110–11
Tintoretto, 167
Titian, 167
totalitarian destruction, 125
transvestism, 34
truth, nature of, 20
Two Lives and a Dream (Yourcenar), 82, 87–88, 94, 95, 98 n. 4

Two Loves of Achilles (Yourcenar), 33, 52, 55 n. 7

Ungaretti, Giuseppe, 168
Universal Man, 23
unlimited desire, 130
Utrillo, Maurice, 168

Valéry, 167
Van Gogh, Vincent, 168
Versailles Peace conference, 127
Vidal-Naquet, Pierre, 34, 56 n. 10
Vigny, Alfred de, 167
Virgil, 167

warfare, 44
Wave of the Future (Lindbergh), 125
Weyergans, François, 12
Whatley, Janet, 148
white supremacy, 133
Whitman, Cedric, 46
Wilson, Jerry, 12
With Open Eyes: Conversations with Matthieu Galey (Galey, Yourcenar), 12–13, 77, 82, 118, 153–54
womb, 19, 20, 102, 106, 108, 110, 113, 117
women. *See also* femininity; feminism; motherhood: defilement rites for, 106–7; fictional novels by, 62; myth of new, 62; political matter of, 15
Woolf, Virginia, 25, 28 n. 26, 204–5
Work in the First Person, A (Carlier), 156
World War I, aftermath of, 127
World War II, 153
writing, process of, 105

Yeux ouverts, Les (Yourcenar), 111, 114. See also *With Open Eyes: Conversations with Matthieu Galey*
Yourcenar: alchemy for, 97; androgynous voice of, 25, 28 n. 20; analogy used by, 23; apolitical stance of, 21; apologia by, 142; approach to writing by, 20, 77–78, 85, 111–12; appropriation of myths by, 33, 55 n. 5; attitude towards men by, 14; as author of own biography, 82; autobiographical trilogy of, 18; commentary by, 179; complexity of, 22, 169; conception *vs.* delivery by, 95; creative process of,

92, 94, 110; death of, 28 n. 17; death/sacrifice themes for, 17, 23–24, 173–74; deconstructive element for, 113–14; denial of feminism by, 33; dialectics of, 64; ecology for, 90–91, 95, 171–72; Embeirikos as companion for, 56 n. 12; essay for, 22–23, 166–75, 184–85, 202 n. 43; European as universal for, 24; evolution of literary characters by, 20, 65–67, 85–86, 91; feminism for, 90, 156–63, 172–73; fictional characters by, 65–67; floating I for, 203; Freud *vs.* Jung for, 23, 56 n. 12; Frick as companion for, 26; gender issues for, 55 n. 9; genealogy and, 96; guilt as writer, 94; historical novel by, 88, 153; hostility for mother by, 71–72; imagery used by, 46–49; incest theme by, 79, 96, 135–36; internal realm for, 20; literary contradictions by, 79–80; literary estate of, 96; literary gestation period for, 20, 97, 110; literary pedagogy by, 82; literary themes of, 170–75; masculine voice for, 25; maternity and, 75; maternity *vs.* paternity of works, 96; matricide used by, 17–18; meditation by, 117–18; memoirs of, 65; metaphors used by, 20; method of delirium by, 117; misogyny for, 54 n. 2; mother of, 18–19; motherhood for, 92–93; mother's death for, 20; mother's wish for, 71–72; narrative strategies by, 76 n. 5; Negro spirituals and, 24; obsession with death by, 17, 23; origins for, 73; paratext for, 78; paratextual writings by, 19; personal experience for, 89; pessimism of, 17, 23, 51; preparation for writing, 20; prose poems of, 16, 25–26; pseudonym of, 18–19, 92, 97; psychology *vs.* politics, 142; realism of characters by, 85–86; reception of works by, 16; repression of maternal by, 19; rule for works of fiction by, 20; search for Universal Man by, 23; sexual identity for, 16; sexual politics of, 16, 21, 54, 125–45; sexual preferences of, 95–96; style of, 95, 114; subjectivity of, 63–64; surplus/excess for, 90; texts of, 9; "the lost center" for, 23; translation of American texts by, 24; Translator's Note by, 179–80; as a universal humanist, 19; writing techniques of, 15–16, 89, 90–91

Yourcenar, works of: *The Abyss*, 79; *Achille ou le mensonge*, 16; *Alceste*, 114; *Alexis*, 79; *Alexis ou le Traité du Vain Combat*, 75 n. 1; *Anna, soror*, 79; *Blues et Gospels*, 179; *A Coin in Nine Hands*, 79; *Crosscurrents*, 84; *Dear Departed*, 18; *Death Drives the Cart*, 94; *Denier du rêve*, 109, 121 n. 19; *Deux amours d'Achille*, 33; *Dreams and Spells*, 83; *En pèlerin et en étranger*, 126; *Entretiens*, 115; *Essais*, 113, 117; *Fires*, 25; *Fleuve profond, sombre rivière*, 24, 179; *Historia Augusta*, 166, 170–71; *La Couronne et la lyre*, 205; *Le labyrinthe du monde*, 20; *Le Temps, ce grand sculpteur*, 101; *Le Temps, ce grand scupteur*, 170; *Les songes et les sorts*, 28 n. 22; *Les yeux ouverts*, 118; *Lettres à ses amis et quelques autres*, 101; *L'oeuvre au noir*, 17; *Memoirs of Hadrian*, 21–22, 75 n. 1, 79–80, 85, 88–89, 99 n. 22, 101; *The Milk of Death*, 70, 71; *Mishima*, 170; *Mystère d'Alceste*, 114; *An Obscure Man*, 81; *Oeuvres romanesques*, 12; *With Open Eyes: Conversations with Matthieu Galey*, 12–13; *Oriental Tales*, 70; *Reflections on the Composition of Memoirs of Hadrian*, 80, 83–85, 99 n. 21; *Sappho et le suicide*, 25; *Sous bénéfice d'inventaire*, 101; *Patrocle ou le destin*, 16; *Théâtre I*, 110; *Théâtre II*, 108; *Two Lives and a Dream*, 98 n. 4; *Un Coup de grâce*, 25; *Un Homme obscur*, 204; *Yeux ouverts*, 114

Žižek, Slavoj, 125
Zola, Emile, 80, 98 n. 12